30-Minute
Money Solutions

Other Books from Morningstar

30-Minute Money Solutions

A Step-by-Step Guide to Managing Your Finances

Christine Benz

WILEY

John Wiley & Sons, Inc.

Published by John Wiley & Sons, Inc., Hoboken, New Jersey.
Published simultaneously in Canada.

Stopwatch courtesy ISTOCK

For general information on our other products and services or for technical support, please contact our Customer Care Department within the United States at (800) 762-2974, outside the United States at (317) 572-3993 or fax (317) 572-4002.

Wiley also publishes its books in a variety of electronic formats. Some content that appears in print may not be available in electronic books. For more information about Wiley products, visit our web site at www.wiley.com.

Library of Congress Cataloging-in-Publication Data:

Benz, Christine.
  30-minute money solutions : a step-by-step guide to managing your finances / Christine Benz.
      p. cm.
  Includes index.
  ISBN 978-0-470-48157-8 (cloth)
  1. Finance, Personal.   2. Investments.   I. Morningstar, Inc.   II. Title.   III. Title: 30-minute money solutions.   IV. Title: Thirty-minute money solutions.
  HG179.B424 2010
  332.024–dc22

                                                                                2009041412

Printed in the United States of America

10 9 8 7 6 5 4 3 2 1

For Greg, my comfort and joy

Contents

Foreword

YOU'D THINK THAT MANAGING YOUR OWN MONEY would be the most elemental of life skills, one we would all master at an early age. You work and are paid money. You spend some and save the rest. You invest some of what you save for higher returns in the future in case you can't work then. It doesn't sound like that difficult a set of skills to develop. Certainly, most of us develop much more complex capabilities for social interaction: how we dress, behave in public, develop a sense of humor, choose friends, maintain relationships, find employment, select a place to live, and so forth. Compared with that, personal finance should be a breeze.

Yet for most people personal finance remains a mystery, leaving far too many of us prone to scams that play on our naïveté. Small wonder—for most of us, the subject of saving and investing wasn't something discussed at home while we were growing up. It most certainly wasn't something taught in our schools. And to compound the problem, the financial services industry seemingly goes out of its way to make the topic impenetrable. What other industry has more needless complexity and more confusing and constantly changing terminology? Did your Fannie Mae ARM get turned into an RMBS or a CMO with a long WAM rated by a NRSRO and sold to a convert/arb shop?

Fortunately, it is possible to cut through the nonsense and forge a sound financial path, even if you're not hip to this week's financial acronym. The basics of personal finance are just that: basic. Buy low, sell high; live within your means; understand your time horizon; set reasonable goals—these are all simple concepts that can be readily grasped and, with effort, mastered by all of us. All you need is a good coach to help you cut through the clutter and keep you on target. *30-Minute Money Solutions* is designed to be just such a guide to get you started or to help you brush up on individual tasks such as saving for college or rolling over a 401(k) plan.

I can think of no finer guide for conquering these tasks than Christine Benz. Christine is a gifted financial analyst—as talented as any we've ever had at Morningstar. She quickly rose through the ranks as an analyst to become director of all our mutual fund analysts. Under her leadership, the team did groundbreaking work and Christine nurtured a team of fine young analysts into seasoned pros. Following the typical Morningstar career path, Christine was poised to run a business unit or to take a central role in corporate management, but she chose to follow her heart. She recognized that her first love was helping investors, so she opted to become Morningstar's in-house financial-planning expert—and she's really run with that mandate, editing our *PracticalFinance* newsletter and contributing regularly to Morningstar.com.

Christine recognizes what far too many people in financial services forget—that it's all about the individual investor. If the investor doesn't win, everyone in and around the investment process has failed, no matter how big a bonus some investment banker or bond trader may walk away with. Personal finance is about people. Helping people navigate this terrain and meet their goals is Christine's passion. You'll see that concern and the human element throughout this book, which centers on real issues faced by real investors. I truly believe that *30-Minute Money Solutions* will help you take control of your financial life and master the elemental skill of personal finance. And by doing that, you'll put your family's security and your own dreams on firmer footing, something we would all define as a winning outcome.

DON PHILLIPS
Managing Director
Morningstar, Inc.

Preface

INVESTORS ARE MOTIVATED by fear and greed, the saying goes. But I saw another emotion on display in the 2008 bear market: grief. And it played out exactly the way psychiatrist Elisabeth Kübler-Ross documented back in the late 1960s.

The first stage, denial, was widespread during the late 2007 through early 2009 downturn. Countless friends, colleagues, and Morningstar readers told me that they weren't opening their investment statements, as if not seeing their losses in black and white would make it all go away.

Others got angry (the next stage), and there were certainly plenty of targets available during the recent debacle. Choose your culprit: reckless lenders, greedy investment firms, and consumers signing up for loans that they knew they couldn't possibly afford. All had a hand in causing the worst stock market calamity since the Great Depression.

Bargaining is the next phase, and while it's less common than the other stages of the grief process, I've seen that in action, too. Many investors have told me that they're hanging on to stocks that they know are too risky for them in the hope of getting back to the price where they bought them. Another couple in their early sixties acknowledged that they have too much of their retirement kitty in stocks but they're determined to hang on. They say that they'll switch to a more age-appropriate mix just as soon as their portfolio gets back to the high point it scaled in 2007.

There have also been plenty of depressed people walking around, not just because of the stock market but because of the overall gloom surrounding the economy. Retirees have had to go back to work, adult kids have had to move in with their parents, and everyone with anything in the stock market has had to recalibrate their dreams. "I'll be working until I'm 95!" one of my friends lamented after taking a pay cut and seeing the value of her 401(k) cut in half.

Finally, there's acceptance, and I think that's where many people are today. With the economy showing signs of life and the market rebounding off its lows, most individuals have made peace with what they've lost. They're ready to get on with the business of their lives, wiser than they were before "subprime" entered the national lexicon, and determined not to get sucked into the next bubble.

At the same time, they're every bit as concerned with meeting their key financial goals—funding comfortable retirements, sending their kids to school, or buying their first homes—as they were before the crisis.

That's where this book comes in. Whether you're a newbie investor or you're trying to revitalize a portfolio that's gone through the wringer, this book is designed to help you meet your financial goals, one step at a time.

Your Get-It-Done Guide

Because you don't have an unlimited amount of time to devote to your financial affairs, *30-Minute Money Solutions* breaks down the broad, daunting goal of getting one's financial house in order into manageable, doable steps. I recognize that most individuals probably can't spend hours at a time tackling financial tasks, and even if they could, they might choose to spend that time another way. Instead, this book is designed to help you use smaller windows of time—30 minutes or an hour—to accomplish a specific financial task, check it off your list, and move on to the next one.

To many in the finance field—including, no doubt, some of my dear colleagues at Morningstar—the very idea of this book is going to seem overly simplistic. How can you possibly do justice to a complicated topic like asset allocation, to which Morningstar affiliate Ibbotson Associates has devoted years of worthwhile study, in a half hour? Surely you can't dig into an issue like selecting good international funds—a topic to which my colleagues Bill Rocco and Gregg Wolper have dedicated much of their careers—in just 30 minutes?

The short answer is that you can't. I'll be the first to acknowledge that this book won't teach you everything that you could possibly want to know about some of these topics.

That doesn't mean, though, that you can't assemble a good, sound portfolio for yourself. You don't need a PhD in finance to achieve your financial goals. You needn't be an expert on the theories behind asset allocation to arrive at a stock/bond/cash mix that's appropriate for you given your age and how long you have until you need to put your hands on that money. You don't have to know a lot about international investing to make room for a slice of foreign stocks in your portfolio and to select a worthwhile mutual fund for the job.

In fact, the more I've studied the topic of personal finance and gotten to know successful investors, the more I've become convinced that the best-laid financial plans are often the most simple. That's something of a revelation to many investors, because financial services providers and the media often work overtime to send the opposite message. Given the legions of financial firms selling their services, many investors assume that creating their own portfolios is a hopelessly complicated endeavor that they couldn't possibly tackle on their own. And minute-by-minute stock market coverage also leads investors to believe that successful investing means making frequent changes to their portfolios based on what's happening in the financial markets throughout the day.

Neither assertion is true. Instead, I firmly believe that successful investing doesn't require complex strategies or an embrace of arcane investment types. If you can get the big-picture decisions right—notably, you save enough and your portfolio is anchored in sensible investments appropriate for your time horizon—you'll be well on your way to financial success. Moreover, tuning out the market's day-to-day gyrations can help, not hinder, your chances of investment success. This book tells you what you need to know to create a simple, straightforward financial plan and how to stick with it through challenging market conditions.

Of course, saving enough and having a good plan are only part of the battle. You need to pick the right investments, too. That's where Morningstar's expertise is a particular advantage. We employ a large group of stock and mutual fund analysts, who spend each day helping our subscribers identify the best stocks and mutual funds. Throughout this book, I won't just provide financial planning guidance, but I've also harnessed our team's top investment recommendations to enable you to put your plan into action.

You may notice that I've relied on a fairly small group of investment picks for various tasks throughout this book. As the former head of Morningstar's fund analyst team and in my current role as Morningstar's director of personal finance, I found myself recommending the same handful of funds again and again. The reason? Because they're so much better than the competition. Those investment recommendations are at the heart of *30-Minute Money Solutions*, and I own many of them in my personal portfolio.

How to Use This Book

30-Minute Money Solutions includes 11 parts. Each of those parts, in turn, is subdivided into chapters that help you accomplish specific financial goals in no more than 30 minutes.

We've also provided a companion web site, www.morningstar.com/goto/30MinuteSolutions. Free and exclusive to readers of this book, the site is an electronic reference guide where you can download worksheets, use financial calculators and other planning tools, and view up-to-date lists of the best investments for various goals and roles in your portfolio. The worksheets provided in the book are for illustration purposes only and aren't meant to be written on. In some cases, the book includes the first page of a worksheet with multiple pages. On *30-Minute Money Solutions'* companion web site, you can download and print out 8.5" × 11" worksheets.

You can use this book in one of two ways. You can, of course, work your way through it from start to finish. The book begins with chapters covering relatively basic financial planning tasks, such as calculating your net worth and budgeting, and then progresses to chapters about tasks that are more sophisticated, such as investing during retirement and rebalancing your portfolio.

However, each of the chapters in this book generally stands on its own, too, so you should also feel free to pick and choose, particularly if you're pressed for time. For example, if college funding is a top priority, by all means start by digging into Part Seven, which focuses on the best strategies for saving for your child's or grandchild's education.

Those who choose to read the book from cover to cover may notice that some concepts are repeated in various spots throughout the book: How to find a stock/bond mix that makes sense for you comes up more than once, as does building yourself a cash cushion to cover emergency expenses, among others. The repetition is intentional: Those concepts underpin a number of financial planning tasks, not just one.

There's No Time Like the Present

Even under the best of circumstances, it can be hard to get motivated to complete financial tasks. That's particularly the case these days, as the recent financial crisis has shaken the faith of even the most seasoned investors. Of course, there's no telling when the market will mount a sustained rebound, and when it does it surely won't go straight up.

Nonetheless, I think that we'll look back on the current environment as one of the most opportune times to invest in a generation. I hope this book provides you with a solid foundation for a lasting and profitable financial plan.

Acknowledgments

ALTHOUGH MY NAME IS ON THE COVER, many individuals contributed to the development of this book.

"Investors First" is one of Morningstar's core tenets, and I have Morningstar founder Joe Mansueto to thank for inspiring me to write a book that helps individuals make better financial decisions.

My crack in-house editing team of Christopher Davis, Susan Dziubinski, Don Phillips, and Gregg Wolper provided invaluable feedback on the content and tone of *30-Minute Money Solutions* as well as moral support along the way. All are superb analysts and writers, and their thoughtful comments improved the content immeasurably.

Maureen Dahlen served as business and project manager for this book. Not only did she keep the project on track, but she also contributed many valuable insights on the book's contents.

Jennifer Gierat and Elizabeth Knapik copyedited *30-Minute Money Solutions*, working into the wee hours to get the manuscript into shape. Christopher Cantore, Mollie Edgar, and Meghan Tweedie did a fabulous job designing the worksheets, tables, and figures that appear in the book and on its companion web site, www.morningstar.com/goto/30MinuteSolutions, all under a tight deadline and with their usual good humor. Matthew Butz and Jun Lin brought creativity and technical know-how to bear as we developed the book's companion web site.

The book also draws on the wisdom and research of many of Morningstar's foremost investment experts, notably managing director Don Phillips, chief of securities research Haywood Kelly, president of equity research Catherine Odelbo, director of mutual fund research Russel Kinnel, and director of mutual fund analysis Karen Dolan.

In addition, I owe thanks to scores of Morningstar analysts, both past and present, especially Scott Berry, Mike Breen, Scott Cooley, Dan Culloton, Paul Herbert, Eric Jacobson, Kunal Kapoor, Dan Lefkovitz, Laura Lutton, Sonya Morris, Jeff Ptak, Bill Rocco, and Christopher Traulsen. Their work, and that of many other Morningstar fund, stock, and exchange-traded fund analysts over the years, gives me great confidence about the investment recommendations contained in this book.

My parents, Richard and Lorraine Smith, as well as my five beautiful sisters, have been an enduring source of love and encouragement for me in this and every other major endeavor I've undertaken. I feel lucky that they all are such a big part of my life.

Last but not least, I owe a huge debt of gratitude to my husband, Greg, who provided crucial feedback and kept our lives on track while I was busy writing. His unflagging support, good sense, and dry wit make every day better.

PART ONE

Find Your Baseline

JIM, ONE OF MY GOOD FRIENDS, had a deathly fear of going to the doctor, as many men do. Having enjoyed his share of beer and rare steaks, he was sure that a diagnosis of sky-high cholesterol would consign him to a life of broccoli and flaxseed. Jim also feared that bad genetics were another strike against him, as his father had encountered several serious health problems before the age of 70. Jim figured that enduring the periodic anxious thought about his health was preferable to visiting the doctor and opening a Pandora's box of health concerns.

Eventually, Jim's chronic heartburn led him to break down and schedule a doctor's appointment. Much to his surprise, Jim was in better shape than he had imagined. Yes, his doctor did recommend that he watch his fat intake, get more exercise, and cut out black coffee. But Jim's cholesterol level was within normal range, his weight was good for someone his age, and his ticker was fine. After hearing this good news, Jim was a little like Mr. Scrooge on Christmas morning. He began running 5 and 10Ks, learned to love oatmeal, and now prides himself on looking a lot younger than his 45 years.

Much like Jim, many people are so terrified about the state of their finances that they don't even want to schedule a checkup. They'd rather not know anything about their financial picture than find out that they're just a few paychecks away from financial ruin.

Yet once they get over the fear of the unknown and see the facts of their money situation laid out in black and white, many individuals find that their finances aren't nearly as bad as they had feared. And even if they do have work to do, they still feel a huge sense of relief—much like Jim did. Rather than worrying constantly that things could get worse, they can rest assured that they know what their problem areas are and are taking action to improve matters.

Finding your financial baseline, which is the focus of the chapters that follow, is a lot like giving yourself a financial checkup. Seeing where you are now—in terms of your assets and liabilities as well as your spending and savings patterns—may seem a little daunting. But it's an essential first step if you want to banish worries and get on the road to improving your finances, something this book is designed to do. I discuss how to calculate your net worth and create a cash-flow statement in Chapters 1 and 2. Chapter 3 helps you set your financial goals and prioritize them, while Chapter 4 demonstrates how to develop a budget that will help you achieve your goals.

Calculate Your Net Worth

FOR MANY PEOPLE, stepping on the scale at the doctor's office can inspire a touch of anxiety.

If you've been eating well and finding time to exercise, the weigh-in can be proof that you're on the right track. But if you've just returned from a vacation where fried shrimp and umbrella drinks were the norm, the scale lets you know you've got some work to do.

Calculating your net worth—summarizing your assets and liabilities, which is the first step in any financial plan—is a lot like stepping on the scale in your doctor's office. (I promise, this is the last time I'll bring up the doctor. But the analogy is particularly apt here.) Your net worth statement (sometimes called a personal balance sheet or statement of financial position), like the scale, provides a clear-eyed look at how well you're doing. Sometimes your net worth isn't pretty—particularly when the stock market isn't cooperating or you've been hit with unexpected expenses. But if you have been watching your expenses, saving regularly, and taken care in your investment selections, it can be pretty gratifying to see your net worth trend up from one year to the next.

Your net worth statement is only a snapshot of where your household's finances stand at a given point in time; your real net worth fluctuates every day, depending on the value of your assets. But that snapshot can go a long way toward helping you identify red flags, plot what your financial priorities should be, and make sure you're on track to reach your goals.

Your net worth statement will also serve as the foundation for other financial-planning-related activities that I discuss in this book. In Chapter 7, I walk you through how to create a master directory so that you will always be able to find important information about your assets: account numbers, passwords, contacts, and so on. Creating a net worth statement will help expedite the process of creating that directory.

Creating and maintaining a net worth statement will also help expedite the estate planning process, because taking a full inventory of your assets and liabilities is usually the first step. (In Chapter 34 you find what you need to know to get started on your estate plan.)

To create a net worth statement, you'll need:

- ▶ Net Worth Worksheet (Worksheet 1.1, available at www.morningstar.com/goto/30MinuteSolutions)
- ▶ Most recent investment statements for taxable investment accounts, retirement accounts, and college savings plans
- ▶ Most recent checking and savings account statements
- ▶ An estimate of the current market value of your home(s). (Be realistic! Unfortunately, homes aren't worth what they were three years ago.)
- ▶ An estimate of the current market value of other assets, including cars, jewelry, artwork, and so on
- ▶ Life insurance policy face values
- ▶ Most recent credit card statement(s), if you have a balance on your account(s)
- ▶ Most recent mortgage and home equity loan statements
- ▶ Most recent statements from any other debts you owe, such as student or auto loans

Start the Clock

Step 1

To create your net worth statement, fill out the information on the Net Worth Worksheet (Worksheet 1.1), available at www.morningstar.com/goto/

Worksheet 1.1

Net Worth Worksheet

PREPARED FOR: _____   DATE: /   /

Find out how much your assets are worth in total by filling out this worksheet. List assets by ownership.

You'll Need:

- Most recent investment statements for taxable accounts, retirement accounts, and college savings plans
- Most recent checking and savings account statements
- An estimate of the current market value of your home(s). (Be realistic! Unfortunately, it's not worth what it was three years ago.)
- An estimate of the current market value of other assets, including cars, jewelry, artwork, etc.
- Life insurance policy face values
- Most recent credit card statement(s), if you have a balance on your account
- Most recent mortgage and home equity loan statements
- Most recent statements from any other debts you owe, such as student or auto loans

NET WORTH: ASSETS

Taxable Accounts:	You	Spouse	Joint	Total
Checking				
Savings				
Credit union				
Money markets				
CDs				
Mutual funds				
Stocks				
Bonds				
Stock options (vested)				
Other				

Retirement Accounts:	You	Spouse	Joint	Total
Annuities				
Traditional IRAs				
Roth IRAs				
401(k), 403(b), 457				
Other				

Print your worksheet at: www.morningstar.com/goto/30MinuteSolutions

30MinuteSolutions. Remember, you're filling in the current market value of your assets, not your purchase price (and not as nice as those memories may be, what the assets were worth at their peak). If you're part of a couple and you and your spouse hold some assets jointly and some separately, note who owns what—and the current value—on the form.

In some cases, like publicly traded securities such as stocks and mutual funds, you'll be able to get a very current, very specific read on what they're worth—for example, if you own 1,000 shares of Microsoft MSFT and the stock closed at $23.45 today, your shares are worth $23,450. For other, less-liquid assets (that is, those that don't trade all the time, such as real estate and automobiles), arriving at their value is more art than science. Web sites like zillow.com can help you make an educated guess about the value of your real estate, while Kelley Blue Book's web site (www.kbb.com) helps you estimate the value of your automobile.

You'll notice that I've included a line for personal assets. Don't get carried away totaling up the value of every pillowcase and pair of shoes that you own. But if you do have other assets of worth, such as artwork or expensive furniture, you can estimate their fair market values and record them here.

Step 2
Next, record your outstanding debts. As with your list of assets, married couples should indicate which spouse owes what (unless the debt is in both people's names).

Step 3
Once you're finished recording your assets and liabilities, total up each column and subtract the smaller sum from the larger one. That amount is your net worth, which you can then track in subsequent years.

Step 4
Now it's time for some analysis. Start by focusing on your bottom line.

- Is your net worth negative or barely positive? If so, you've got work to do; I discuss how to set up a budget in Chapter 4.
- Even if your net worth is positive, spend some time scrutinizing the underlying numbers. Check to see whether a big share of your net worth

is tied up in a single asset or two, such as your house or stock issued by your employer. Of course, homes are the largest asset for many households, and there's nothing inherently wrong with that. But it does mean that your future savings should go toward building up your investment assets.

Step 5

Next, check out whether your cash cushion is sufficient. By cash cushion, I mean any money you have stashed in safe, liquid securities such as CDs, money market funds, and checking and savings accounts. The right amount to hold in these investments will vary depending on your circumstances.

▶ If you're already retired and relying on your own assets to cover your living expenses, strive to keep two to five years' worth of living expenses in safe, highly liquid vehicles. If you're retired and relying on other sources of income, such as a pension, to fund your day-to-day expenses, your cash cushion can be at the low end of this range.

▶ If you're still working, you, too, should maintain a cash cushion so that you can get by in case of a financial emergency like a big home repair or the loss of a job. The usual rule of thumb is that you should have three to six months' worth of living expenses in your emergency fund, but I think that figure may be too low for many individuals. If you have any reason to be nervous about your job security (and these days, that's just about everyone) or you're a higher-income earner, plan to save closer to a year's worth of living expenses. I show you how to create an emergency fund, and recommend what to put in it, in Chapter 10.

Next Steps

▶ Financial decision making isn't always rational. (The whole field of what's called *behavioral finance*, in fact, addresses how investors often make decisions that aren't in their best interests when deciding what to buy and sell and when.) Combat that tendency by thinking about allocating your own financial capital just as a good businessperson would: You scout around for the best use of your assets at that particular point in time.

As with a businessperson assessing the company balance sheet, your net worth statement can provide you with important direction in allocating your capital and can help alert you to potential problem spots. In

Chapters 8 and 9 I coach you on taking a logical approach to deploying your hard-earned money.

Don't worry, you won't be reduced to a robot—you'll allocate some capital to fun and allow room for the inevitable so-called irrational purchase. The point is that by making the effort to understand your overall financial position, you'll be able to do these more enjoyable things while still being confident that you're in good financial shape.

▶ Assessing your net worth periodically—I recommend doing so once a year—can also provide a window into trends in your financial picture and whether you're on track to meet your goals. Of course, it's better to see your assets outweigh your liabilities no matter what your life stage or age, but that's particularly true as you get older. You'll want to see your financial assets trending up and eventually far outweighing your liabilities. The reason is pretty straightforward and intuitive. As humans, we come into this world with a lot of what my colleagues at Ibbotson Associates call human capital—essentially, our own earning power, or ability to earn and create financial capital, or assets. But as we age and near retirement, our human capital diminishes and we need to rely more on our financial capital to meet our daily living expenses.

2

See Where Your Money Goes

While balancing the family checkbook one day, one of my friends looked at her husband and said, "We're broke." Their baby daughter, sitting on the floor and soaking up every new word like a sponge, repeated: "We're broke." The one-year-old said it over and over—"Broke broke broke broke"—until my friend and her husband dissolved into laughter.

Unfortunately, assessing your household's inflows and outflows won't always be as lighthearted, and you may need to adjust your lifestyle to create a healthier pattern. (Thankfully, my friend's financial pickle was short-lived, and her daughter picked up a new word.) But checking up on where your money goes over a specific period of time—often referred to as creating a personal cash-flow statement—is an essential step when creating a financial plan. Your personal cash-flow statement can help you spot trends in how you're spending your money and whether you're saving enough, make sure your spending is aligned with your priorities, and develop a budget.

Whereas your net worth statement (Chapter 1) summarizes the assets and liabilities that you've accumulated to date, your cash-flow statement captures how you use your money on an ongoing basis. The cash-flow statement shows you what cash comes into your household—through the income from your job and other sources—and what money you're spending or saving.

You can create a cash-flow statement for one month, one year, or any other period you like. Many financial planners use a one-year period, because longer-term cash-flow patterns can smooth out "lumpy" spending that can occur from month to month. However, unless you've been tracking each and every expenditure you've made over the past year, it may be more realistic to create a cash-flow statement for a one-month period. (You can use the Personal Cash-Flow Statement Worksheet, available at www.morningstar.com/goto/30MinuteSolutions, for either time period.)

To create your personal cash-flow statement, you'll need:

▶ Personal Cash-Flow Statement Worksheet (Worksheet 2.1), available at www.morningstar.com/goto/30MinuteSolutions

▶ Most recent paycheck. (If your salary is variable, because you're self-employed or work on a commission basis, use an average of your pay over the past 6 to 12 months.)

▶ Statements showing income from other sources, such as pensions, Social Security, or savings/investment interest

▶ Most recent bank and investment statements

▶ Most recent credit card statement(s)

▶ Statements for other debts, such as student or auto loans

▶ A record of your discretionary expenditures over the past month

Start the Clock

Step 1

Start by recording your income on the Personal Cash-Flow Statement Worksheet (Worksheet 2.1), available at www.morningstar.com/goto/30MinuteSolutions. For most of you, your monthly income is pretty easy to quantify; it's your net income from your job, plus income you receive from other sources, such as investment interest or Social Security.

Step 2

Next, use the worksheet to record your fixed expenses, such as your mortgage or rent payments and utility bills.

Worksheet 2.1

Personal Cash-Flow Statement

PREPARED FOR: DATE: /   /

You'll Need:
- Most recent paycheck. (If your salary is variable, because you're self-employed or work on a commission basis, use an average of your pay over the past 6–12 months.)
- Statements showing income from income sources, such as pensions, Social Security, or savings/investment interest
- Most recent bank and investment statements
- Most recent credit card statement(s)
- Statements for other debts, such as student or auto loans
- Most recent checking and savings account statements
- A record of your discretionary expenditures over the past month

INCOME: MONTHLY AMOUNT

Salary (net: after taxes and benefits)	
Spouse's salary (net: after taxes and benefits)	
Pension income	
Social Security income	
Interest/investment income	
Other income (specify)	
Other income (specify)	
Other income (specify)	
TOTAL: Monthly Income Amount	

EXPENSES: MONTHLY AMOUNT

Fixed:	
Mortgage or rent	
Other real estate payments (taxes, assessments, etc.)	
Auto loan	
Student loan	
Credit card payment	
Utilities	
Tuition	
Child care	
Food	
Clothing	
Other expenses (specify)	
Other expenses (specify)	
Other expenses (specify)	
Other expenses (specify)	

Print your worksheet at: www.morningstar.com/goto/30MinuteSolutions

Step 3

Now move on to discretionary expenses. These outlays, clothing, chai lattes, and movie rentals, can complicate matters. Unless you track your expenses on an ongoing basis using a service like Quicken or charge nearly everything on your credit card, you simply won't have the same paper trail that you will for your fixed expenses.

Say you've tried to total your discretionary expenses over the past month and find that you have a large category of "miscellaneous"—money you've spent that's unaccounted for. If that's the case, keep track of your discretionary expenses over the next month. (You may find that having to write every expense down has the positive side effect of deterring you from spending money on things you don't really need.)

Also document your monthly savings and investments in this area, apart from any company retirement plan contributions that are currently being deducted from your paycheck. Your investment and bank statements should also provide you with a clear view of what you've been able to save or invest over the past month.

Step 4

Subtract your expenses from your income to arrive at your monthly cash-flow surplus (if it's a positive number) or deficit.

Step 5

Analyze your cash-flow statement to see if you're in positive territory. If you're landing in the red, Chapter 4 can help you set up a budget.

If you're in the black, pat yourself on the back and check to see if you're saving and investing enough. Total up monthly contributions to your company retirement plan as well as contributions to other accounts.

The right amount will depend on your income: As you earn more, you should also be able to sock more away. But as a very general rule of thumb, you should be saving a *minimum* of 10 percent of your income if you're still working, and preferably much more than that. (In Chapter 4 I discuss how to increase your savings rate by creating a budget; a cash-flow statement is the ideal way to start that process.)

Step 6

Finally, assess whether your borrowing levels are within reasonable ranges. Of course, what's "reasonable" is completely subjective. Loan officers look for monthly housing costs to be less than 28 percent of the borrower's pretax income and total monthly payments on all debts to be less than 36 percent of pretax income. (Be careful: You'll use your aftertax income for your cash-flow statement, but these ratios use pretax income to help determine whether your debt load is manageable.) Your debt-servicing expenses should fall well under these ranges; if they don't, that's a red flag that your current lifestyle could be unsustainable.

Next Steps

▶ Almost everyone who creates a personal cash-flow statement sees a surprise or two when all of their discretionary expenses are grouped together and laid out in black and white. You might be perfectly comfortable with some of these expenses; for example, you pay your dog walker the princely sum of $320 a month, but you would feel terrible if Daisy didn't get her daily walk while you're at work. However, you may find other expenses excessive or even altogether unnecessary. The process of creating a budget (Chapter 4) helps you bring your priorities and your spending into sync with one another.

▶ If you're saving and investing in some months and not others, one way to add some discipline to the process is to put your investments on autopilot. Most mutual fund companies and investment supermarkets allow you to set up a plan whereby you invest a fixed amount each month, so the money comes right out of your checking account and gets deployed into the investments of your choice. Establishing such a program, usually called an automatic investment plan, is similar to how a 401(k) plan works. Because you never put your hands on that money, it helps ensure that you keep investing in a variety of market environments, which is a recipe for successful investment results. Part Four has many more tips for getting started in investing.

3
———

Set Your Financial Goals

WHEN MY HUSBAND AND I started to think about remodeling our octogenarian home a few years ago, our heads were filled with HGTV-fueled visions of what we could accomplish. A steam shower in our bathroom to create a spa-like experience at home. A beverage bar in our home office to satisfy the occasional urge for an espresso without having to trek the whole 12 feet into the kitchen. Radiant-heat flooring in numerous spots to ensure warm tootsies year-round.

The first builder's bid hit our e-mail box with a thud, however, followed by another and another. Much to our chagrin, outfitting our old house with every bell and whistle that we had dreamed of was going to cost much more than we had originally budgeted for the renovations. Meanwhile, the real estate market was sinking like a stone, making it less and less likely that we'd ever see a decent return on our copious upgrades.

Our choices were twofold. We could either plow ahead with everything that we wanted, budget and sinking housing market be damned, or we could get real and scale back the project.

We decided to do the latter and went back to the drawing board. Renovating our circa 1972 kitchen was on both of our "must-do" lists, as was improving our bathrooms (adios faux oak vanities!). Some of the other improvements that we had envisioned, however, easily fell into the category of "nice to have" rather than "must-do." We might consider them again some day, but for now we will concentrate on the improvements that will have the most impact on our daily lives.

You need to take a similar approach when setting your financial goals. It's fine to start by dreaming big: a lovely home and maybe even a vacation home, top colleges for the kids and grandkids, a comfortable retirement, lots of travel, and so on.

From there, however, it's important to look at what those goals will actually cost you—not just in today's dollars but in real, inflation-adjusted greenbacks. If it looks like you won't be able to achieve them all (and that's a reality for most of us), you'll have to make choices. Through this process, you may decide that spending on a near-term goal, such as a new car or a bigger home, isn't worth giving the kids' college funds short shrift.

Specifying your financial goals has another beneficial side effect. By quantifying your goals, you anchor them in reality. It's easy to say, "I know that I want to retire when I'm young enough to enjoy all that free time." But if you take the next step and look at what an early retirement will actually cost you, you may find out that it's just not practical. Knowing the real costs of a big goal like retirement may also prompt you to pause before spending on wants rather than real necessities.

To set your financial goals, you'll need:

▶ Goal Planning Worksheet (Worksheet 3.1, available at www.morningstar. com/goto/30MinuteSolutions)
▶ Net Worth Worksheet from Chapter 1 (optional; available at www. morningstar.com/goto/30MinuteSolutions)
▶ Personal Cash-Flow Statement Worksheet 2.1 from Chapter 2 (optional; available at www.morningstar.com/goto/30MinuteSolutions)

Start the Clock
Step 1

Using the Goal Planning Worksheet (Worksheet 3.1), write down your short-, intermediate-, and long-term goals. Don't censor yourself: Include goals that

Worksheet 3.1

Goal Planning Worksheet

PREPARED FOR: _____   DATE: _____ / _____ / _____

You'll Need:
- Net Worth Worksheet (Worksheet 1.1), if completed
- Personal Cash-Flow Statement (Worksheet 2.1), if completed

Calculators:
To estimate future costs for retirement, college, and other financial goals, go to: www.morningstar.com/goto/30MinuteSolutions

GOAL: SHORT-TERM (5 years or fewer)

Goal Priority:

Goal _____

Date	Duration	Expected Cost($)	

Goal Priority:

Goal _____

Date	Duration	Expected Cost($)	

Goal Priority:

Goal _____

Date	Duration	Expected Cost($)	

Goal Priority:

Goal _____

Date	Duration	Expected Cost($)	

Goal Priority:

Goal _____

Date	Duration	Expected Cost($)	

Goal Priority:

Goal _____

Date	Duration	Expected Cost($)	

Goal Priority:

Goal _____

Date	Duration	Expected Cost($)	

Goal Priority:

Goal _____

Date	Duration	Expected Cost($)	

TOTAL: Short-Term Goals

Print your worksheet at: www.morningstar.com/goto/30MinuteSolutions

you are likely to achieve as well as those you're dreaming of. Also factor in paying off your mortgage as well as getting rid of more nefarious types of debt such as credit card bills.

Group your goals into one of three bands based on time horizon: goals you'd like to achieve in 5 years or fewer, goals you'd like to achieve in the next 5 to 15 years, and goals you'd like to achieve in 15 years or more. Your age, and the ages of your children, will determine your time horizon for some of your goals. For example, if funding your child's education is on the list and your child is 11 now, you can put that savings goal in the 5- to 15-year bucket. Indicate the year in which you'd like to achieve it.

If it's a goal that you will pay for over a number of years, such as retirement or college, indicate the year in which you'd need to begin tapping your assets to fund the goal, and also fill out the Duration field. Of course, when it comes to retirement, filling out this field means quantifying your own longevity. That's tricky, but the actuarial tables on the Social Security Administration's web site can help you arrive at a reasonable estimate: www.ssa.gov/OACT/STATS/table4c6.html. From there, I think it's helpful to be optimistic and assume even greater longevity: Add at least a few years. Also factor in your family history: If most of your relatives lived to be 90, that increases the chance that you will, too.

Be as granular as you can be: For example, if you have three children who will start college in three different years, make three separate entries. If you'd like to make a down payment on a house in the next two years and have it paid for by the time you retire in 2045, include those as two separate goals: amassing the down payment and paying it off.

Step 2

Next, prioritize your goals by numbering them in the left-hand column on the Goal Planning Worksheet. If you've completed the worksheets in Chapters 1 and 2, the data you've gathered can help in this process. For example, if you have a lot of debt that's holding you back from saving for other goals, reducing or eliminating that debt should be at the top of your list of financial priorities. It's also essential that you plan to have an emergency fund if you don't already have one—6 to 12 months' worth of living expenses in a highly liquid account such as a savings account or money market fund. (Creating an emergency fund and finding the right investments for it is the focus of Chapter 10.) You'll also want to set a goal for when you hope to have your mortgage paid off. If you're in your fifties and your retirement nest egg has shrunk substantially in the recent bear market, a key goal for you will be to bulk up your savings.

Step 3

The next step is to quantify how much your goals will cost. Start by writing down the expected cost of your financial goals that are close at hand. This should be pretty straightforward: If you aim to amass a 20 percent down payment for a home that will cost $250,000 in two years, your goal is $50,000 in 2012.

Unfortunately, quantifying most goals isn't as simple. Inflation ebbs and flows but almost always goes up over long periods of time. The net result is that something that costs $50,000 today is almost sure to cost substantially more 20 years from now.

If you have a financial goal that's more than a year or two away, it's important to adjust the cost upward to reflect what you'll actually pay once inflation is factored in. That gets even more complicated for goals that you expect to fund over several years, such as retirement or college.

To help simplify the task, the 30-Minute Money Solutions web site (www.morningstar.com/goto/30MinuteSolutions) includes several different inflation calculators to help you quantify the cost, in real dollars, of retirement, college, and other goals.

Next Steps

► Most households wrestle with whether to prioritize paying off debt or investing in the market. Chapter 8 helps anchor your decision making by looking at which use of your money gives you the greatest bang for your buck. Individuals often have a tough time prioritizing retirement savings over college savings. In almost every situation, however, funding your retirement should take precedence over college savings. As the saying goes, your child can get a loan to pay for college, but no one will give you a loan to pay for retirement.

▶ If you're part of a couple, it's important that you're both involved in the process of financial goal setting. You can complete the worksheet together or identify goals separately and then compare notes.

4
_____

Create a Budget

IN MID-2009, I received an e-mail from a couple seeking a portfolio makeover in my newsletter, *Morningstar PracticalFinance*. They were in their mid-fifties, and they had seen their investment portfolio shrink by nearly half during the bear market of 2008. That, in turn, had scuttled their hopes for retirement in less than a decade, and they were wondering how they could make up the lost ground.

This couple's investment portfolio, with more than 80 percent in stocks, was clearly too aggressive given their life stage. In talking with them about their finances, however, I discovered that their investments weren't their main problem. Their spending was.

The couple had scrimped and saved to buy a carpet-cleaning business in the early 1990s and went through some lean years while they were building up their clientele. Thanks to their sacrifices and hard work, the business was generating more than $200,000 in take-home income for them per year.

As is so often the case, however, this couple's spending went up right along with their pay, and their savings slowed to a trickle. They bought a bigger home, took regular trips to Las Vegas, and were in the habit of spending money on nearly anything they wanted, from flat-screen TVs to catered family parties.

When I asked them if they had a budget, they said that they once had. While they were buying and building up their business, they even lived in a two-bedroom apartment with their two children. But after their income had increased to a more comfortable level, they didn't see as much need for budgeting and eventually stopped tracking their expenses altogether. When they tried to look back on what they had spent over the past month, more than $1,500 was unaccounted for. I pointed out that if they were to save that amount each month rather than spend it on stuff that they couldn't remember, that would do far more to get their portfolio back on track than selecting the right investments ever could.

Because we all have a natural tendency to spend what we have, everyone needs a budget, regardless of age, life stage, or whether we think we've "made it" or not. The key point about a budget is that it helps ensure that your spending syncs up with your priorities. This couple wanted to balance their here-and-now goals of travel and fun with their long-term goals of funding a comfortable retirement and perhaps leaving a legacy for their children.

Below, I've detailed a 30-minute approach to budgeting, but there are whole books, plus web sites and software packages devoted to this topic. If your Net Worth Worksheet (Worksheet 1.1) and Personal Cash-Flow Statement (Worksheet 2.1) showed that you're bleeding red ink, it's worth devoting a fair amount of time and attention to creating and staying on a budget.

To establish a budget, you'll need:

- ▶ Budget Worksheet (Worksheet 4.1, available at www.morningstar.com/goto/30MinuteSolutions)
- ▶ A record of your monthly income and expenses. If you completed the Personal Cash-Flow Statement (Worksheet 2.1, available at www.morning star.com/goto/30MinuteSolutions), you'll already have compiled this information
- ▶ A list of your goals, along with when you hope to achieve them and how much they'll cost. (Chapter 3 helps you prioritize and quantify your goals.)

Worksheet 4.1

Budget Worksheet

PREPARED FOR: DATE: /   /

You'll Need:
- A record of your monthly income and expenses
- A list of your goals, along with when you hope to achieve them and how much they'll cost

INCOME: MONTHLY AMOUNT

Salary (net: after taxes and benefits)	
Spouse's salary (net: after taxes and benefits)	
Pension income	
Social Security income	
Interest/investment income	
Other income (specify)	
Other income (specify)	
Other income (specify)	
TOTAL: Monthly Income Amount	

EXPENSES: MONTHLY AMOUNT

Fixed:	Spent	Budget
Mortgage or rent		
Other real estate payments (taxes, assessments, etc.)		
Auto loan		
Student loan		
Credit card payment		
Utilities		
Tuition		
Child care		
Food		
Clothing		
Insurance		
Other expenses (specify)		
Other expenses (specify)		
Other expenses (specify)		

Print your worksheet at: www.morningstar.com/goto/30MinuteSolutions

Start the Clock

Step 1

Enter your current fixed and variable expenses, as well as information about your sources of income, on the Budget Worksheet (Worksheet 4.1, available at www.morningstar.com/goto/30MinuteSolutions). For expenses and income sources that don't fit neatly into the categories provided, use the "other" lines. If you have several expenses of a given type, make a note alongside the line item—for example, "DVD Rentals" or "Toiletries/Makeup."

Also record any savings that you're typically able to set aside each month.

Step 2

Start the budgeting process by scrutinizing your variable (or discretionary) expenses over the past month(s). Because you have the most control over this set of costs, making adjustments here is the fastest way to improve your household's financial picture.

Be forward looking as you evaluate your variable expenses. The data you've supplied about your income and spending provides a snapshot of the money you have coming in and going out. But your budget gives you a chance to shape your spending to fit with your goals, both personal and financial. For example, you may have spent a lot on carryout and restaurant meals over the past month. But if getting in shape is on your list of personal priorities, you can tweak your budget to reduce your spending on restaurant meals and increase the dollars that you're allocating toward food from the grocery store so you can prepare healthy meals at home.

As you go through the process of evaluating your variable expenses, it's also essential to be realistic. Just as dieters can't stick with the plan if it doesn't allow for the occasional piece of birthday cake or glass of wine, it's also unrealistic to plot out a budget with no room for the occasional movie or lunch with friends. Using your real past expenses as a template for your budget helps anchor you in reality, not a pipe dream.

If you anticipate expenses that are predictable but not necessarily monthly—such as holiday and birthday gifts—it's a good idea to distribute those costs throughout the year. Look back on the past year's worth of gift giving, estimate your expenditures, and adjust downward or upward as you see fit. Then divide by 12 to arrive at your monthly budgeted amount.

Record your target expenditures for each line item in the Budget column on the Budget Worksheet.

Step 3

Next turn your attention to your fixed expenses on the Budget Worksheet. Although household necessities are usually referred to as fixed costs, that's a bit of a misnomer. Yes, these items are necessities, but you may be able to adjust them somewhat. Among the areas where it's possible to reduce your fixed costs are:

- ▶ Food
- ▶ Clothing
- ▶ Credit card interest rates (sometimes, but not always, negotiable)
- ▶ Mortgage payments (if refinancing is an option)
- ▶ Telecom services such as landline phones, cellular phones, Internet service, and cable TV/satellite. (You may be able to change providers or negotiate a lower rate with your current provider, especially if you're purchasing more than one service.)

Take note of the areas where you may be able to reduce your fixed costs and plan to follow up on them. If you are able to obtain reductions in these areas, adjust your budget accordingly.

Step 4

As you tweak your target expenditures, pay attention to how the changes affect your bottom line. Your goal should be not only to balance your household budget but also increase the amount you have earmarked for saving and investing each month.

Step 5

Finally, put in place a plan to check your real-life spending versus your budget on an ongoing basis. One of the key mistakes that people make when budgeting is that they create a budget and then put it in the drawer.

Start by finding a place to record your household's expenses. Software programs like Quicken can help you track your expenses, but you can also track them with a pen and paper. Be sure to ask your spouse to do the same.

Next, block out time on your calendar each month (ideally, one hour per month over the next three to six months) to check up on your actual expenses versus your budget. If your first budget assumptions were unrealistic or if something material has changed in your household's financial picture, adjust your budget accordingly.

Next Steps

▶ If you're looking to implement a budget right away, it's best to concentrate your energies on reducing your variable costs, which are easier to adjust, rather than trying to cut fixed costs such as your mortgage. However, the process of evaluating your net worth (Chapter 1), creating a cash-flow statement (Chapter 2), and budgeting may have revealed that reducing your variable costs won't be enough to move the needle. In the case of the couple I mentioned earlier in this chapter, for example, it was clear to me that their housing costs were much higher than they needed to be, given that their children were all grown and out of the house. They didn't have to move right away, but I recommended that they consider downsizing to a smaller home, thereby reducing their monthly fixed outlay.

▶ Don't worry about budgeting for expenses that are truly unknowable in advance, such as medical bills or big home or car repairs. By creating an emergency fund (Chapter 10), you'll create a cushion that will allow you to pay these bills without throwing your budget out of whack.

PART TWO

Get Organized

AMID THE FINANCIAL CRISIS THAT BEGAN IN 2007, pundits have pondered the many factors that contributed to American consumers letting their finances get so far out of whack. Some conjectured that Americans have an emptiness in their lives that led them to seek solace in stuff: ever-larger houses, expensive cars, storage lockers full of possessions that they didn't really need. Others chalked it up to our culture's emphasis on immediate gratification: Buy it today and worry about paying for it later.

But one factor has gone completely unheralded, maybe because it's so mundane: paperwork. As anyone who has ever closed on a home loan or tried to read investment statements knows, the financial services industry cranks out a voluminous amount of paper. Some of it is boilerplate legalese that you don't really need, while other forms and statements are more important but inscrutable if you're not steeped in the business. The net result is that many people tend to ignore their financial statements altogether, thereby losing track of their monthly inflows and outflows.

By contrast, if you know what to focus on and what to tune out, and manage your financial documents as you receive them, you'll be forced to reckon with how much you have in assets and how much you owe. You will thus have a better sense of your household's cash flows and balance sheet, as well as where any potential trouble spots might lurk.

There are other concrete reasons to keep your financial documents in order. It's a given that you'll have to put your hands on some of these papers in the future—to file your taxes or an insurance claim, for example—so it makes good sense to keep them in a logical and readily accessible location. It's also essential that your heirs be able to locate your important financial documents.

Of course, with any self-improvement project, the chasm separating reason and action can seem as wide as the Grand Canyon. When it comes to getting your financial house in order, however, you can take a few easy steps that will get you well on your way to becoming truly organized. That's the focus of this section.

First, create a system for paying your bills on time. Whether you opt for online banking or decide to keep it old school, I walk you through a logical system for bill-paying in Chapter 5.

Chapter 6 focuses on which financial documents you need to keep and which you can safely toss. The good news is that, thanks to technology, you don't need to save nearly as many financial papers as you once did, because you can readily retrieve much of what you need by going online or by scanning important documents and saving them on your computer. But you do need to have a system for the items you keep, and I'll help you create one.

Finally, the linchpin of an organized financial household is a document that amalgamates key information about each of your accounts. In Chapter 7, I show you how to create such a document and keep this sensitive information safe.

5

Create a Bill-Paying System

DURING THE RECENT FINANCIAL CRISIS, I worked with a local television channel to provide on-air financial coaching for families who needed it. In the course of that project, I counseled a thirty-something couple who, in most important ways, had it all together: two good jobs, two beautiful young daughters, a great extended family support system, and a condo in a desirable neighborhood of Chicago.

They needed help, though, with the details. Although they were comfortable, not rich, they routinely dropped several hundred dollars a week on restaurant and carryout meals, and they were paying for two health club memberships that they didn't use. They also admitted to having a hard time keeping track of their bills, sometimes incurring late fees for not paying on time. Their lack of attention to details was hindering their ability to get ahead financially, despite the fact that they earned two good paychecks.

Curbing a tendency to overspend can be tough, particularly when habits such as the daily latte are so ingrained. At the end of our meeting, I walked away not completely sure that this couple would implement most of the spending cutbacks I recommended.

But I hope that I got through to them on the subject of paying their bills on time, because doing so would arguably have just as big an impact on their financial well-being as reducing their spending. Although the $15 late charge on their Sears credit card seemed innocuous to them and was a drop in the bucket relative to their monthly outlay, repeated late charges, along with any interest charges they might rack up, could add up to some serious money and would begin affecting their credit rating. That, in turn, could seriously impair their ability to borrow money at a favorable rate in the future, and if things got really bad it could also affect their ability to land new jobs. (Many employers conduct credit checks on prospective employees.)

I urged them to investigate online banking, either through their bank or through an outside service like Quicken, and I recommend that avenue for all those trying to simplify their financial lives. (Just to clarify: To conduct online banking, you don't need to deal with an online-only bank. Most banks with bricks-and-mortar offices now extend online banking services to their customers.)

If you're busy and want to make sure your bills never slip through the cracks, banking online can help you put recurring bills on autopilot; it can also be a great time-saver. Online banking can also be a money-saver: At many banks, you'll pay lower (or no) fees for managing your business online than you will if you're writing physical checks. The fact that you're not dealing with the mail can also help ensure that your creditors receive your payments on time. Finally, online banking and bill paying help reduce the chances of identity theft, presuming that you've set up a solid online security system. For all these reasons, online banking is a great choice for bill paying.

Whether you use online banking or write physical checks to pay your bills, as this couple did, it's important to set up a system to make sure that you pay them on time.

To create a bill-paying system, you'll need:

► A calendar, either electronic or paper, that you check frequently

 Start the Clock—For Online Bill Paying

Step 1

If you decide to set up an online bill-paying system, your first step is to verify that your computer's security system is up-to-date, including firewalls, antivirus software, and spyware. If you haven't downloaded an update for this software for some time, it's probably time to do so. Also make sure you have downloaded the latest version of your web browser, as it will include the most current encryption technology to ensure the safety of your data.

Step 2

Next, decide what type of online bill-paying system you'd like to use. You can work directly with each separate utility or credit card company to have the payment extracted from your account, but that's cumbersome. A better choice is to contact your bank to find out if it offers online banking (most do at this point) or to use a third-party vendor such as Quicken.

Quicken and other bill-paying software packages offer some nice personal-accounting features that help you keep track of your expenses and see your accounts aggregated together, but there's usually a monthly charge associated with those packages. Online bill paying, on the other hand, is apt to be free through your bank. (Some of the big banks offer the best of both worlds: free online banking that harnesses Quicken's features.)

Step 3

After that, go online to set up your online banking system or call your bank to determine how to proceed. You'll have to set a password to log on in the future; use a combination of numbers and letters to help prevent identity theft. Once you're set up with an online banking system, you can take advantage of the various features available, including automating the payment of recurring bills. (These features vary by bank.)

Start the Clock—For Paying Bills the Old-Fashioned Way

Step 1

If you opt for pen-and-paper bill paying—or if you're primarily using online banking but have to pay the periodic bill the old-fashioned way—set up a system to ensure that you're paying on time but not too early. Paying your bills as soon as you receive them is a surefire way to avoid late fees and keep your credit record in tiptop shape, but it also means that you'll be giving the credit card company or utility free use of your money up until the time when your bill is officially due.

The most straightforward way to keep track of your bills is to log incoming bills on a calendar, either print or electronic. Plan to mail upcoming bills at least seven days before their due dates. Mark the due date, as well as the recipient's name, on the calendar on that date; you can also include the amount. Then write the mail date on the outside of the envelope. Store all bills to be paid in a single spot within your house or home office; make sure your spouse knows the system and is putting bills there, too. Once a week, check your calendar and bill holder for the bills that need to be paid in the week ahead.

Step 2

In addition to setting up a system for paying your bills in a timely fashion, you also need to have a system for dealing with your bills after you've paid them. If the bill is related to your tax return—for example, it's your mortgage statement or a utility bill for the home office that you write off on your taxes—be sure to save it in a file.

After you've paid bills unrelated to your tax return, err on the side of caution and shred anything that has identifying information on it. Chapter 6 includes details about which financial paperwork to save and which you should shred.

Next Steps

▶ Limiting the number of credit cards in your household not only reduces the chances that you'll spend more than you can afford and rack up interest charges, but it also has beneficial side effects. It lowers the number of bills that you have to contend with, can help improve your credit rating, and reduces your vulnerability to identity theft. One or two credit cards per person are sufficient to establish and maintain credit.

▶ Online bill paying is generally preferable to snail mail, for the reasons I outlined above. Because you're not writing physical checks, though, you may lose that tangible sense of where your money is going. To help you keep track, many online bill-paying systems group your expenses into categories; you can then compare your actual spending within each of these categories with the amount that you had budgeted.

6

Create a Filing System

ONE OF MY LONGTIME COWORKERS IS, without a doubt, the most organized person I've ever known. With the exception of a couple of snapshots of her kids, her desk is so clean and clutter-free that it might as well belong to an intern. And while many of us shipped several huge boxes of documents to Morningstar's new office when we moved last December, Bridget sent just a few.

So, what's her secret? Like all truly organized people, she never has to put "get organized" on her to-do list. When it comes to paperwork, she deals with it as soon as she puts her hands on it rather than setting it in a "deal with this later" pile. She either takes action with the item—by reading it or forwarding it—files it, or recycles or shreds it. That's precisely the strategy that you should use to stay on top of your financial paperwork.

Technology can be your friend when it comes to reducing clutter and staying organized. Most financial services providers will give you the option to receive your statements electronically; not only is that the green alternative, but it also reduces the amount of paper that you'll have to deal with. (I discussed online bill paying in Chapter 5.) And for those documents that you'd like to save, you can scan them and store them on your computer rather than having to find a home for a piece of paper. As we all become more comfortable with technology, I expect that households will save less and less financial paperwork.

The specific system you use for organizing your financial paperwork is a matter of personal preference. What's crucial, though, is that you store truly important documents in a safe place, such as a safe-deposit box at your bank or a fireproof box that you keep in your home. You'll also want to set up some storage at home, either physical or electronic, to keep other documents, such as financial statements related to the current tax year. Finally, you need to destroy sensitive documents and make sure that someone other than you is able to locate your important documents in a pinch. (In Chapter 7 I discuss how to create a master directory of your financial assets.)

You'll find that there's a lot of conflicting advice on what to save, toss/recycle, and shred. If you needed to, you could very likely find duplicates for some of the items that I've suggested you save at home or in your safe-deposit box. I have tended to err on the side of caution with my advice.

To create a filing system, you'll need:

- ▶ A shredder
- ▶ A filing cabinet or file box
- ▶ File folders and file labels (accordion-type files work well for large files)
- ▶ A safe-deposit box at your local bank and/or in-home fireproof box

 Start the Clock
Step 1

Print out the "Save, Shred, or Recycle?" guidelines (Worksheet 6.1) and refer to them frequently as you deal with the paperwork in your home office.

Step 2

Create files (either physical or electronic) for your in-home storage. You can also create subfolders within these files. Just be careful not to create so many individual files that you begin questioning where something is stored. The following categories will make sense for most households.

- ▶ Home (can include home repair/upgrade receipts, property tax bills, and so on)

Worksheet 6.1

Save, Shred, or Recycle?

PREPARED FOR: _____   DATE: _____ / _____ / _____

You'll Need:
- A shredder
- A filing cabinet or file box
- File folders and file labels (accordion-type files work well for large files)
- A safe-deposit box at your local bank or in-home fireproof box

SAVE: IN YOUR SAFE-DEPOSIT BOX OR IN AN IN-HOME FIREPROOF BOX

- Certificates of birth, death, marriage, and adoption
- Social Security card
- Deeds
- Car titles
- An inventory—either written or video—of your household possessions, especially electronics, expensive appliances, collectibles, and jewelry
- Tax returns for the past seven years, as well as any receipts, statements, and other documents that relate to those returns
- Insurance policies
- Estate documents such as wills, trusts, and powers of attorney (keep additional copies with your estate planning attorney and in a safe place at home)
- Contracts
- Important medical records

SAVE: IN YOUR IN-HOME STORAGE

- Paper bank statements (if you still receive them) after you've balanced your checkbook
- Receipts related to major home improvements (but not routine home maintenance such as fertilizing the lawn)
- Receipts, credit card statements, and utility bills if related to the current tax year
- Warranties, user manuals, and receipts related to household appliances and equipment (you may want to store these unwieldy items in separate boxes)
- Investment statements
- Trade confirmations for securities that you still own
- Copies of estate documents such as wills, trusts, and powers of attorney

SHRED IT:

- Credit card offers and other solicitations with your name preprinted on them
- Canceled checks related to non-tax-deductible items
- Deposit slips that accompany your bank and investment statements
- Credit card receipts if they don't have your account number on them
- Paid utility bills, if unrelated to the current tax year
- Paid credit card bills, if unrelated to the current tax year

RECYCLE IT:

- Marketing materials that accompany your bank and investment statements
- Prospectuses and annual and semiannual reports related to your investments (after you've read them, of course!)
- Warranties and manuals for items that you no longer own

Print your worksheet at: www.morningstar.com/goto/30MinuteSolutions

- ► Warranties and Owners Manuals (can be combined with "Home Improvements" documents in an accordion file)
- ► Auto
- ► Current Tax Year (store receipts, charitable receipts, canceled checks, and bills related to the current tax year)
- ► Investment Statements (you'll probably want to create a separate file for each individual provider or account type—for example, "College Savings" and "Retirement Savings")
- ► Bank Statements
- ► Estate Documents

Step 3

Gather the following items and plan to put them in your safe-deposit box or fireproof box, if they're not in there already. If you suspect you'd have a hard time replacing a document, your safe-deposit box or fireproof box is probably the right place for it.

- ► Certificates of birth, death, marriage, and adoption
- ► Social Security card. (Get it out of your wallet!)
- ► Deeds
- ► Car titles
- ► An inventory—either written or video—of your household possessions, especially electronics, expensive appliances, collectibles, and jewelry
- ► Tax returns for the past seven years, as well as any receipts, statements, and other documents that relate to those returns
- ► Insurance policies
- ► Copies of estate documents such as wills, trusts, and powers of attorney (and keep additional copies with your estate-planning attorney and in a safe place at home)
- ► Contracts
- ► Important medical records

Next Steps
- ► The information provided in this chapter will help you set up a system for dealing with your paperwork, but if you have a big backlog of unfiled

papers, it's going to take you more than 30 minutes to get them all filed in the right spot. Plan to do it in stages rather than tackling this task all in one go.

▶ The files I outlined in Step 2 above will apply to most households. However, you will probably want to customize your filing categories based on your own household—for example, if you have a child in college, you will want to set up a separate file to stash college-related financial paperwork.

▶ Once you've set up a filing system, get in the habit of dealing with your mail as soon as it arrives. Put it with other bills to be paid, file it, shred it, or recycle it.

7

Create a Master Directory

When it came to creating passwords for logging on to various sites on the Internet, my default password was always pretty simple: the name of my dear yellow Labrador, now an old lady, plus the street number of my husband's and my first house. With the exception of the occasional stumble (case-sensitivity!), that system worked pretty well.

At least it did for a while. At some point, though, we got a second dog and moved to a different house. Some passwords expired, or I was issued temporary ones like XJLZ3677 that I never got around to customizing. And I also began managing more of my business online, from making my 401(k) elections to putting my newspapers on vacation hold. My user names and passwords multiplied exponentially, seemingly overnight. In short order, my once-straightforward system for managing my user names and passwords became a convoluted muddle of multiple house numbers, two different dogs' names, and temporary passwords.

One day when I had a few extra minutes to spare, I decided that it was time to mop up my self-made mess. I created a simple Microsoft Word document that I store on my laptop at home as well as my PC at work; I also password-protected it to ensure its safety. On it, I put the URLs of all the web sites I visit, as well as my user names and passwords. If I need to create or change any of the information, I simply crack open the file and resave it. I can't claim that the system is perfect—I occasionally update my at-work online directory and fail to do so at home. I can say, however, that I'm not clicking the dreaded "Lost Your Password?" link with nearly the frequency that I once was.

Along those same lines, creating a master directory of your financial information can greatly simplify your financial life. Your directory won't replace individual files that you keep for each of your financial accounts, but it will serve as a valuable central repository for all of your salient financial information, including account numbers, URLs, passwords, financial advisors, and phone numbers.

Creating a master directory has a key secondary benefit, too: By pulling together all your crucial information into a single document, you spare your loved ones the time and expense of having to hunt around for various bits of information if something should happen to you.

Your master directory can be either an electronic or print document. (Because the information in your directory may change over time, using an electronic document is preferable.)

To create a master directory, you'll need:

- ▶ Master Directory Worksheet (Worksheet 7.1, available at www.morning star.com/goto/30MinuteSolutions)
- ▶ Net Worth Worksheet, if you've completed it (see Worksheet 1.1, available at www.morningstar.com/goto/30MinuteSolutions)
- ▶ Financial account numbers, as well as passwords and the names and phone numbers of any advisors you use

Start the Clock

Step 1

Fill in the Master Directory Worksheet provided (Worksheet 7.1, available at www.morningstar.com/goto/30MinuteSolutions). If you completed the Net Worth Worksheet in Chapter 1, you'll have a good head start on completing this document.

Worksheet 7.1

Master Directory

PREPARED FOR: DATE: /   /

You'll Need:

■ Net Worth Statement if you've completed it

■ All of your financial account numbers, as well as passwords and the names and phone numbers of any advisors you use

DIRECTORY: KEY INDIVIDUALS

Attorney

Name	Firm
Phone Number	E-mail Address

Accountant

Name	Firm
Phone Number	E-mail Address

Insurance Agent

Name	Firm
Phone Number	E-mail Address

Financial Advisor

Name	Firm
Phone Number	E-mail Address

Human Resources Contact

Name	Firm
Phone Number	E-mail Address

Banker

Name	Firm
Phone Number	E-mail Address
Safe-Deposit Box	Key Location

Print your worksheet at: www.morningstar.com/goto/30MinuteSolutions

Step 2

Because your master directory contains information that could be extremely valuable to identity thieves, it's essential that you take steps to ensure the security of this document, whether you've created a print document, an electronic document, or both. (No matter which format you use, I recommend that you create a backup version of this document in case you lose or misplace your original.)

If you've created an electronic master directory, password-protect the document. Be sure to use a combination of numbers and letters for your password. (For a document this sensitive, the last thing you want to do is use a password that someone could readily guess.) If you've created a print version of your master directory, save the document in a secure place, such as a locked drawer or home safe.

Step 3

The next step is to alert your spouse or a trusted family member, friend, or financial advisor of the document's existence, as well as to provide instructions on how to gain access to your master directory if you become incapacitated. (If you've created an estate plan, you should be sure to notify your agents—your executor and/or the person to whom you've granted financial power of attorney—of the existence of your master directory.)

If you choose to provide a copy of this document to anyone else, be sure to underscore the importance of keeping it in a safe location. Use an encrypted (password-protected) electronic file or, if sharing a printed version, advise your friend, relative, or advisor to store it in a locked location.

Next Steps

▶ Once you've created your master directory, be sure to keep it up-to-date as your account numbers, passwords, and contact information change. And if you create an electronic master directory, be sure to regularly back up your files. (You are backing up your files, right?)

▶ If you've created a master directory, you have an excellent head start on the estate-planning process. I discuss estate planning in Part Eleven.

PART THREE

Find the Best Use of Your Money

AT MORNINGSTAR, we spend most of our time trying to help investors identify the best stocks and mutual funds for their goals.

That's a worthwhile endeavor—no doubt about it. But in talking to more and more people about their money, I've realized their make-or-break financial decisions came well before they began selecting investments. Did they save enough? Did they rack up big debts? Did they short-shrift their retirement plans in exchange for saving for their kids' college educations?

All these decisions boil down to a central question: What's the best allocation of my household's precious financial resources? Should you pay down your outstanding debts, even so-called good debt like your mortgage? Or invest in the market? Are you better off saving in your company retirement plan, an IRA, or a plain old taxable account?

In some cases, the decision is obvious. For example, if you've got high-interest credit card debt, the best use of your money, by far, is to pay it off, because it's outlandish to assume that any investment could possibly generate an annual percentage return to rival what you're paying to service that debt.

In most cases, though, finding the best return on your money is more art than science. For example, say you have a 5 percent mortgage. Can you reasonably expect your investments to return 5 percent a year, thereby making that a better use of your cash than prepaying the home loan? Possibly. The decision rests on several factors, including whether the loan's interest is tax-deductible, whether you're saving in a tax-favored investment vehicle like an IRA, and so forth.

Because the decision about whether to pay down debt or to invest is an important one in every household, in Chapter 8 I discuss how to add rigor to your decision-making process. Of course, the decision rests partly on your own disposition, as well as your return expectations for your investments. I discuss realistic return expectations for various types of assets in this chapter.

And if you've decided to invest, you also need to think about what type of vehicle to use for the job. Every investor is confronted with a bewildering array of choices, ranging from company retirement plans to various types of IRAs to taxable accounts, and the appropriateness of these vehicles will depend on a range of different factors. Chapter 9 is designed to help you think through the variables before committing to one or more of these investment vehicles.

8

Determine Whether to Pay Down Debt or Invest

"IF I HAVE A MORTGAGE, am I better off paying it down as soon as I possibly can, or should I use that money to invest in the market instead?"

One of my neighbors asked me that question a few years ago, and I instantly knew that the topic would strike a chord with the readers of my column on Morningstar.com.

After all, the shelves of your local bookstore are full of tomes that coach consumers on how to get the credit card monkey off their backs, and there's universal agreement that if you're carrying a balance on your credit card, the best thing that you can possibly do is get rid of it as soon as possible. The mortgage crisis also provided countless examples that taking on more mortgage-related debt than you can afford is a one-way ticket to financial ruin.

But other types of debt, such as a manageable mortgage, home equity-related debt, and student loans, occupy an underanalyzed middle ground. Interest rates on these types of debt are often substantially lower than credit card rates, and that interest may, in some cases, be tax-deductible. For those reasons, it's worth analyzing whether the aggressive paydown of that debt is the best use of your money or whether you should invest in the market.

Ultimately, it's a truly personal decision that's affected as much by your own personality as it is by math. I know several financially savvy individuals, including some of my Morningstar colleagues, who prioritized paying down their mortgages (or even paid them off altogether) over putting even more money into their investments. They wanted to reduce their households' fixed costs, and they've told me that step helped buy them peace of mind and gave them greater flexibility. Other people, particularly those who are just starting out and want to take maximum advantage of the compounding that long-term investing affords, may choose to invest in the market rather than prepaying their mortgages on an aggressive schedule.

Here are some of the key factors that affect the decision about whether to pay off debt or to invest. Some of these variables, as you'll see, are difficult to quantify with precision.

▶ **Anticipated return on investment:** You might think you can easily out-earn your mortgage interest rate, particularly given how low interest rates have gone over the past few years. However, bear in mind that paying off your mortgage offers a knowable rate of return (assuming it's a fixed-rate loan), whereas investing in almost anything else does not. Even if you're investing in a CD that pays you a fixed rate of interest, you may have to settle for a different, lower rate in the future. (And in any case, CD rates are currently well below mortgage rates.)

Your time horizon for your investments will also likely have a significant impact on the combination of investments you choose and that, in turn, will affect the rate of return that you're able to earn. If you're a younger investor with a long anticipated time in the market and a high percentage of your portfolio in stocks, which have historically garnered better returns than bonds and cash, you could make a stronger case for paying less on your mortgage while putting more money into the stock market. Because of compounding, a dollar saved today is worth substantially more than one saved 20 years from now. Moreover, the larger your portfolio's equity stake, the more likely you are to be able to earn back your borrowing costs.

(There are no guarantees, though. While stocks have returned more than bonds over very long periods, there's no telling whether that will be the case in the future.)

If, on the other hand, you have a big percentage of your portfolio in bonds because you hope to retire within the next 15 years, you have a smaller chance of recouping your borrowing costs and should think about paying down your mortgage on a more aggressive schedule.

▶ **Interest rate to service your debt:** This factor seems straightforward, right? Yes, if you have a fixed-rate loan. But if you have an adjustable-rate loan, calculating your borrowing costs is more complicated. Adjustable-rate mortgages typically fluctuate in line with prevailing market interest rates, which makes it tricky to forecast long-term borrowing costs. While interest rates are currently quite low relative to historic norms, which in turn benefits borrowers with variable-rate loans, that may not always be the case.

▶ **Number of years until retirement:** One of the best things pre-retirees can do is to reduce their fixed costs going into retirement. Doing so buys them more flexibility and reduces the income they'll need to take from their portfolios once they retire. That, in turn, improves the odds that their portfolios will last throughout their lives. So if you're getting close to retirement, reducing or eliminating debt should top your list of priorities.

▶ **Tax benefits associated with your debt:** Credit card debt has been rightly demonized as having no redeeming qualities whatsoever—unless you're the credit card issuer, that is. But other types of debt may receive tax breaks that can help reduce your overall borrowing costs. For example, you're typically able to deduct any mortgage interest, as well as the interest on some types of home equity loans, on your tax return. This can be a particularly big advantage early in the life of your mortgage, when most of your payments go toward interest expenses. Say that your annual mortgage interest outlay is $20,000. If you're deducting that interest, your real mortgage cost is substantially lower.

You can also deduct student loan interest payments, up to a certain amount, provided your income falls below a certain threshold and you meet other requirements.

However, it's worth noting that taxpayers have a choice of either item-izing deductions or claiming a standard deduction on their income tax forms; in 2009 the standard deduction for single filers was $5,700 and $11,400 for married couples filing jointly. If your itemized deductions aren't substantially higher than your standard deduction, your tax savings from interest-payment deductions may not amount to much.

▶ **Tax advantages associated with investing:** Just as certain types of debt are tax-deductible, you're also able to take advantage of tax breaks when you sock away money for retirement and college in certain types of vehicles. Those tax breaks can add to the return that you're able to pocket from those investments. Savers in 401(k)s and traditional IRAs enjoy tax-deferred compounding, while investors in Roth IRAs and 529 plans enjoy tax-free withdrawals when they use the money to pay for retirement and college, respectively. Therefore, the actual returns that you earn by saving in these types of vehicles are higher than what you earn on taxable investments. (I discuss the pros and cons of these various types of vehicles in Chapter 9.)

▶ **Matching contributions:** Some employers match a portion of employees' contributions to their company retirement plans. That obviously enhances the attractiveness of investing at least enough to earn any matching funds that your employer has promised.

▶ **Private mortgage insurance:** Private mortgage insurance is another factor to consider when deciding whether to invest in the market or to pay down your mortgage. Lenders typically require you to pay for this insurance if you have less than 20 percent equity in your home. Thus, if you're on the hook for PMI, you have a strong incentive to get rid of it as soon as you possibly can, either by paying down your principal value aggressively (and thereby building up your equity in the home) or by having your home reappraised if you've made substantial improvements to it.

To determine whether to pay down debt or to invest, you'll need:

▶ Expected Return Worksheet (Worksheet 8.1, available at www.morningstar .com/goto/30MinuteSolutions)
▶ Morningstar's Instant X-Ray tool (available at www.morningstar.com/ goto/30MinuteSolutions)

Worksheet 8.1

Expected Return Worksheet

PREPARED FOR: DATE: /   /

You'll Need:
- Morningstar's Instant X-Ray tool, available at www.morningstar.com/goto/30MinuteSolutions

- The current interest rates of your debt, whether credit card, mortgage-related, or student-loan related

- Current investment statements

- Most recent tax return

Prioritize Your Spending:
First Priority (tie): Debt with high interest rate relative to what your investments are apt to earn and interest is not deductible and/or you're paying private mortgage insurance.

First Priority (tie): 401(k) contributions that your employer is matching.

Second Priority: Debt with high interest rates relative to what your investments are apt to earn and interest is tax-deductible or debt with reasonable interest rates (4%-5%) and interest is not tax-deductible.

Third Priority (tie): Investments with reasonable expected rates of return (4%-5%) and that also enjoy tax-favored status (IRAs and 401(k)s).

Third Priority (tie): Debt with reasonable interest rates (4%-5%) and interest is tax-deductible.

Fourth Priority: Investments whose expected rates of return are in line with interest on debt and that enjoy no tax benefits.

CURRENT DEBTS

Debts:	Variable Rate	Deductible Intrst	PMI	Interest Rate (%)	Priority
Home loan	○ Yes ○ No	○ Yes ○ No	○ Yes ○ No		
Home equity loan/line of credit	○ Yes ○ No	○ Yes ○ No			
Student loan	○ Yes ○ No	○ Yes ○ No			
Auto loan					
Credit card balance					
Credit card balance					
Credit card balance					
Other debt	○ Yes ○ No	○ Yes ○ No	○ Yes ○ No		

CURRENT INVESTMENTS

Investments	Tax Benefits (check)	Matching Contributions	Expected Return (%)	Priority
Company retirement plan	○ Yes ○ No	○ Yes ○ No		
IRA	○ Yes ○ No			
IRA	○ Yes ○ No			
College savings	○ Yes ○ No			
Taxable account				
Checking/savings				
Other savings/investments				
Other savings/investments				
Other savings/investments				

Print your worksheet at: www.morningstar.com/goto/30MinuteSolutions

▶ Current interest rates of your debt, whether credit card, mortgage/home equity, or student loan

▶ Current investment statements

▶ Most recent tax return

 Start the Clock

Step 1

Using the Expected Return Worksheet (Worksheet 8.1), write down any debts you have outstanding, including mortgages, home equity loans or lines of credit (if you currently have a balance), student loans, or credit cards. Fill in the Interest Rate % column; indicate if your rate is variable.

Note whether any part of that interest is tax-deductible. Also take note of whether you're paying private mortgage insurance on your home loan.

Step 2

Now write down your current investment accounts. Indicate whether you're receiving any tax benefits by investing in that type of account, as well as whether you're earning any matching contributions. Leave the Expected Return % column blank.

Step 3

Use Morningstar's Instant X-Ray tool, available at www.morningstar.com/goto/30MinuteSolutions, to identify the stock/bond/cash mix for each of your investment accounts: 401(k)s, IRAs, and any taxable accounts. Start by entering each of your holdings into the tool, then click Show Instant X-Ray to see the stock/bond/cash mix (also called an asset allocation) for that account.

Step 4

After you've found a stock/bond/cash breakdown for each of your accounts, calculate an expected return for each of your accounts. Of course, you can't be certain about the expected returns of any asset class, but I think that it pays to be conservative and also take into account the effects of inflation. I would use 2 percent for cash, 4 percent for bonds, and 6 percent for stock holdings.

If your account consists of some combination of stocks, bonds, and cash, you'll need to come up with a combined expected return. For example, if

Instant X-Ray says that one of your accounts consists of 10 percent cash, 50 percent bonds, and 40 percent stock, you'd calculate the expected return as follows: 2.4 percent return from the stock portion of your portfolio (6% × .40), 2.0 percent return from the bond portion of your portfolio (4% × .50), and 0.2 percent return from the cash portion of your portfolio (2% × .10). The aggregate expected return for such a portfolio would be 4.6 percent (2.4% + 2.0% + 0.2%).

Step 5

Compare the potential rates of return for your investment assets with the interest that you're paying to service your debt. Prioritize your spending in the following sequence:

First priority (tie): Debt with high interest rate relative to what your investments are apt to earn, where interest is not deductible and/or you're paying private mortgage insurance

First priority (tie): Company retirement plan contributions that your employer is matching

Second priority: Debt with high interest rates relative to what your investments are apt to earn, where interest is tax-deductible—or, debt with reasonable interest rates (4 percent to 5 percent), where interest is not tax-deductible

Third priority (tie): Investments with reasonable expected rates of return (4 percent to 5 percent) that also enjoy tax-favored status—IRAs and 401(k)s

Third priority (tie): Debt with reasonable interest rates (4 percent to 5 percent) and tax-deductible interest

Fourth priority: Investments whose expected rates of return are in line with interest on debt and that enjoy no tax benefits

Next Steps

▶ As you go through this exercise, you're almost certain to encounter one or two toss-ups. When you do, the tie should go to the investment that offers you the most certain return. For example, say your mortgage interest is 5.5 percent and you're forecasting a similar return on your IRA. Because the return on your mortgage paydown is certain, whereas your investment's return is not, it makes sense to prepay at least some of your mortgage each month before putting cash to work in the IRA.

▶ As you evaluate the decision about whether to pay down debt or invest, take care to ensure that your opinion isn't clouded by what behavioral finance experts call *recency bias,* the tendency to have your decision making be unduly influenced by recent events. As stocks have performed abysmally over the past decade, it's tempting to prefer an ultra-low but knowable return over one that is more unpredictable but potentially higher.

▶ Deciding whether to pay down debt or invest isn't the only capital allocation question you'll have to resolve. If you decide to invest, you also have to determine what type of vehicle to invest in. That's the focus of Chapter 9.

9

Decide Where to Invest for Retirement

"My company just cut our 401(k) match. Should I continue to invest in the plan, or am I better off starting a Roth IRA?"

Shannon, a graphic designer in her mid-twenties, wasn't the only one who wrote me with that question in 2009. Amid the economic downturn, many companies cut employee benefits instead of—or in some cases in addition to—eliminating jobs. That left employees like Shannon in a quandary.

Chapter 8 covered the decision about whether to pay off debt or invest. But assuming that your debt is under control and you've decided to invest for retirement, your next step is to look for the vehicle with the greatest bang for your buck, just as Shannon was doing. Should funding your 401(k) be your top priority, given that your money goes in on a pretax basis and you may earn a match? How do Roth or traditional IRAs fit into the picture? Or perhaps it makes sense to simply save in your taxable account so you can readily put your hands on the money if you need it.

Thinking through your best options can be tricky. Just how good is the tax break you're earning by investing in a company retirement plan or IRA? Your tax brackets—the one you're in now and the one you will be in at the time you expect to retire—are one factor to consider when prioritizing the various tax-advantaged investment vehicles: Is it better to pay tax now or later? (And, unless you're very near retirement, it can be difficult to guesstimate what your in-retirement tax bracket will be.)

Your income level could also put certain investment options, such as the Roth IRA or a deductible IRA, off-limits. The decision also depends on how much you have available to invest. If you plan to make substantial contributions, you may invest in a few separate tax-sheltered options as well as your taxable account.

The ability to tap any retirement assets prior to retiring is also important: Of course, it's always better to leave your retirement money in place so that it can grow, but you have to be realistic, too. If you think that you might need the money sooner rather than later, you'll need to avoid vehicles that carry penalties for early withdrawal. Finally, if you're investing in an employee retirement plan with a limited menu of choices and/or an additional layer of costs, you'll also have to weigh how good that lineup is. In the face of all of these choices, it's no wonder so many people decide to do nothing.

In the case of Shannon and other individuals who aren't earning any matching funds for their 401(k)s, I'd recommend maxing out Roth IRA contributions before putting money into the 401(k). For most individuals with a fixed pool of investment assets, the following sequence will make sense:

First priority: Invest enough in company retirement plan to earn company match
Second priority: Invest in IRA (Roth or deductible) or Roth 401(k)
Third priority: Invest in company retirement plan to maximum
Fourth priority: Invest in traditional nondeductible IRA
Fifth priority: Invest in taxable account

To determine where to invest for retirement, you'll need:

► Details on your company's retirement plan (usually available in a Summary Plan Description; ask your HR administrator for this document)
► An estimate of your income for the current year

Start the Clock

Step 1

Begin by checking your employee handbook or your company retirement plan's Summary Plan Description to find out whether your company matches any portion of your retirement plan contributions. If so, plan to invest at least that much in your plan. For example, if your employer is making a matching contribution of 3 percent of your salary and you make $50,000 a year, you'll need to contribute at least $1,500 of your own money to your 401(k) to be entitled to your employer's full matching contribution. Doing otherwise is like leaving free money on the table.

If you're not earning matching contributions on investments in your company retirement plan or still have money to invest once you're investing enough to meet the match, move on to the next step.

Step 2

Next, determine what type of IRA you're eligible to contribute to. Morningstar's IRA Calculator, available at www.morningstar.com/goto/30Minute Solutions, can help you determine eligibility based on your income and other factors, such as your ability to contribute to a company retirement plan.

If you can contribute to a Roth, that's usually preferable to contributing to a traditional IRA, even if you can deduct your IRA contributions. (In Part Six I discuss IRAs in depth.) The key advantage is flexibility. Whereas you must begin taking distributions from a traditional IRA at age $70\frac{1}{2}$, there are no such requirements governing Roth IRA withdrawals. You can let the money compound for as long as you like, and you can continue investing at any age. (With most other tax-sheltered vehicles, you can't make contributions once you hit age $70\frac{1}{2}$.) In addition, withdrawals are tax-free, assuming you've reached age $59\frac{1}{2}$ and you've held the account for at least five years. The Roth is also the much better option if there's a chance you may need to pull your money out before you're $59\frac{1}{2}$, because you can withdraw your contributions at any time and for any reason without having to pay taxes or a penalty.

In certain situations it might make sense for investors to avail themselves of traditional deductible IRAs (presuming they're eligible) before contributing to a Roth IRA. For example, if you expect to be in a lower tax bracket when you retire than when you were working, that's an argument for funding a

401(k) or deductible IRA before the Roth. That's because you'll pay taxes on your 401(k) and deductible IRA when you withdraw the money, whereas you contribute after-tax dollars to the Roth. (Unless you're very close to retirement, however, you won't likely know what your tax bracket will be. If you're not sure, I'd opt for the Roth.)

Step 3

Once you've met your employer's matching contribution and set aside enough money to fully fund a Roth or deductible IRA, go back to your company retirement plan and take a closer look at the options and the fees associated with your plan. Chapter 15 provides you with guidance on conducting a quick due diligence check on your plan. Provided it's decent or better, plan to invest the maximum allowable amount in the plan. Remember that contribution limits are higher if you're over 50; also consider a Roth 401(k) if one is available to you.

Step 4

If you've maxed out your 401(k) and earn too much to contribute to a Roth IRA (and therefore a deductible IRA is also out of reach), consider investing in a traditional nondeductible IRA. True, you won't be able to deduct your contribution from your taxable income—unlike a deductible IRA—and you'll also have to pay taxes on your account's investment earnings when you withdraw money. But you will enjoy the benefit of tax-deferred compounding.

One other argument for opening a traditional nondeductible IRA in 2010 or earlier is that investors of all income levels will be able to convert their traditional IRAs to Roth IRAs in that year. So if you earn too much to contribute to a Roth, a traditional nondeductible IRA is one way to get in through the back door. (In Chapter 21 I discuss the ins and outs of conversions.)

If you open a traditional nondeductible IRA and don't convert to a Roth, bear in mind that this vehicle carries all of the same restrictions that accompany a deductible IRA—in particular, you must begin taking distributions at age $70^{1}/_{2}$, whether you're ready or not.

Step 5

If you've exhausted your key tax-advantaged options, turn your attention to saving money in your taxable accounts. From here on out, you'll want to stay hyperattuned to the tax efficiency of any investments you select. In Part Eight the focus is on managing and selecting investments for your taxable account.

Next Step

▶ Most 401(k) plans allow you to put your contributions on autopilot, so that you're investing a specific dollar amount or percentage per paycheck. In addition to enforcing discipline, such a system can help you avoid one of the biggest pitfalls of investing: putting a lot of money to work when stocks are expensive. You can put in place a similar program with your IRA or taxable investments using what's called an automatic investment plan, whereby your investment is automatically deducted from your checking account each month. Many mutual fund companies and brokerage firms offer these plans. You can change or suspend the autopilot option at any time, so setting up such a program allows more flexibility than you might think.

PART FOUR

Get Started in Investing

"Just pick up a dish."

One of my high school teachers shared that seemingly frivolous bit of wisdom years ago, and it has stuck with me ever since. It was from an article in a women's magazine she had read in the 1950s, about how to clean up after a dinner party when your house is full of dirty dishes and glassware. The idea was that if you pick up one dish, and then another and another, soon you'll find that you're making real, measurable progress toward your goal. For my teacher, "just pick up a dish" became a metaphor for tackling any task that seemed overwhelming, whether writing her master's thesis or helping students learn trigonometry.

This section, about how to get started in investing, is the equivalent of picking up that first dish. No, it won't teach you everything that you need to know about investing, but it covers the essential first steps to getting started.

In Chapter 10, I discuss an essential precursor to creating a long-term portfolio: creating an emergency fund. Setting some money aside in ultrasafe investments is a must-do before you begin investing in stocks or other long-term securities. This cushion will provide a safety net in case you lose your job, and it will also prevent you from having to tap your long-term investments in case of a financial emergency. In this chapter, I talk about how to determine how much to set aside in your emergency fund, as well as how to select appropriate investments for it.

Once you start putting together your investment portfolio for longer-term goals like retirement, the most essential of these steps, covered in Chapter 11, is finding an appropriate asset allocation, or, in layperson's terms, identifying the right mix of stocks and bonds for your portfolio. It's a complicated topic that has sparked much academic research and debate over the years. After the recent bear market, some pundits have questioned whether it even makes sense to invest in stocks at all. Still, there are some rules of thumb that you can use to stack the odds in your favor. Ibbotson Associates, part of Morningstar, is the leader in the field of asset allocation, and, in Chapter 11, I've supplied its guidance on appropriate stock/bond mixes for investors with varying time horizons.

Once you've articulated your asset allocation, it's time to write an investment policy statement, in which you state your goals for your portfolio and the parameters you'll use to select and monitor your holdings. When the market is tossing about your investments and you're tempted to make big changes, your investment policy statement, which I discuss in Chapter 12, can help ensure that you act with a cool head.

In Chapter 13 I focus on investing for short- and intermediate-term goals—not retirement or college for your infant, but goals you expect to achieve within the next several years. I discuss how to find the right investments for goals that are fairly close at hand, and also share some of Morningstar's best specific investment ideas for near-term goals.

Creating a long-term portfolio is the focus of Chapter 14. Many investors overcomplicate long-term investing by buying specific investments for every nook and cranny of the market or making frequent changes based on their best guesses about the market's direction. But creating a sturdy, low-maintenance, long-term portfolio can also be extremely simple, particularly if you focus on high-quality, broad-based mutual funds. Because I think the latter route is best for most investors, I provide some specific recommendations for streamlined and simple portfolios. Index mutual funds and target-date mutual funds have grown in popularity in recent years, largely because they can help simplify your investment life. I discuss these two types of vehicles in Chapter 14.

10

Create an Emergency Fund

In EARLY 2009, I met a lovely couple in their early fifties who were struggling with more than $20,000 in credit card debt. When I visited them at their home in a Chicago suburb, it was obvious that they weren't profligate spenders; their home was modest, and they said that they hadn't taken a real vacation in years.

Rather, their credit card problems began once their children started college. Although they were able to cover the tuition costs and typical monthly living expenses with their salaries, their monthly outlay on those two expense categories left no room for error. As a result, they began charging unexpected expenses like car repairs and veterinary care on their cards, incurring exorbitant interest fees along the way.

They were clearly troubled about having dug themselves into such a deep hole, and they were eager to do everything that they could to pay off the debt as soon as possible. We discussed various ideas for reducing their financing costs, such as transferring the debt to a home equity line of credit or borrowing from one of their 401(k) plans, both of which are preferable to high-interest credit card debt.

What I think surprised them, though, was that I didn't suggest that they put every extra penny toward paying down their debt. Rather, I urged them to simultaneously set up an emergency savings fund. True, setting up an emergency fund would probably mean that it would take them longer to pay off all of their debt, but it would also guard against the prospect of taking on any more debt than they already had. Not only could they use their emergency fund to pay unexpected bills, but it would also provide a needed cushion should one of them lose their job.

In fact, creating a safety net in case of job loss is the key reason to set up an emergency fund. Conventional financial planning wisdom holds that you should have three to six months' worth of household living expenses tucked away in your emergency fund, with the thought being that it would take you that long to find a new job if you should lose yours. However, I would recommend building yourself an even more generous cushion if you can swing it, preferably nine months' to a year's worth of living expenses. That's particularly true if you're highly paid or work in a highly specialized field, because it's usually more difficult to replace such jobs. And of course, if you have any reason to believe that your job is in jeopardy—either because of problems in the economy at large or at your own company—you should also aim to build a larger emergency fund.

In addition to determining the right amount for your emergency fund, you also have to take care in selecting the investments that you put inside it. As a general rule of thumb, your emergency fund should consist of investments with maturities of less than one year, including checking and savings accounts, money market accounts, and CDs. This is money that you could need to tap in a pinch, so you want to steer clear of higher-yielding investments that could be tough to sell or that you might have to sell at a loss if you needed to get out in a hurry. Instead, you need to stick with vehicles that ensure you'll be able to take out as much as you put in.

Here's an overview of the types of savings and investment vehicles that are acceptable for your emergency fund:

▶ **Checking and savings accounts:** Convenience is the big plus here, but rates may be rock-bottom. Deposits of up to $250,000 per institution will be covered by FDIC insurance.

▶ **Money market deposit accounts:** These interest-bearing savings accounts typically offer a limited number of transactions per month, and deposits of as much as $250,000 per institution are FDIC-insured.

▶ **Certificates of deposit:** CDs are apt to have a higher yield than checking, savings, or money market accounts. They also carry FDIC insurance for deposits of as much as $250,000 per institution. The big drawback to holding CDs in your emergency fund, however, is that you'll pay a penalty to withdraw money from a CD prematurely. So if you hold CDs as part of your emergency fund, you'll have to weigh the higher yield against the risk of having to pay a penalty to pull money out.

▶ **Money market funds:** A money market mutual fund can be a good option for an emergency fund, and yields are apt to be higher than what you'd earn on your checking, savings, or money market account. Because money funds buy very short-term bonds, they can readily swap into newer, higher-yielding securities when interest rates edge up. The big downside relative to the checking and savings accounts, CDs, and money market accounts is that money market fund assets are not FDIC-insured.

If you opt for a money market fund, low costs should be your key consideration. That's because the amount that you pay in expenses will be the key determinant of the yield that you get to pocket. (Expenses are deducted directly from yield.) You should pay no more—and preferably much less—than 0.50 percent in expenses for your money market fund. One other tip: If you do spy a fund with very low fees, make sure that the fund company isn't temporarily waiving part of its expenses in an effort to attract new investors. Such waivers can readily be reversed. Also be wary of a fund with a yield that's substantially higher than that of the competition, especially if the fund doesn't have very low fees. It could be investing in lower-quality securities to pump up its yield and pumping up its risk level at the same time.

Also bear in mind your tax bracket when shopping for a money fund for your taxable account. Even if you're not in the highest tax bracket, it may make sense to opt for a tax-free money market fund over a taxable one. That's because the muni fund's yield may actually be higher than the taxable fund's once you factor in taxes. To quickly compare the aftertax yields of taxable and tax-free funds, use the Tax-Equivalent Yield function

of the Morningstar Bond Calculator, available at www.morningstar.
com/goto/30MinuteSolutions.

To create an emergency fund, you'll need:

▶ Credit card statements and other documents to help determine your
monthly living expenses. (If you completed a cash-flow statement [Work-
sheet 2.1] or a budget in Chapter 4, you'll already have a very specific idea
of your spending needs.)
▶ Current statements for all of your liquid accounts, including checking,
savings, money market accounts, and CDs
▶ Morningstar's Bond Calculator (available at www.morningstar.com/goto/
30MinuteSolutions)

 Start the Clock

Step 1

Determine your monthly living expenses. Don't include nonessential items
that you could live without in a pinch, such as housecleaning and discretionary
clothing purchases. Multiply that number by three months. This is your
absolute minimum savings target for your emergency fund.

Step 2

Add up the aggregate investments that you hold in your checking and savings
accounts, money market accounts and funds, and CDs. Exclude any assets
that you have earmarked for other purposes, such as money that you're saving
for a car down payment or college tuition; also exclude any cash holdings in
your stock or bond mutual funds. This is your current emergency fund.

Step 3

Subtract the figure in Step 2 (your current emergency fund) from the figure in
Step 1 (your target emergency fund). This is how much you need to save at a
bare minimum—it should be double this level or more. Setting money aside
to hit this savings target should be your main savings priority in the months
ahead. (If you're also paying off high-interest credit card debt, you should try
to build up your emergency fund at the same time.)

Step 4

To home in on the best investments for your emergency fund, start by looking at the yields for your current investments. Then go to www.bankrate.com to find current yields for CDs, money market deposit accounts, and money market mutual funds; compare them with what you're earning currently. Bearing in mind the guidelines earlier in this chapter about FDIC insurance and liquidity, also remember that it's fine to use a combination of these vehicles rather than holding your entire emergency fund in one place. For example, you may choose to keep two months' worth of living expenses in your checking account and the rest of your emergency fund in a higher-yielding CD or money market fund.

Next Steps

► If you're a homeowner, it makes sense to augment (but not replace) your emergency fund by setting up a home equity line of credit to use in case of emergency. That way, should you find yourself in a real bind and have to exhaust your emergency fund, you'll have another safety net in place. Interest rates on HELOCs are usually quite low relative to other forms of financing, and the interest is tax-deductible in most situations. Set up a HELOC while you're employed, because it's much harder to secure this type of financing if you're not.

► Although it's not ideal to use your retirement savings as a piggy bank, your Roth IRA can help back up your emergency fund if need be. You can tap Roth IRA contributions at any time and for any reason; because of that flexibility, setting one up is a great first step when you get started in investing. I discuss Roth IRAs in-depth in Part Six.

► Yields on money market funds and CDs are currently very low relative to historical norms. You may be able to obtain a slightly higher rate by using an online-only bank for your emergency fund.

11

Find the Right Stock/Bond Mix

Are you a stock or a bond?

You may not be accustomed to comparing yourself to a financial security, but it may be useful when you're trying to figure out your portfolio's optimal stock/bond mix.

The thinking goes like this: If your own earning power—which Morningstar affiliate Ibbotson Associates calls human capital—is very stable and predictable, then you're like a bond. Think of a tenured college professor, whose income is secure for the rest of his life, or a senior who's drawing upon a pension from a financially stable company. Because such an individual has a predictable income, he could keep a larger share of his portfolio in stocks than someone with less stable human capital. He's a bond.

At the opposite end of the spectrum would be an investment broker whose income depends completely on the stock market. When the market is going up and the broker's clients are clamoring to invest, her commissions are high and she may also earn a bonus. But when the market is down, so is her income, and her bonus may be nonexistent. She's a stock. She'd want to hold much more in bonds than stocks, because her earnings are so dependent on the stock market.

Just as our career paths affect how we view our own human capital, so do our ages. When you're young and in the accumulation phase, you're long on human capital and short on financial capital—meaning that you have many working years ahead of you but you haven't yet amassed much in financial assets. Because you can expect a steady income stream from work, you can afford to take more risk by holding equities. As you approach retirement, however, you need to find ways to supplant the income that you earned while working. As a result, you'll want to shift your financial assets away from equities and into income-producing assets such as bonds or annuities.

Of course, there are no guarantees that stocks will return more than bonds, even though they have done so over very long periods of time. In fact, in the 10 years from August 1999 through August 2009, stocks eked out a small gain per year, on average, whereas bondholders gained an average of 6 percent per year. Against that backdrop, it might be tempting to ignore stocks altogether.

At the same time, however, it stands to reason that over very long periods of time, various asset classes will generate returns that compensate investors for their risks. Because investors in stocks shoulder more risk than bondholders, and bondholders take on more risk than investors in ultrasafe investments like CDs, you can reasonably expect stocks to beat bonds and bonds to beat CDs and other cash-type investments over very long periods of time. (Of course there are no guarantees that will be the case, as the past decade shows.) In turn, that suggests that younger investors with long time frames should have the majority of their investments in stocks, whereas those who are close to needing their money should have the bulk of their assets in safer investments like bonds and CDs.

What I've discussed so far is called strategic asset allocation—meaning that you arrive at a sensible stock/bond/cash mix and then gradually shift more of your portfolio into bonds and cash as you get older. Of course, it would be ideal if we could all position our portfolios to capture stocks' returns when they're going up and then move into safe investments right before stocks go down. In reality, however, timing the market by, say, selling stocks today and then buying them back at a later date is impossible to pull off with any degree of accuracy—so much so that most professional investors don't try it.

Maintaining a fairly stable asset allocation has a couple of other big benefits: It keeps your portfolio diversified, thereby reducing its ups and downs, and it also keeps you from getting whipped around by the market's day-to-day gyrations. An asset-allocation plan provides your portfolio with its own true north. If your portfolio's allocations veer meaningfully from your targets, then and only then should you make big changes.

To find the right stock/bond mix, you'll need:

▶ A list of your current investments. (If you prepared a Net Worth Worksheet [Worksheet 1.1, available at www.morningstar.com/goto/30Minute Solutions], you already have this information.)
▶ An estimate of the year in which you plan to retire
▶ Morningstar's Instant X-Ray tool (available at www.morningstar.com/goto/30MinuteSolutions)

Start the Clock

Step 1

Before determining a target asset allocation, start by checking out where you are now. Log on to Morningstar's Instant X-Ray tool, available at www.morningstar.com/goto/30MinuteSolutions. Enter each of your holdings, as well as the amount that you hold in each. (Don't include any assets you have earmarked for short-term needs, such as your emergency fund.) Then click Show Instant X-Ray. You'll be able to see your allocations to stocks (both domestic and international), bonds, cash, and "other" (usually securities such as convertibles and preferred stock), as well as your sector and investment-style positioning.

Step 2

The next step is to get some guidance on where you should be. Find the asset allocation in Figure 11.1 that corresponds to your anticipated retirement date. Remember, this allocation corresponds to your long-term goals (for example, retirement assets), not your emergency fund or any shorter-term savings that you've earmarked for purchases that are close at hand.

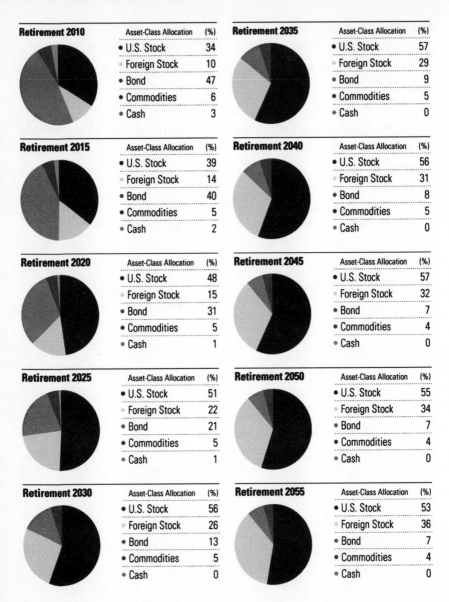

Retirement 2010	Asset-Class Allocation	(%)
• U.S. Stock		34
• Foreign Stock		10
• Bond		47
• Commodities		6
• Cash		3

Retirement 2035	Asset-Class Allocation	(%)
• U.S. Stock		57
• Foreign Stock		29
• Bond		9
• Commodities		5
• Cash		0

Retirement 2015	Asset-Class Allocation	(%)
• U.S. Stock		39
• Foreign Stock		14
• Bond		40
• Commodities		5
• Cash		2

Retirement 2040	Asset-Class Allocation	(%)
• U.S. Stock		56
• Foreign Stock		31
• Bond		8
• Commodities		5
• Cash		0

Retirement 2020	Asset-Class Allocation	(%)
• U.S. Stock		48
• Foreign Stock		15
• Bond		31
• Commodities		5
• Cash		1

Retirement 2045	Asset-Class Allocation	(%)
• U.S. Stock		57
• Foreign Stock		32
• Bond		7
• Commodities		4
• Cash		0

Retirement 2025	Asset-Class Allocation	(%)
• U.S. Stock		51
• Foreign Stock		22
• Bond		21
• Commodities		5
• Cash		1

Retirement 2050	Asset-Class Allocation	(%)
• U.S. Stock		55
• Foreign Stock		34
• Bond		7
• Commodities		4
• Cash		0

Retirement 2030	Asset-Class Allocation	(%)
• U.S. Stock		56
• Foreign Stock		26
• Bond		13
• Commodities		5
• Cash		0

Retirement 2055	Asset-Class Allocation	(%)
• U.S. Stock		53
• Foreign Stock		36
• Bond		7
• Commodities		4
• Cash		0

Allocations of Morningstar's Lifetime Allocation Indexes, developed in conjunction with asset-allocation expert Ibbotson Associates. Note that even long-dated portfolios contain some bonds and near-dated portfolios include some stocks.

Figure 11.1   How Does Your Stock/Bond Mix Stack Up?

Step 3

The allocations in Figure 11.1 are a good starting point, but you can further fine-tune your asset allocation by asking yourself the following questions:

▶ **Are you expecting other sources of income during retirement, such as a pension?**
   Yes: More equities
   No: Fewer equities
▶ **Does longevity run in your family?**
   Yes: More equities
   No: Fewer equities
▶ **Are you expecting to need a fairly high level of income during retirement?**
   Yes: More equities
   No: Fewer equities
▶ **Have you already accumulated a large nest egg?**
   Yes: Fewer equities
   No: More equities
▶ **Is your savings rate high?**
   Yes: Fewer equities
   No: More equities
▶ **Is there a chance that you'll need to tap your assets for some other goal prior to retirement?**
   Yes: Fewer equities
   No: More equities
▶ **Do you want to leave assets behind for your children or other loved ones?**
   Yes: More equities
   No: Fewer equities
▶ **If still working, are you in a very stable career with little chance of income disruption?**
   Yes: More equities
   No: Fewer equities

Next Steps

▶ The Internet is chock-full of worthwhile tools to help you arrive at an appropriate asset allocation. If you've saved your portfolio on Morningstar .com, Morningstar's Asset Allocator tool can help you optimize your current portfolio's asset mix to give it a better shot at reaching your financial goals. T. Rowe Price's Retirement Income Calculator www3.troweprice .com/ric/ric/public/ric.do provides another way to see whether you're on track to meet your retirement income goals.

▶ Are you already retired or getting close to it? Chapter 29 includes a helpful worksheet that factors in your asset allocation to provide guidance on an optimal in-retirement portfolio withdrawal rate.

12

Create an Investment Policy Statement

ONE OF MY FAVORITE PROGRAMS on National Public Radio is *This I Believe*, a series of spoken essays in which individuals articulate the beliefs that have helped shape their lives. The essays, based on a 1950s' radio program hosted by Edward R. Murrow, include thoughts about birth and death, baseball and driving. Big names like Muhammad Ali and John Updike have contributed essays to *This I Believe*, as have schoolteachers and attorneys. The series consistently demonstrates the value of having an overarching set of beliefs that can help you appreciate what's important to you and navigate tumultuous times.

Think of your investment policy statement, the subject of this chapter, as your own, investment-related version of *This I Believe*. In it, you'll articulate the key reasons why you're investing, what you're hoping to gain from your investments, whether you're on track to meet your goals, and how often you'll make changes. Once you've created one, you can use your investment policy statement as your compass, a check to keep your investment portfolio on course to meet its goals even when the market and your emotions are telling you to run for the hills. Referring to your investment policy statement before you make any investment decisions can help ensure that you're investing with your head, not your gut.

Corporations and big institutional investors like pension plans create elaborate, 20-page investment policy statements. However, you needn't hire a consultant to develop your investment policy statement, and you don't have to use consultant-ish terms like "Executive Summary" and "Reporting Requirements," even though they appear in a lot of investment policy statements prepared by the pros.

In fact, I think the best investment policy statements for individuals are fairly stripped down and written in plain English; that way, you'll be able to easily identify the things that you should be focusing on.

If you have separate investment portfolios geared toward different investment goals—for example, you have your own retirement assets that you expect to tap in 20 years as well as a college savings plan for your 15-year-old—you may find it helpful to create separate investment policy statements for each sleeve of your portfolio. Don't get too carried away, though. By getting too complicated and creating too many sleeves of your portfolio, you risk getting bogged down in paperwork and missing the big picture about whether your investments are on track to get you to your goals.

You'll notice that other chapters have covered some of the same ground as your investment policy statement. That's by design. The investment policy statement is there to document, in black and white, the key aspects of your investment plan.

To create an investment policy statement, you'll need:

- ▶ Most recent statements for all of your investment accounts
- ▶ Investment Policy Statement Worksheet (Worksheet 12.1, available at www .morningstar.com/goto/30MinuteSolutions)
- ▶ Inflation calculators (available at www.morningstar.com/goto/30Minute Solutions)
- ▶ Goal Planning Worksheet (Worksheet 3.1), if completed
- ▶ Net Worth Worksheet (Worksheet 1.1), if completed
- ▶ Expected Return Worksheet (Worksheet 8.1), if completed

Worksheet 12.1

Investment Policy Statement

PREPARED FOR: _____ DATE: ____ / ____ / ____

You'll Need:

- Most recent statements for all of your investment accounts
- Inflation calculators, available at www.morningstar.com/goto/30MinuteSolutions
- Net Worth Worksheet (Worksheet 1.1), if completed
- Goal Planning Worksheet (Worksheet 3.1), if completed
- Expected Return Worksheet (Worksheet 8.1), if completed

IDENTIFY INVESTING GOALS

Investing Goal	When
Duration	Estimated Cost
Current Assets	Additional Contributions/Frequency /

SPECIFY ASSET-ALLOCATION RANGES

Domestic Equity		% to	
Large Cap (optional)		% to	
Mid-Cap (optional)		% to	
Small Cap (optional)		% to	
Foreign Equity		**% to**	
Developed Markets (optional)		% to	
Developing Markets (optional)		% to	
Bond		**% to**	
Short Term (optional)		% to	
Intermediate Term (optional)		% to	
Long Term (optional)		% to	
Cash		**% to**	

PROJECT RATE OF RETURN

Equity	%	
Bond	%	
Cash	%	
Combined	%	

Print your worksheet at: www.morningstar.com/goto/30MinuteSolutions

Start the Clock

Step 1

Using the Investment Policy Statement Worksheet (available at www. morningstar.com/goto/30MinuteSolutions) as your template, start by writing down your key investing goal and the year in which you hope to reach it. If it's a goal that you will pay for over a number of years, such as retirement or college, fill out the Duration field. Of course, when it comes to retirement, filling out this field means quantifying your own longevity. That's tricky, but the actuarial tables on the Social Security Administration's web site can help you arrive at a reasonable estimate: www.ssa.gov/OACT/STATS/table4c6.html. From there, I think it's helpful to be optimistic and assume even greater longevity: Add at least a few years.

If you completed the Goal Planning Worksheet (Worksheet 3.1), you'll have already completed this step, as well as Step 2.

Step 2

To the extent that you can, quantify how much your goal will cost. If you have a financial goal that's more than a year or two away, it's important to adjust the cost upward to reflect what you'll actually pay once inflation is factored in. That gets even more complicated for goals you expect to fund over several years, such as retirement or college. To help simplify the task, the 30-Minute Money Solutions web site (www.morningstar.com/goto/30MinuteSolutions) includes several different inflation calculators to help you quantify the cost, in real dollars, of retirement, college, and other goals.

Step 3

Go online or refer to your most recent statements to arrive at the current value of the investment assets you have earmarked for that specific goal. Also indicate how much you plan to invest toward this goal on an ongoing basis. (If you completed the Net Worth Worksheet, Worksheet 1.1, you will have already completed this step.)

Step 4

Next, document your asset-allocation targets for these investments. If you aren't sure what they should be, refer to Chapter 11.

Because your portfolio's asset allocation will ebb and flow based on how stocks are performing versus bonds and cash, your investment policy statement should set a range for your asset allocation rather than targeting a static figure for each asset class. After all, you don't want to have to make changes to your portfolio just because stocks went up 5 percent over the past month; that kind of trading can be costly and time-consuming.

For the broad asset classes, a range of 10 percentage points (or even 15 or 20 percentage points if you'd like to be a hands-off investor) is reasonable. For example, say your asset-allocation target for your retirement portfolio is 55 percent stock, 40 percent bonds, and 5 percent cash. In your investment policy statement, you'd set out the ranges as follows:

▶ **Stocks:** 50 percent to 60 percent
▶ **Bonds:** 35 percent to 45 percent
▶ **Cash:** 0 to 10 percent

Some investment policy statements include sub-asset class breakdowns, setting parameters for large-, mid-, and small-cap stock exposure; you can also break out U.S. and foreign stock exposure. There's nothing wrong with that, but you don't need to get too fancy. Setting your exposure to the broad asset classes and keeping your portfolio in line with those parameters is most important.

Step 5

Based on your asset-allocation parameters, project a rate of return for your portfolio. That will require you to forecast rates of return for various asset classes, a task that's certainly more art than science. (If you completed the Expected Return Worksheet [Worksheet 8.1], you will already have completed this calculation.) I like to be conservative and assume a 6 percent return for stocks, a 4 percent return for bonds, and a 2 percent rate of return for cash.

If your account consists of some combination of stocks, bonds, and cash (and you assume the forecasted rates of return I just laid out), you'll need to come up with a combined expected return. For example, if your accounts consist of 10 percent cash, 50 percent bonds, and 40 percent stocks, you'd calculate the expected return as follows: 2.4 percent return from the stock portion of your portfolio (6% × .40), 2.0 percent return from the bond portion of your portfolio (4% × .50), and 0.2 percent return from the cash portion of your portfolio (2% × .10). The aggregate expected return for such a portfolio would be 4.6 percent (2.4% + 2.0% + 0.2%).

Step 6

Next, document what you're looking for in your individual investments: the criteria you used when you selected the securities in your portfolio and what you'll use to judge them on an ongoing basis.

Some worthwhile criteria for do-it-yourselfers include:

▶ No-load funds only
▶ Expense ratios of less than 1 percent for stock funds, less than 0.75 percent for bond funds
▶ Manager tenure of more than five years
▶ Holds up well in down markets
▶ Average credit quality of A or better (for bond funds)
▶ History of good tax efficiency (for investments you hold in your taxable account)
▶ Long-term (10-year or more) returns in top half of peer group or beating appropriate market benchmark

Step 7

Once you've set your asset-allocation parameters and your criteria for individual security selection, your next step is to specify how often you'll check up on your portfolio and when you'll make changes. In my experience, less is usually more when it comes to checking up on your holdings and your portfolio's performance.

Semiannual or quarterly (at most) portfolio checkups are more than adequate. When it comes to making changes, I'd recommend doing so when your checkups indicate that your portfolio's allocations to the broad asset classes have diverged from your target range by 5 or 10 percentage points or more. Part Ten of this book provides guidance on monitoring your investments.

Step 8

The final step in creating an investment policy statement is to specify what your checkups will consist of and how you'll evaluate whether you're on track to meet your goals.

You can do so in a few separate ways:

- ▶ Monitor individual holdings versus the criteria you laid out in Step 6.
- ▶ Monitor portfolio's asset allocation versus target allocation. (This will be the main trigger for your rebalancing efforts.)
- ▶ Monitor individual holdings' performances versus style-appropriate benchmarks.
- ▶ Monitor aggregate performance of holdings within an asset class versus a benchmark geared toward that asset class (for example, all U.S. stock funds' performance versus a broad-market benchmark like the Dow Jones Wilshire 500 Index).
- ▶ Monitor entire portfolio's performance versus a blended benchmark. For example, say your portfolio's asset-allocation target is 55 percent stocks and 45 percent bonds. You can benchmark your portfolio's return versus the return of a blended portfolio consisting of 55 percent in Vanguard Total Stock Market Index VTSMX and 45 percent in Vanguard Total Bond Market Index VBMFX.
- ▶ Monitor portfolio's rate of return versus the projected rate of return you articulated in Step 5.
- ▶ Monitor assets accumulated versus your goal.

Next Steps

- ▶ If you're familiar with investment policy statements, you know that they often include a couple of features that I've omitted here. For starters, they often include an investor's assessment of his or her own risk tolerance. In reality, however, most investors are very poor judges of their own ability to tolerate risk; when stocks are going up they rate their risk tolerance as very high, but when everything's going down they feel more conservative. Because it's not very useful, I didn't include risk tolerance here.

▶ Many investment policy statements also focus on performance, setting out rigid parameters such as "fund must be in top half of peer group over trailing three-year period." I think that, too, is misguided, because most investments lag their peer groups from time to time, and short-term underperformance can have a big effect on a holding's longer-term numbers. I've also learned that investments often start to perform best after a period of terrible performance. To the extent that your investment policy statement mentions performance, it should be very long-term.

13

Invest for Short- and Intermediate-Term Goals

"I'm hoping you can give my new wife and me some recommendations for where to invest the money we're saving for a down payment for our first house. We hope to buy in about five years and we'd like to keep our money safe, but CD rates are so low."

Eric's e-mail seemed positively quaint when I received it in early 2005. The housing market wasn't a fully formed bubble yet, but signs of froth were everywhere. Aided and abetted by lax lending standards, young people and grandparents alike were rushing headlong into the world of home-buying, financing condos and houses with little or no money down and, in the worst instances, poor credit and shaky employment histories. Why wait to save up for a down payment when someone will finance the whole thing right away and you're guaranteed to double your money in the space of a few years?

We now know why. As the subprime crisis morphed into a housing market crisis, a financial freeze-up, and, eventually, a full-blown global economic recession, many individuals gained a newfound appreciation for the merits of deferring gratification and saving for their futures. The household savings rate in the United States rose to 6.9 percent in mid-2009, its highest level since 1993, after dipping into negative territory just a year earlier. Individuals like Eric and his wife are still planning to buy houses and cars and take trips, but, like Eric and his wife, they're doing it the old-fashioned way: They're saving the money first.

Much of this book centers around how to meet your long-term investing goals—for most people, that means funding a comfortable retirement and paying for college. But what about those in-between goals, like amassing a down payment for a home, funding big home improvements, or buying a car? Stocks are too risky, but if you want to save toward your goal for a few years or more, you'd hate to have that money just sitting in your checking account, earning little or no return.

Helping you steer a safe middle course is the focus of this chapter. If you know how much you need to save to reach your goal, how much you have saved already, and how much you plan to save, you can then determine how long it will take you to reach it. In turn, you can identify appropriate investments given your time horizon. The closer at hand your financial goal is, the more conservative your investments should be.

To invest for short- and intermediate-term goals, you'll need:

▶ A list of your financial goals. (If you completed the Goal Planning Worksheet [Worksheet 3.1], you will have already defined and quantified your financial goals.)

▶ Current investment statements for assets you have earmarked for short- and intermediate-term goals

▶ Inflation calculators (available at www.morningstar.com/goto/30Minute Solutions)

Start the Clock

Step 1

Begin by quantifying what your financial goal will cost in today's dollars. Go to www.morningstar.com/goto/30MinuteSolutions for several calculators to determine how much your financial goals will cost in tomorrow's dollars.

If you completed the Goal Planning Worksheet (Worksheet 3.1), you will have already done this.

Step 2

Next, check your progress toward this goal. How much have you saved, and how much will you save on an ongoing basis?

Step 3

With those variables in hand, you should be able to determine how long it will take you to reach your goal. So, for example, if you have $10,000 saved, you're saving an additional $200 a month, and you'd like to amass $20,000, it will take you roughly four years to hit your goal amount.

Don't assume any return on your investments at this point. With a little help from the market, it will take even less time to hit your goal than you've calculated it will. But if you're saving and investing for a goal that's close at hand, your own savings rate is going to be a much bigger determinant of whether and when you reach your financial goal than any return you'll earn from your investments.

Step 4

Once you know your time horizon, you can identify the right investments. The shorter the time horizon, the safer the investments should be.

Fewer than Two Years from Goal   If your goal amount is this close at hand, my advice is straightforward: Play it safe. Yes, yields on CDs and money market funds are low; interest on savings and checking accounts may be nonexistent. But when you're this close to needing the money, you can't afford to lose any part of what you've saved. If you're running behind your target amount, taking on more risk isn't the answer. Instead, you may have to delay your goal or save more in the interim in order to hit your goal amount.

Here's an overview of the key investment types available to you:

- ▶ **Checking and savings accounts:** Convenience is the big plus here, but rates are apt to be rock-bottom. Deposits of up to $250,000 per institution will be covered by FDIC insurance.
- ▶ **Money market deposit accounts:** These interest-bearing savings accounts typically offer a limited number of transactions per month, and deposits of as much as $250,000 per institution are FDIC-insured.

▶ **Certificates of deposit:** CDs usually offer higher yields than you can earn on a money market fund. If you have saved an amount that's close to your target, why not lock it up and earn the highest possible rate you can? CDs also carry FDIC insurance for deposits of as much as $250,000 per institution. On the flip side, CDs require that you leave your money in them for a fixed period—one month, one year, or even longer. (You'll pay a penalty to withdraw money from a CD prematurely.)

▶ **Money market funds:** Although rates aren't as high as you're apt to earn with a CD, a money market mutual fund can be a good option if there's a chance you'll need to withdraw the money. Also, when interest rates go back up, money funds can quickly translate higher interest rates into higher take-home yields. Because money funds buy short-term bonds, they can readily swap into newer, higher-yielding securities when interest rates edge up. The big downside in comparison to the checking and savings accounts, CDs, and money market accounts is that money market fund assets are not FDIC-insured.

If you opt for a money market fund, cheaping out should be your key consideration. That's because the amount you pay in expenses will be the key determinant of the yield that you get to pocket. (Expenses are deducted directly from yield.) You should pay no more—and preferably much less—than 0.50 percent in expenses for your money market fund. One other tip: If you do spy a fund with very low fees, make sure that the fund company isn't temporarily waiving part of its expenses in an effort to attract new investors. Such waivers can readily be reversed. Also be wary of a fund with a yield that's substantially higher than the competition, especially if the fund doesn't have very low fees. It could be investing in lower-quality securities to pump up its yield, and pumping up its risk level at the same time.

Also bear in mind your tax bracket when shopping for a money fund for your taxable account. Even if you're not in the highest tax bracket, it may make sense to opt for a tax-free money market fund over a taxable one. That's because the muni fund's yield may actually be higher than the taxable fund's once you factor in taxes. To quickly compare the after-tax yields of taxable and tax-free funds, use the Tax-Equivalent Yield function of the Morningstar Bond Calculator, available at www.morningstar.com/goto/30MinuteSolutions.

Table 13.1   Top Money Market Funds

Name	Ticker	Taxable or Tax-Exempt	Investment Minimum ($)
Fidelity Cash Reserves	FDRXX	Taxable	2,500
Fidelity Municipal Money Market	FTEXX	Tax-Exempt	5,000
Fidelity AMT Tax-Free Money Market	FIMXX	Tax-Exempt	25,000
Payden Cash Reserves	PBHXX	Taxable	5,000
TIAA-CREF Money Market	TIRXX	Taxable	2,500
Vanguard Prime Money Market	VMMXX	Taxable	3,000
Vanguard Tax-Exempt Money Market	VMSXX	Tax-Exempt	3,000

Low expense ratios help these funds deliver competitive yields without taking on extra risk.

Table 13.1 features some solid money market options.

Two to Five Years from Goal   Because your time horizon is further away, you can consider taking on a little more risk than you would with money that you might need within the next few years. In turn, you'll be able to garner a slightly higher yield than you could with a money market fund or a CD. Stock funds—even conservative ones—are off-limits, as it's possible that you might need to tap your money when stocks are at a low ebb. Instead, stick with a short-term bond fund or even a conservatively positioned intermediate-term bond fund. Table 13.2 has Morningstar's favorite investments for the job. When you come within two years of hitting your goal amount, shift the assets into an ultrasafe investment like a CD or money market fund.

As with your savings for very short-term goals, it also makes sense to investigate tax-free alternatives. You'll earn a lower yield, but that yield may trump the taxable fund's payout once taxes are taken into account. To compare the after-tax yields on taxable and muni funds, check out the Tax-Equivalent Yield function of the Morningstar Bond Calculator.

Five to Ten Years from Goal   Although safety is still important, you can afford to take a bit more risk in the hope of generating a higher return if you have a time horizon of 5 to 10 years. You can hold a small amount in stocks to generate decent capital appreciation and enough bonds to stabilize the portfolio. I also

Table 13.2   Morningstar's Top Picks for Short Time Horizons

Name	Ticker	Category	Taxable or Tax-Exempt	Investment Minimum ($)
Dodge & Cox Income	DODIX	Int-Term Bond	Taxable	2,500
Fidelity Short-Intermediate Muni Income	FSTFX	Muni Short	Tax-Exempt	10,000
Fidelity Intermediate Municipal	FLTMX	Muni Intermediate	Tax-Exempt	10,000
Harbor Bond	HABDX	Int-Term Bond	Taxable	1,000
iShares Barclays 1-3 Years Credit Bond (ETF)	CSJ	Short-Term Bond	Taxable	N/A
T. Rowe Price Short-Term Bond	PRWBX	Short-Term Bond	Taxable	2,500
T. Rowe Price Tax-Free Short-Intermediate	PRFSX	Muni Short	Tax-Exempt	2,500
Vanguard GNMA	VFIIX	Int-Term Gov	Taxable	3,000
Vanguard Intermediate-Term Tax-Exempt	VWITX	Muni Intermediate	Tax-Exempt	3,000
Vanguard Limited-Term Tax-Exempt	VMLTX	Muni Short	Tax-Exempt	3,000
Vanguard Short-Term Bond Index	VBISX	Short-Term Bond	Taxable	3,000
Vanguard Total Bond Market Index	VBMFX	Int-Term Bond	Taxable	3,000
Vanguard Short-Term Tax-Exempt	VWSTX	Muni Short	Tax-Exempt	3,000

All of these funds have been able to deliver solid long-term returns while limiting losses. Focus on funds that land in our short-term categories if you're closer to two years from needing your money, and intermediate-term funds if your time horizon is closer to five years.

urge investors to pay close attention to tax efficiency when assembling an intermediate-term portfolio. If you plan to tap these assets within the next 10 years, before you're ready for retirement, it would be impractical to save in a 401(k), an IRA, or some other tax-advantaged vehicle.

Table 13.3 includes some of Morningstar's favorites for intermediate-term time horizons. Most of these funds land in our conservative-allocation category, meaning that they hold the majority of their assets in bonds but also hold some stocks.

Next Steps

▶ Once you've squared away your short- and intermediate-term savings goals—what you're saving for, how much it will cost you, and what you'll be investing in—you can turn your attention to longer-term goals like retirement and college savings. Chapter 14 shows you how to create a basic long-term portfolio. Parts Five and Six tackle the ins and outs of retirement saving, while Part Seven coaches you on investing for college.

Table 13.3   Morningstar's Top Picks for Intermediate-Term Time Horizons

Name	Ticker	Category	Investment Minimum ($)
Dodge & Cox Balanced	DODBX	Moderate Allocation	2,500
T. Rowe Price Personal Strategy Income	PRSIX	Conservative Allocation	2,500
T. Rowe Price Spectrum Income	RPSIX	Multisector Bond	2,500
Vanguard Tax-Managed Balanced	VTMFX	Conservative Allocation	10,000
Vanguard Wellesley Income	VWINX	Conservative Allocation	3,000
Vanguard Wellington	VWELX	Moderate Allocation	10,000
Vanguard STAR	VGSTX	Moderate Allocation	1,000

These funds all own varying combinations of stocks and bonds. T. Rowe Price Spectrum is the most conservative and bond-heavy, whereas Dodge & Cox Balanced is among the more aggressive funds listed here.

▶ Amid the credit crisis, Congress increased the limit on assets covered by FDIC insurance from $100,000 to $250,000 per depositor per institution. That increase will remain in effect through 2013. So if you're concerned about the safety of your money, investing in an FDIC-insured vehicle is the way to go. Go to the FDIC's web site for a broad array of information about this type of insurance and what it covers.

Create a Hands-Off Long-Term Portfolio

ONE OF THE MOST POPULAR FEATURES in my newsletter, *Morningstar PracticalFinance,* is called "Portfolio Makeover," featuring the before and after portfolios of real-life individuals. Some of the portfolio submissions I receive need a complete overhaul, while others feature well-thought-out asset allocations and topnotch stocks and funds.

Nearly all the portfolios have one thing in common, though: They're way more complicated than they need to be. Most portfolios feature upward of 25 stock and fund holdings, and I've even seen portfolios with 70 or more individual stocks and funds.

It's easy to see how that happens: Many couples are investing in more than one company retirement plan, and they may also have a few different IRAs and taxable accounts. And most investors, knowing that diversification is desirable, layer on multiple holdings within those accounts. Wall Street's tendency to peddle the hot investment du jour doesn't help matters. People own niche offerings that they easily could do without, such as funds that focus on a single market sector or geographic region. In the late 1990s, every other portfolio seemed to feature a technology or Internet fund; over the past five years, energy and commodities have been de rigueur.

Of course, diversification *is* good, but it can get out of hand. The big drawback to an excessively large portfolio: You could end up with more investments than you could realistically keep track of. If you own individual stocks, you need to stay up-to-date on what's happening at every company. Even if you own mutual funds, which allow you to be more hands-off, you still need to pay attention to who's managing your fund, whether its strategy or costs have changed, and so forth. If you have 25 holdings in your portfolio, that adds up to a lot of research hours—more than many investors care to spend.

Also, if your portfolio is hyper-diversified, it may generate returns much like the broad market's. If that's the case, you're better off going with a cheap index fund rather than painstakingly assembling a portfolio of many individual investments and paying much more for it.

For all these reasons, I'm strongly in favor of building and maintaining the most streamlined portfolio that you can. It's inevitable that you'll have multiple accounts, given the complexities of the retirement savings system, but you can easily get away with just a handful of holdings within each of those accounts. Here are three key ways to create simple portfolios:

Option 1—Target-date funds: For investors looking to build simple, hands-off portfolios, target-date funds are a welcome development. The funds are designed as one-stop investment vehicles composed of what the fund company thinks is an appropriate mix of investments for someone with your anticipated retirement date. The manager or fund company gradually adjusts the investments in target-date funds to become more conservative as retirement draws near.

Unfortunately, the risks of some target-date funds were exposed in 2008: Some had sunk far too much into the stock market for portfolios geared toward older investors, while others put too much money into individual funds whose risks came back to haunt them when the housing market collapsed. So if you opt for one of these funds, it's important to do your homework up front. Morningstar's favorite target-date series are run by Vanguard (more conservative, bond-heavy asset allocations) and T. Rowe Price (more aggressive stock/bond mixes).

One other important caveat is that nearly all target-date funds are "funds of funds" run by a single fund company. Although such a portfolio might be diversified, in another way you're putting all your eggs in one basket by entrusting your money to a single firm. It had better have a sensible asset-allocation plan and the firm should also do a good job of running money in all the major asset classes: domestic and international stocks as well as bonds. Not many meet that test. Morningstar analysts began rating target-date programs in 2009, and Vanguard's plan came out on top.

Option 2—Index: Target-date funds provide an easy way to simplify your investment life, but they're blunt instruments. They feature the same allocations for all investors with the same retirement date. If you'd like to simplify your portfolio but exert more control over your stock/bond mix, index funds can be a logical place to start building your portfolio. Index funds don't have a stock- or bond-picker at the helm who's aiming to beat a market benchmark, such as the S&P 500 Index; instead, the index fund manager is simply trying to match the index's returns, minus the costs associated with running the fund.

That might not sound terribly ambitious (one of my colleagues once jokingly called it "un-American"!). But over long periods of time, index funds that track broad stock and bond market indexes have been able to beat the average fund with an active stock- and bond-picker at the helm. Costs are the secret. Because they don't have to employ a fund manager or analysts to pick stocks and bonds, index funds can be run on a shoestring, often charging 0.25 percent per year or less. (The typical actively managed U.S. stock fund charges 1.2 percent, and the typical active bond fund has a 0.8 percent expense ratio.) Index funds don't have to make many trades, either, so that, too, reduces the drag of trading-related costs on your bottom line. A few large fund families offer extremely low-cost index funds, with Fidelity, Vanguard, and, more recently, Schwab continuously competing for "cheapest index fund" rights. Some exchange-traded funds—essentially index funds that you can buy and sell throughout the day, much like a stock—also have very low expense ratios.

In addition to competitive performance, index funds are ideal for simplifiers. A single, broadly based index fund can give you exposure to the whole stock or bond market, enabling you to build an entire portfolio with just two or three funds. Index funds from reliable firms also need very little baby-sitting, so once you've set up an index-based portfolio, your only job is to keep your stock/bond mix in line with your targets. Finally, broad-market index funds and exchange-traded funds tend to be a particularly good option if you're saving outside your company retirement plan or IRA, because they generate few taxable capital gains. (I detail the ins and outs of saving in your taxable account in Part Eight.)

Table 14.1 includes Morningstar's favorite broad-market index funds and exchange-traded funds. (Index funds are best if you plan to invest more money on an ongoing basis, while ETFs can be more cost-effective if you're making a one-time, lump-sum purchase.)

Option 3—Index funds complemented by sturdy active funds or all active funds: All-index portfolios can be highly effective, but if you'd like a chance to juice returns a bit, building a portfolio to do that is still simple. You can

Table 14.1   Morningstar's Favorite Core Index Funds

Name	Ticker	Category	Investment Minimum ($)
U.S. Stock Funds			
Fidelity Spartan 500 Index	FSMKX	Large Blend	10,000
Fidelity Spartan Total Market	FSTMX	Large Blend	10,000
iShares S&P 500 (ETF)	IVV	Large Blend	N/A
Schwab S&P 500	SWPPX	Large Blend	100
Schwab Total Stock Market Index	SWTIX	Large Blend	100
Vanguard Dividend Appreciation (ETF)	VIG	Large Blend	N/A
Vanguard 500 Index	VFINX	Large Blend	3,000
Vanguard Total Stock Market Index	VTSMX	Large Blend	3,000
Foreign-Stock Funds			
Fidelity Spartan International Index	FSIIX	Foreign Lrg Blend	10,000
Vanguard All-World ex-US (ETF)	VEU	Foreign Lrg Blend	N/A
Vanguard Total Intl Stock Market Index	VGTSX	Foreign Lrg Blend	3,000
Bond Funds			
Vanguard Total Bond Market Index	VBMFX	Int-Term Bond	3,000

Combining these funds based on your target asset allocation is a simple way to create a no-maintenance portfolio. Exchange-traded funds are best for those who plan to make one large purchase; traditional index funds are better for those who invest smaller sums over a period of time. (Note that all of the Vanguard funds are available in a traditional and ETF format.)

use index funds complemented by a few topnotch active funds, or else you can create a portfolio that's composed entirely of actively managed funds.

The jury is still out when it comes to determining where to use active funds and where to use index funds in your portfolio. During the recent bear market, for example, active managers using value-oriented strategies were, on average, able to beat their benchmarks. (There are different shades of value investing, but in general it means that a manager looks for stocks that are trading cheaply relative to what he or she thinks they're worth.) Growth-oriented managers, particularly those who focus on small and midsize stocks, had a harder time beating their benchmarks. However, those results tend to change depending on the time period you examine.

Table 14.2 includes Morningstar's favorite actively managed core funds.

To create a hands-off long-term portfolio, you'll need:

▶ A target asset allocation. (Chapter 11, and Figure 11.1 in particular, provide you asset-allocation guidance.)

Start the Clock

Step 1

Start by considering whether you'd like to invest in a target-date fund for all or a portion of your portfolio. If not, move on to the next step.

If you like the target-date concept, you'll need to simply choose the target-date fund that corresponds with your expected retirement date. Morningstar's favorite target-date funds are from Vanguard (more conservative/bond-heavy portfolios) and T. Rowe Price (more stock-heavy portfolios).

If your menu of fund choices includes target-date funds run by firms other than T. Rowe Price and Vanguard, look for overall expense ratios that are less than 1.00 percent per year—preferably much less. Also check to see how a prospective target-date fund's asset allocation compares with the asset allocations provided in Figure 11.1. If it's far off, opt for a portfolio that gives you more control over your asset mix.

Step 2

If you like the simplicity of target-date vehicles but would like to maintain more control over your stock/bond mix, consider a portfolio composed

Table 14.2   Morningstar's Favorite Actively Managed Core Funds

Name	Ticker	Category	Investment Minimum ($)
U.S. Stock Funds			
Dodge & Cox Stock	DODGX	Large Value	2,500
Fairholme	FAIRX	Large Blend	2,500
Fidelity Contrafund	FCNTX	Large Blend	2,500
Oakmark	OAKMX	Large Blend	1,000
Oakmark Select	OAKLX	Large Blend	1,000
Selected American	SLADX	Large Blend	10,000
Sequoia	SEQUX	Large Blend	5,000
Sound Shore	SSHFX	Large Value	10,000
T. Rowe Price Equity Income	PRFDX	Large Value	2,500
T. Rowe Price New America Growth	PRWAX	Large Growth	2,500
Foreign-Stock Funds			
Artio International Equity II	JETAX	Foreign Lrg Blend	1,000
Artisan International	ARTIX	Foreign Lrg Growth	1,000
Dodge & Cox Global Stock	DODWX	World Stock	2,500
Dodge & Cox International	DODFX	Foreign Lrg Value	2,500
Harbor International	HIINX	Foreign Lrg Value	2,500
Harbor International Growth	HIIGX	Foreign Lrg Growth	2,500
Masters' Select International	MSILX	Foreign Lrg Blend	10,000
Oakmark Global	OAKGX	World Stock	1,000
T. Rowe Price Global Stock	PRGSX	World Stock	2,500
Bond Funds			
Dodge & Cox Income	DODIX	Int-Term Bond	2,500
Fidelity Intermediate Muni Income	FLTMX	Muni Intermediate	10,000
Fidelity Municipal Income	FHIGX	Muni Long	10,000
Fidelity Tax-Free Bond	FTABX	Muni Long	25,000
Fidelity Total Bond	FTBFX	Int-Term Bond	2,500
Harbor Bond	HABDX	Int-Term Bond	1,000
Metropolitan West Total Return Bond	MWTRX	Int-Term Bond	5,000
T. Rowe Price Spectrum Income	RPSIX	Multisector Bond	2,500
Vanguard Intermediate-Term Tax-Exempt	VWITX	Muni Intermediate	3,000

These broadly diversified actively managed funds could work well instead of—or in addition to—the index funds shown in Table 14.1. All feature seasoned management teams and relatively low expenses, giving their managers a fighting shot at beating the index over time.

entirely of index funds or exchange-traded funds. (If the target-date or all-index portfolios don't appeal to you, move on to the next step.)

Table 14.1 shows Morningstar's favorite core index funds and exchange-traded funds. Use the target asset allocations in Chapter 11/Figure 11.1 to determine how much to invest in each of the index funds shown in Table 14.1.

Step 3

If you'd like a shot at beating a market index rather than just matching it, build a portfolio that combines index funds with active funds or consists entirely of active funds. Use the portfolio allocations in Figure 11.1 as a starting point, then populate them with active funds from Table 14.2 or a combination of active and index funds (Table 14.1). For example, for your domestic-stock weighting, you could include a 50 percent stake in Vanguard Total Stock Market Index VTSMX and a 50 percent stake in Dodge & Cox Stock DODGX. Don't go overboard; a handful of stock and bond funds is all you need to build a well-diversified portfolio.

Next Steps

▶ Even if you'd like to focus primarily on actively managed funds for your investments, you may still want to complement them with small positions in index funds. Research by Vanguard involving millions of portfolio combinations found that even portfolios with topnotch active funds improve their risk/return profiles by holding at least a little in index funds.

▶ This chapter was designed to help you create a simple, straightforward portfolio and therefore focuses entirely on funds. It's possible to create extremely effective portfolios using individual stocks, but it will take you more than a half hour to put such a portfolio together, and it will also require more in the way of ongoing monitoring. Of course, there are many wonderful resources for stock investors, but I'm partial to Pat Dorsey's book, *The Five Rules for Successful Stock Investing* (John Wiley & Sons, 2004).

PART FIVE

Invest in Your Company Retirement Plan

A BEAR MARKET IS NEVER WELCOME, but the one that rocked investors in late 2007 and 2008 was particularly ill-timed. That's because it clobbered the account balances of the first wave of 401(k) investors, many of whom were newly retired or getting set to retire.

The number of employees who are managing their own retirement plans has climbed steadily over the past few decades. As the costs of providing pensions, which offer steady income streams, have skyrocketed, many companies switched from offering so-called defined-benefit (that is, pension) plans to defined-contribution plans: 401(k)s, 457s, and 403(b)s. (401(k) plans are mainly for private sector employees, whereas 457s are for government employees and workers at some not-for-profit firms. 403(b)s are mainly for educators and also may be set up for employees in the not-for-profit sector.) In 1980, the Department of Labor estimated that 40 percent of all workers in the private sector had a defined-benefit plan, 19 percent were participating in a defined-contribution plan, and 11 percent participated in both types of plans. By 2004, that mix had shifted substantially: The percentage of employees participating in defined-benefit plans had shrunk to 21 percent, whereas 42 percent were participating in defined-contribution plans, and 13 percent were participating in both.

Unfortunately, roughly a fourth of employees who have 401(k) plans don't participate because they don't think that they can afford it, they don't recognize the importance of saving on their own behalf, or they feel that they don't have the time or knowledge to make good investment choices.

If you're one of the many individuals bewildered by the process of steering the investments in your company retirement plan, this section is designed to help. One of the first steps is to determine whether your company plan is a worthwhile repository for your hard-earned investment dollars: In Chapter 15 I show you how to determine how good your company retirement plan is. (For an overview of the pros and cons of saving in your company retirement plan versus other types of investment vehicles, read Chapter 9.)

In Chapter 16, I coach you on how to determine whether to invest in a traditional 401(k) plan or a Roth 401(k). Roth 401(k)s have been around only since 2006, and the vast majority of 401(k) savers still use the traditional 401(k) type, which allows you to make pretax deposits. But I think the Roth, to which you contribute aftertax dollars in exchange for tax-free withdrawals during retirement, can make sense for a couple of different types of investors, notably those who are just starting out and higher-income earners who have already amassed a lot of assets in a traditional 401(k).

If you're already contributing to your company retirement plan, the next step is to select the optimal mix of investments. As I discuss in Chapter 17, this process can be as simple as selecting a single, all-in-one fund, but you can also build a portfolio consisting of multiple complementary investments.

Finally, this section addresses what to do if you've gone through the steps in Chapter 15 and have determined that your company retirement plan is a stinker. You may decide to invest in another vehicle, such as a Roth IRA, particularly if you're not earning a match on your contributions. But if you decide to go ahead and invest in a subpar 401(k) because you want to take advantage of the tax benefits, Chapter 18 shows you how to make lemonade out of those lemons.

15

Determine How Good Your Company Retirement Plan Is

ONE OF MY CLOSE FRIENDS, a single mom, held various part-time jobs throughout her career, living frugally but always struggling to make ends meet. Now that her daughter is grown, however, she's been able to obtain full-time work in a field that she's passionate about, assisting in a veterinary clinic. Not only is she able to spend her days nurturing the animals she loves, but she's also enjoying full-time benefits for the first time in her working life, including a solid health-care plan and the opportunity to contribute to a 401(k).

As I helped her review the options available in her new retirement plan, I was struck by how little information the investment provider had made available. All my friend had to go on were the fund names, their general objectives (for example, "Growth"), and their one-, three-, and five-year returns. There were no manager names, no expense information, no clues about whether the funds buy stocks of tiny, risky companies or bonds issued by the U.S. Treasury.

Unfortunately, retirement plan participants are often flying blind when it comes to evaluating their plans and selecting investments. There's no easy way to evaluate the quality of a plan overall, and some of the administrative costs associated with retirement plans are buried in a document called the Summary Plan Description that's available only on request by participants. In addition, some plans provide very little information about the individual investment options and retirement plan participants do not necessarily receive annual reports and documents that are available to other fund shareholders.

This information is essential not only for selecting the right investments, but also in helping determine whether investing in the company retirement plan is the right use of a participant's money. Participants with weak plans who aren't earning any matching contributions from their employers might in fact be better off striking out on their own, ideally by saving in a Roth IRA, than they would be investing in their company plans.

Unfortunately, a little bit of digging revealed that my friend's plan is one of the stinkers. Although I was initially heartened to see that her plan is managed by one of the top fund companies in the business, her individual fund options are costly—more than twice as expensive as the share classes that non-retirement-plan investors can obtain by going outside the plan. (Some investments are explicitly created for 401(k) plans, and investors in them may have to pay administrative costs that aren't borne by investors in other versions of the same fund. This is particularly common for plans offered by smaller employers.) Investing the percentage my friend needed to earn the company match—in this case, 3 percent of her paycheck—would be worthwhile. Beyond that, however, her plan's high costs would quickly erode the tax-deferred compounding that she'd enjoy by saving within the confines of the plan. If she wanted to put more dollars away for her retirement, she'd be better off setting up a Roth IRA.

If you're employed and eligible to contribute to a company retirement plan, conducting some basic due diligence about the plan's quality is an essential first step as you determine whether your company plan is the best use of your hard-earned investment assets.

To determine how good your company retirement plan is, you'll need:

▶ The Summary Plan Description for your 401(k). (Ask your human resources administrator to provide you with one.)
▶ The plan's annual report. (HR should also be able to provide this.)
▶ A list of the investment options available to you

Start the Clock

Step 1

Refer to your 401(k) plan's Summary Plan Description or your employee handbook to see if your employer matches any portion of your contributions. If so, you'll want to contribute at least that percentage to your plan. (Doing otherwise is like turning down free money.)

If your company isn't matching any portion of your contributions, you should still consider investing in your 401(k) because you'll be able to enjoy tax-free compounding—that is, your contributions will grow based on how your investments perform and you won't owe any taxes on those gains until you withdraw the money in retirement. There's also an advantage to making contributions automatically, which is what most 401(k) plans allow you to do. However, you'll want to carefully research the quality of your plan before you make contributions that exceed the amount on which you're being matched.

Step 2

Also in the Summary Plan Description, check how your company handles the administrative costs associated with running the plan. Some companies defray all these administrative costs for their employees; others pass them on to plan participants. A company retirement plan's investment costs are usually separate from its administrative costs, but sometimes the administrative costs of the plan are bundled into the fund expense ratio. (See the next step for details on checking individual fund costs.)

If your company is not covering the plan's administrative costs, check up on how much you're paying. Within the Summary Plan Description, you may see your plan's administrative costs expressed in percentage terms or dollars and cents, neither of which will be too useful without some context. To help gauge the reasonableness of your plan's administrative costs, divide your plan's costs by the total dollars in the plan to arrive at a percentage. If your plan's administrative costs are higher than 0.5 percent per year, that's a red flag that your plan is costly. Proceed to the next step to see if your individual fund choices are also costly.

If you can't find administrative expenses in the Summary Plan Description, ask your company's human resources group for help in digging up this number. It may appear in your plan's annual report (Form 5500).

Step 3

If your plan holds mutual funds, you can find detailed information about the funds in your plan by entering their tickers on Morningstar.com. If the investments in your plan don't have tickers or don't register on Morningstar.com when you type their names in the ticker box, move on to the next step.

As you go about finding information on Morningstar.com, be sure that the share classes of the funds you find on the site (share classes are usually identified by a tagline after the fund's name, for example, Institutional, A, or Retirement I) match the share classes of the funds in your plan.

If Morningstar.com has a report for one of the funds in your plan, you'll see an array of information on that fund's home page. As you peruse the data, pay particular attention to the following items:

▶ **Expense ratio:** This statistic encompasses the management and administrative costs associated with that particular fund, and, depending on the share class in your plan, it may also encompass some of the management fees associated with your company retirement plan. Look for funds with expense ratios that fall below the following thresholds:
  ▶ **U.S. stock funds:** Less than 1.25 percent
  ▶ **Bond funds:** Less than 0.75 percent
  ▶ **Foreign stock funds:** Less than 1.5 percent
  If your plan's investments are appreciably higher than these thresholds, that's another red flag that your plan is pricey.
▶ **Category:** In addition to checking the expense ratios for each of the funds in your plan, also look to make sure that your plan has a decent number of "core" funds from which to choose. Core investments usually land in one of the following Morningstar categories:
  ▶ Large Blend
  ▶ Large Value
  ▶ Large Growth
  ▶ Foreign Large Blend
  ▶ Foreign Large Value
  ▶ Foreign Large Growth
  ▶ Moderate Allocation

- ▶ Conservative Allocation
- ▶ Target Date
- ▶ Intermediate-Term Bond

An array of funds in other categories, such as specialty and/or regional funds, can be valuable, but you'll probably want to keep the bulk of your retirement plan assets in one of the aforementioned core categories.

- ▶ **Manager start date:** Also check how long the managers have been running the fund. When selecting mutual funds, there's almost never a good reason to settle for a newbie manager. Look for manager tenures of five years at a minimum.

  Of course, it is possible for a manager to be new to a specific fund but still have a lot of experience overall. However, if your plan has a number of funds with short manager tenures, it can be a red flag that the fund company is experiencing companywide upheaval or relies heavily on the skills of relatively inexperienced skippers.

- ▶ **Returns relative to category:** Returns aren't the be-all and end-all of fund selection, but they are the only quantifiable measure of how a fund has delivered for its shareholders in the past. Check out a fund's 5- and 10-year return ranking versus its category peers. (Lower numbers are better here.) Not every fund in your plan has to be at the top of the charts, but look for a good number of funds whose returns land in the category's top half or better.

Step 4

If you can't find information on Morningstar.com about the investments in your plan, you'll have to do a bit more homework. Company retirement plans are increasingly offering non-mutual fund investments such as separately managed accounts in their menu of choices. Such investment options aren't necessarily worse than mutual funds and in fact may be quite strong and inexpensive, but they don't have to provide the same level of disclosure that mutual funds do. (One caveat: If you find yourself in the position of having to dig up details on a lot of non-mutual funds, the research process can be arduous and you may end up spending more than the half hour I've allotted for this process.)

Start by requesting more information from your company and/or investment provider about your plan's investment options: Ask for details on the fund company running the investments, strategy, top 10 holdings, manager tenure, and costs. If you are able to get your hands on this information, you can conduct the same due diligence process that I outlined above for mutual funds.

If you're able to find out only who's running the fund but can't find any other details, you may be able to do a little bit of sleuthing to identify a mutual fund that's a near-clone of the investment in your plan—for example, if you find out that a firm such as Dodge & Cox is running a fund called "Core Stock" for your company, it's a good bet that the fund is nearly identical to Dodge & Cox Stock DODGX. Use any other information that you have—such as manager names, return histories, or top 10 holdings—to corroborate that the mutual fund is a good proxy for the investment in your plan. If it is, you can conduct the due diligence outlined in the previous step.

Step 5

Finally, it's time to decide on your course of action. Consider the following as you weigh your options.

▶ If your plan scores poorly on the above items, you can still make a save. In Chapter 18 I discuss how to take the best and leave the rest in a subpar company retirement plan.

▶ If your plan is truly a stinker, consider other sources of retirement funding. Are you eligible to contribute to a Roth IRA or a traditional deductible IRA, for example? That may be preferable to putting the full amount in your company retirement plan. (In Part Six I discuss IRAs in detail.)

▶ Are you a high-income earner who is already maxing out other tax-sheltered options such as IRAs? If so, that argues for contributing the maximum to your 401(k), even if you don't particularly like the investment options and/or you're not earning a match. Contribution limits are much higher for 401(k)s than IRAs, allowing you to shelter more of your investment income from taxes. Those tax savings can be valuable if you're in a high tax bracket, even if the individual options in your plan are only so-so.

Next Steps

▶ Also conduct the due diligence on your spouse's plan. If that plan rates better than yours on the above metrics and your spouse is not currently maxing out his or her contributions, you might consider diverting a higher share of your household's investment assets to that plan before focusing on your own.

▶ If you have more time to spend with the Summary Plan Description, check the other features of your plan. For example, are 401(k) loans permitted, and if so, what are the rules governing them? It's particularly important to check these details if there's any chance that you may need to tap your assets prior to retirement.

16

Decide between a Traditional and Roth 401(k)

I'M NO RETAIL ANALYST, but I think there's a logical reason why department stores like Macy's and Sears have been losing ground to specialty retailers like Williams-Sonoma and J. Crew for the past few decades. It's what behavioral finance pros call *choice overload*. Consumers have a dizzying array of selections for nearly every product, and that sense of having too many options can be exacerbated in department stores. Specialty retailers, by contrast, provide an edited-down menu of choices, helping ease decision making for time-pressed consumers.

A similar phenomenon exists in the realm of finance, where choice overload can lead to ill-considered decision making or, worse yet, no decision making at all. A study by the Wharton School's Pension Research Council, for example, found that 401(k) participation rates fall as the number of funds increase. A host of other studies have reached similar conclusions.

For that reason, I had a hard time getting excited about the Roth 401(k) when some companies began offering the option in 2006. I know firsthand that 401(k) participants often have a difficult time making decisions, so I was concerned that this new vehicle could further clutter their thought processes, providing yet another disincentive to save.

The jury's still out on whether this is the case, but in the meantime, I've warmed up to the Roth 401(k) as an option for certain investors, especially young people just starting out in their careers as well as higher-income earners who already have a lot stashed in traditional 401(k)s. Meanwhile, the Roth 401(k) has also begun to pop up as an option in more and more company retirement plans. I've begun to direct my own 401(k) contributions to a Roth.

If you're familiar with how a Roth IRA works, it's easy to get your arms around how a Roth 401(k) operates. As is the case with a Roth IRA, you'll contribute after-tax dollars to a Roth 401(k). The trade-off for taking the tax hit sooner rather than later is that you'll be able to withdraw your contributions and any earnings without having to pay taxes.

That's just the opposite of the tax treatment your traditional 401(k) contributions and withdrawals receive. You invest pretax dollars in a traditional 401(k) and therefore have more investment dollars working for you from the get-go, but you'll pay income tax on your withdrawals.

Other than the basic differences in tax treatment, Roth 401(k)s are quite similar to traditional 401(k)s, and most companies that offer the Roth option will probably offer the Roth and traditional 401(k)s in tandem. (Educational and charitable institutions that currently offer 403(b)s may also add a Roth option to their plans; as of mid-2009, Congress was debating a bill that would allow Roth contributions to a 457 plan. The concepts in this chapter also apply to other types of company retirement plans that offer a Roth option.)

There's no income limitation governing who can contribute to either type of account, and the same contribution limits that apply to a traditional 401(k) will also apply to a Roth 401(k). The limit applies to your total contributions to both accounts; that is, you won't be able to contribute the maximum to both a Roth and a traditional 401(k).

Once you've told your 401(k) provider whether you want your investment dollars to go to the traditional 401(k) or to the Roth 401(k) (and you may have the option of sending part of each contribution to each vehicle), you'll be able to allocate your investment dollars among a menu of investment choices. Finally, you generally can't withdraw your investment earnings on a tax-free basis until you reach age $59\frac{1}{2}$, and you'll be required to begin taking distributions from the Roth 401(k) when you're age $70\frac{1}{2}$, just as you have to do with a traditional 401(k) plan. (You can avoid taking distributions by rolling your Roth 401(k) into a Roth IRA, however. I discuss the ins and outs of rollovers in Chapter 22.)

The rules regarding Roth 401(k)s are pretty straightforward, but the calculus about whether to invest in one versus a traditional IRA is more art than science.

To determine whether to invest in a traditional or Roth 401(k), you'll need:

▶ Roth vs. Traditional 401(k) Worksheet (Worksheet 16.1, available at www.morningstar.com/goto/30MinuteSolutions)
▶ The company retirement plan's Summary Plan Description or your employee handbook
▶ Most recent tax return
▶ Current 401(k) balance, as well as your balances in other retirement accounts such as IRAs

Start the Clock

Step 1

Refer to your 401(k) plan's Summary Plan Description or other literature about your company's 401(k) plan to see whether your employer offers a Roth 401(k) option. Even if your employer doesn't currently offer this option, you may still want to go through the following steps. If you determine that a Roth 401(k) is a good bet for you, you can lobby your company to add this option to your plan.

Step 2

Next, complete the Roth vs. Traditional 401(k) Worksheet (Worksheet 16.1), available at www.morningstar.com/goto/30MinuteSolutions. Here are some details on the questions and why they're relevant to the decision about whether to invest in a Roth or traditional 401(k).

1. **Are you just starting out a career in a lucrative field?**

     If so, it's a good bet that your income in retirement will be higher than what it is now. If that's the case, a Roth 401(k) may be a better option than a traditional 401(k).

Worksheet 16.1

Roth vs. Traditional 401(k) Worksheet

PREPARED FOR: DATE: /   /

An increasing number of 401(k) plans are offering a Roth option. The key differences are as follows:

Traditional 401(k)
- Pretax contributions
- Tax-deferred compounding
- Taxed upon withdrawal in retirement

Roth 401(k)
- After-tax contributions
- Tax-free compounding
- Tax-free withdrawals

You'll Need:
- Company retirement plan's Summary Plan Description or employee handbook
- Most recent tax return
- Current 401(k) balance, as well as balances in other retirement accounts such as IRAs

DETERMINE TRADITIONAL VS. ROTH 401(K)

	Traditional 401(k)	Roth 401(k)
Are you just starting out in a career in a lucrative field?	○ No	○ Yes
Have you recently completed a course of study that is apt to boost your earnings potential?	○ No	○ Yes
Do you take a lot of tax credits and deductions?	○ Yes	○ Yes
Are you within five years of retirement?	○ Yes	○ Yes
Is your income apt to be higher or lower in retirement than it is now?	○ Lower	○ Higher
Do you already have a lot of assets in a traditional IRA and/or 401(k)?	○ No	○ Yes
Are you maxing out your 401(k) contributions? *	○ No	○ Yes
Will you be able to fund your retirement without your 401(k) assets?	○ No	○ Yes
Does your income level disqualify you from contributing to a Roth IRA?	○ No	○ Yes

RESULTS

- If most of your answers fell under the Traditional 401(k) column, that's likely the better option for you.
- If most of your answers fell under the Roth 401(k) column, you're a good candidate for Roth 401(k) contributions.
- If your answers were evenly divided among the two columns, consider splitting your contributions between the two vehicles.

TO CONTRIBUTE THE MAXIMUM ALLOWABLE AMOUNT:

- Traditional 401(k): Divide the maximum allowable 401(k) contribution by your annual salary to arrive at percentage.
- Roth 401(k): Multiply the maximum allowable amount by 1 plus your tax rate (for example, 1.28 if you're in the 28% tax bracket). Then divide that amount by your total salary to arrive at your desired percentage contribution per check.

Print your worksheet at: www.morningstar.com/goto/30MinuteSolutions

2. **Have you recently completed a course of study that is apt to boost your earnings potential?**

   As with the question above, this suggests that you're better off paying taxes on your retirement plan contributions now than you are by waiting to pay tax during retirement.

3. **Does your most recent tax return show a lot of tax credits and deductions that are based on income?**

   With a Roth 401(k), your contributions are included in that year's income, whereas traditional 401(k) contributions aren't included in income, thereby increasing your eligibility for tax breaks. Take a look at last year's tax return. If you took advantage of a lot of credits and deductions in the past, such as the child tax credit or the earned income tax credit, and think that you may still be eligible for them in the future, increasing your income level by adding Roth 401(k) contributions probably isn't a great idea.

4. **Are you within five years of retirement?**

   If you plan to retire within the next five years or so, the tax-free compounding that the Roth affords won't be as beneficial as it would be if you have a longer time horizon until retirement.

5. **Is your income apt to be higher or lower in retirement than it is now?**

   If you have many years until retirement, you're probably going to have to give it your best guess. However, your income is apt to be lower in retirement if you're close to retirement and you haven't yet saved much.

6. **Do you already have a lot of assets in a traditional 401(k) or IRA?**

   One of the key advantages of obtaining Roth treatment for your retirement assets is that it allows you to pay a knowable tax rate (today's) in exchange for tax-free withdrawals in the future.

   Of course, none of us knows what future tax rates will look like, but as I write this in mid-2009, the government is spending at a prodigious pace. In addition, the Economic Growth and Tax Relief Reconciliation Act of 2001 had some pretty generous provisions, especially for investors, and many of them are set to expire in 2010.

   For those who have a large share of their retirement portfolios in a traditional 401(k) or a traditional IRA, a Roth 401(k) provides a good way to hedge one's bets against higher rates in the future. Contributing to a Roth 401(k) can make even more sense if you've amassed a large traditional 401(k) nest egg and you've not been able to contribute to a Roth IRA because you earn too much. Even if you have no idea whether your income level and tax bracket in retirement will be higher or lower than they are now, the Roth 401(k) provides a good opportunity to diversify the tax treatment of your retirement kitty: You'll pay some taxes now (on the Roth 401(k)) and some later (on the money you withdraw from your traditional 401(k)).

7. **Are you currently maxing out your 401(k) contributions?**

If so and you're in a position to contribute even more, bear in mind that the Roth 401(k) actually has a higher effective contribution rate than does a traditional 401(k). On paper, the contribution limits are identical—in 2009, the limit is $16,500 for those younger than 50 and $22,000 for those over 50. (Those figures will rise in line with inflation in 2010 and thereafter.) But you make after-tax contributions to a Roth 401(k), whereas your entire traditional 401(k) kitty will eventually be taxed. That means that once taxes are factored in, the Roth 401(k) actually allows you to contribute a larger sum.

8. **Will you be able to fund your retirement without using all or some of your 401(k) assets?**

If so, the Roth 401(k) offers an important feature: the ability to roll over those assets to a Roth IRA once you've retired or left your employer. Unlike with a traditional 401(k), Roth 401(k), or traditional IRA, you're not required to take distributions from a Roth IRA once you are age $70^{1}/_{2}$. That allows you to stretch out the tax benefits of the IRA for a longer period of time, giving your assets more time to grow.

9. **Does your income level disqualify you from contributing to a Roth IRA?**

If you haven't been able to contribute to a Roth IRA because you earn too much, investing in a Roth 401(k) is one way to ensure that you can take tax-free withdrawals from at least a portion of your retirement kitty.

Step 3

Once you've completed the worksheet, look at whether most of your responses land in the Traditional 401(k) or Roth 401(k) column; that will help you determine what type of 401(k) contributions you should be making. If your responses were mixed, that's probably an argument for splitting future contributions between the two types of vehicles.

Step 4

Once you've made a decision about whether to invest in a traditional or Roth 401(k), it's time to execute your plan.

If you want to contribute the maximum to a traditional 401(k), the math is pretty simple: Divide the maximum contribution amount by your annual salary to arrive at a percentage, then instruct your 401(k) provider to take out that percentage per check.

The calculation is a touch more complicated for Roth 401(k) contributions. To arrive at the right amount, multiply the current contribution limit by 1 plus your tax rate—for example, if you want to make the maximum contribution and you're in the 28 percent tax bracket and under 50, multiply $16,500 (the max for 2009) by 1.28. Then divide that amount ($21,120) by your total salary to come up with your desired percentage contribution per check.

Next Step

▶ Employees mulling future Roth 401(k) contributions should bear in mind that the Roth 401(k) provision is set to expire in 2010 unless Congress takes further action to keep it alive. That sounds ominous, but an expiration of the Roth 401(k) would most likely mean that employees wouldn't be able to make fresh contributions to their Roth 401(k)s; the existing money would stay in the account and withdrawals would likely still be tax-free. Most tax experts agree that it is extremely unlikely that Congress would vote to tax withdrawals on current Roth balances, given that 401(k)s are the savings vehicle of choice for most middle-class investors and that would amount to taxing the same assets twice.

17

Select the Best Investments for Your Company Retirement Plan

In talking with friends and family members about how they manage their 401(k) investments, it's clear that investment styles are highly personal, reflecting both disposition and how much time a person has on his or her hands.

A small percentage of the 401(k) investing population is what I would classify as downright hyperactive, exemplified by my engineer neighbor, who used to spend part of his workdays day trading stocks with his buddies. Taking cues from a computer program that one of them had written, they'd jump into a stock when the market opened and be out of it later in the afternoon. (I haven't heard much about this pastime recently, so it's a good bet that the bear market has cooled the engineers' enthusiasm for day trading.)

Then there's the commitment-phobe, who's so worried about making poor choices or so unsure about her abilities that she takes tiny positions in many different investments. I've even seen 401(k) plans in which the participant selected funds geared toward multiple target dates: for example, a 10 percent position in the 2020 fund, a 10 percent stake in the 2030 fund, and so on. You can do worse things than overdiversify, and this investor may ultimately be better off than the day trader, but the commitment-phobe's strategy clearly isn't ideal, either.

Another segment of the 401(k) investing population falls into the "just can't be bothered" camp. Because of their own real or perceived lack of investment knowledge, choice overload, or time constraints (or most likely a combination of the three), many would-be 401(k) participants have made no choices at all. Research into 401(k) investor behavior shows that roughly one fourth of those eligible to participate in 401(k)s do not, even when their employers are offering matching contributions. That well-documented inertia prompted the passage of the Pension Protection Act of 2006, which allowed companies to automatically opt their employees into the company retirement plan. For those employees who are automatically opted in, the vast majority of folks stay in, stick with the default option, and continue to contribute at whatever the default rate is.

For most investors, the best strategy for managing a retirement portfolio falls somewhere between the do-nothings and the hyperactive traders. The following steps will help you identify a comfortable middle course that also fits with your disposition, knowledge level, and the amount of time you have for managing your 401(k).

To select the best investments in your company retirement plan, you'll need:

▶ A menu of the choices available to you in your 401(k) or other company retirement plan
▶ A rough idea of when you expect to retire. (If you're young and have no idea, you can use age 65 as a default. If you're closer to retirement, you should have a clearer idea of what's realistic for you.)
▶ An idea of an appropriate stock/bond mix for you given the number of years you have until retirement. (Chapter 11 covers this topic in-depth, and I've also provided some sample asset allocations in Figure 17.1.)

 Start the Clock

Step 1

Take a moment to think about how much time you'd like to devote to creating and maintaining your company retirement plan. If the answer is "very little,"

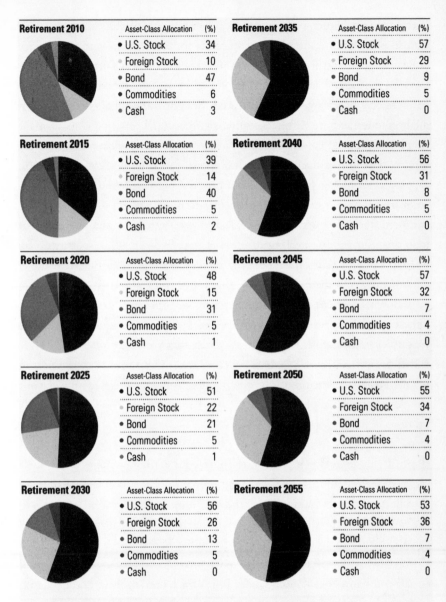

Retirement 2010	Asset-Class Allocation	(%)
	• U.S. Stock	34
	○ Foreign Stock	10
	• Bond	47
	• Commodities	6
	• Cash	3

Retirement 2035	Asset-Class Allocation	(%)
	• U.S. Stock	57
	○ Foreign Stock	29
	• Bond	9
	• Commodities	5
	• Cash	0

Retirement 2015	Asset-Class Allocation	(%)
	• U.S. Stock	39
	○ Foreign Stock	14
	• Bond	40
	• Commodities	5
	• Cash	2

Retirement 2040	Asset-Class Allocation	(%)
	• U.S. Stock	56
	○ Foreign Stock	31
	• Bond	8
	• Commodities	5
	• Cash	0

Retirement 2020	Asset-Class Allocation	(%)
	• U.S. Stock	48
	○ Foreign Stock	15
	• Bond	31
	• Commodities	5
	• Cash	1

Retirement 2045	Asset-Class Allocation	(%)
	• U.S. Stock	57
	○ Foreign Stock	32
	• Bond	7
	• Commodities	4
	• Cash	0

Retirement 2025	Asset-Class Allocation	(%)
	• U.S. Stock	51
	○ Foreign Stock	22
	• Bond	21
	• Commodities	5
	• Cash	1

Retirement 2050	Asset-Class Allocation	(%)
	• U.S. Stock	55
	○ Foreign Stock	34
	• Bond	7
	• Commodities	4
	• Cash	0

Retirement 2030	Asset-Class Allocation	(%)
	• U.S. Stock	56
	○ Foreign Stock	26
	• Bond	13
	• Commodities	5
	• Cash	0

Retirement 2055	Asset-Class Allocation	(%)
	• U.S. Stock	53
	○ Foreign Stock	36
	• Bond	7
	• Commodities	4
	• Cash	0

Allocations of Morningstar's Lifetime Allocation Indexes, developed in conjunction with asset-allocation expert Ibbotson Associates. Note that even long-dated portfolios contain some bonds and near-dated portfolios include some stocks.

Figure 17.1   How Should You Allocate Your Company Retirement Plan?

check to see whether your company offers a target-date fund. Such funds feature a stock/bond mix that's appropriate for someone in your general age range and gradually become more conservative as you get closer to retirement. Some of the biggest 401(k) providers, including Vanguard and T. Rowe Price, have created target-date funds with well-thought-out asset allocations, high-quality underlying investments, and low costs overall.

As good as the concept behind target-date funds is, however, not every fund company has executed it well. Some of these funds are too costly: An expense ratio higher than 1 percent a year is a big red flag; over time, those costs are apt to be a big drag on your long-term returns.

Also, the funds may have stock/bond mixes that are too aggressive or too conservative. To check up on how a fund looks on that score, hop on www.morningstar.com and type in the name of the target-date fund that you're investigating. On the main page for that fund, you'll see its Asset-Allocation breakdown. Compare that with the pie chart for your target date in Figure 17.1. (These stock/bond/cash mixes were created by Ibbotson Associates, which is part of Morningstar.) If the target-date fund that you're considering diverges widely from the asset allocations provided here, that should prompt you to investigate further before using one of these funds as the linchpin of your company retirement plan.

Step 2

If you'd like to retain more control over your retirement portfolio than a target-date fund affords, or if the target-date funds offered in your retirement plan don't appear to be very good, the next most straightforward option is to use index funds for all or part of your company retirement portfolio. Index funds don't try to beat the market; instead, they invest in every stock or bond within a benchmark like the S&P 500 (large-company stocks) or Russell 2000 (small-company stocks). Some index funds track narrow slices of the market, such as wind-power stocks or Latin America, but the index funds that are appropriate for most 401(k) investors track broad swaths of the market. For example, "total market" U.S. stock index funds try to approximate the returns of all publicly traded companies in the United States, whereas "total market" bond index funds try to replicate the returns of the investment-grade (that is, no junk bonds) bond market in the United States.

You might assume that index funds would be weak performers alongside funds run by fund managers who are actively selecting stocks and bonds, but you'd be wrong. Because they feature very low costs and many actively managed funds do not, index funds have delivered solid performance versus the average fund with an active stock-picker at the helm. Index funds also have a lot of appeal for minimalists: You won't have to worry about whether your manager has left for another firm or has shifted part of the portfolio into cash and thrown off your target stock/bond/cash mix.

If you want to build an all-index-fund 401(k) plan, you would simply identify an appropriate asset allocation (see Figure 17.1 for some ideas) and then direct the appropriate percentage of your contributions to the corresponding index funds. For example, say you're planning to retire in 2040. You could put 55 percent of your assets in a total U.S. stock market index fund, another 30 percent in a total foreign stock market index fund, and the remainder in a total U.S. bond market index fund. You would need to make changes to your portfolio only when your asset allocations got out of whack with your targets and in order to make your portfolio more conservative as you near retirement. (You can find details on how to do that in Chapter 33.)

Step 3

Of course, a simple, all-index plan won't work if you don't have any broad-based indexes from which to choose. Or perhaps you'd like to try to beat the market rather than merely track it. Another popular and worthwhile strategy is to use index funds for the core of your portfolio and actively managed funds to supplement them.

If you do decide to opt for active management for all or part of your portfolio, you'll have to invest more time at the outset than you will if you go the all-index route. You'll have to do some homework to identify worthy active managers, and you'll also need to conduct some ongoing oversight to make sure that they are meeting your expectations or are still at the helm.

Still, there's no doubt that some active stock- and bond-pickers have been able to solidly beat their benchmarks over time. So, while an all-index portfolio can be a sturdy and low-maintenance way to go, you may be able to give your portfolio some oomph by adding some funds run by active stock-pickers.

When selecting active funds, you might be tempted to invest in the ones that have posted the best returns over the past several years, or simply focus on those with 4- or 5-star ratings. Don't make that mistake. Yes, returns and star ratings are among the few quantifiable ways to judge how effective a manager has been, and Morningstar's star ratings have also shown some predictive ability. But your analysis shouldn't stop there. Check up on how much experience the manager has; look for at least a five-year tenure. And with expenses being among the most reliable predictors of long-term performance, it makes sense to gravitate toward the lowest-cost options in your plan. Look for stock funds with expense ratios of less than 1.25 percent, and preferably much lower than that, and bond funds that cost less than 0.75 percent.

Next Steps

- ► The investment options that I've outlined above focus on using your 401(k) plan's preset menu of choices. If you'd like to exert more control over your plan by selecting individual stocks or using mutual funds and exchange-traded funds outside of your plan, that may be an option; an increasing number of employers are allowing participants to invest outside of their plans using their provider's self-directed brokerage option, or window. Using self-directed brokerage, participants can put part or all of their assets in investment vehicles of any kind. You'll be in complete control of your 401(k), but remember that with freedom comes responsibility. Selecting individual stocks, funds, and ETFs will require a greater investment of your time, and you may not be able to make automatic contributions as is the case in a company retirement plan.

- ► In September 2009, Morningstar's fund analyst team began providing research reports on individual target-date programs. Premium Members of Morningstar.com can see a snapshot of the asset-allocation framework of each plan, as well as ratings of the plan's managers, parent company, costs, and a host of other factors.

18

Make the Most of a Subpar 401(k) Plan

I'VE LEARNED a lot of life lessons from my mother, but one of the most important is the ability to make the best of what seems like a lousy break. When I was in third grade and the eye doctor was outfitting me with my first pair of glasses (gold wire frames, no less), Mom confidently assured me that some fashion models actually *chose* to wear spectacles. When my father was too busy to take a family vacation one summer, she invented the "staycation" long before that word existed, carting my sisters and me to Chicago museums, restaurants, and a matinee of *A Chorus Line*. When the chicken pox kept me from seeing my beloved Chicago Cubs on my birthday, she and Dad donated our tickets to a local children's home and asked the folks at Wrigley Field to say my name over the PA system. They did, and I swelled with pride as I watched the game from our rec room that afternoon. Who knew that being a benefactor could be just as much fun as being there in person?

In a similar vein, if you've checked your company retirement plan (see Chapter 15 for details on how to do this) and determined that it's subpar, you can take steps to make the most of it. Of course, if it's really a stinker and you're not earning any matching contributions, you may be better off avoiding it and investing through a vehicle like a Roth IRA; Chapter 9 includes guidance on how to prioritize various retirement savings vehicles.

But 401(k) contribution limits are much more generous than IRA limits. Add in the benefits of tax-free compounding and automated investing that 401(k)s confer, and I think you're usually better off investing something in your 401(k) than you are forgoing it altogether.

To help optimize your investment choices in a subpar 401(k) plan, you'll need:

▶ A list of the investment options in your 401(k) plan
▶ A list of the investment options in your spouse's 401(k) plan, if applicable
▶ A list of your household's other retirement assets
▶ A target asset allocation for your retirement savings. (See Chapter 11 for a how-to guide.)
▶ Morningstar's Instant X-Ray tool (available at www.morningstar.com/goto/30MinuteSolutions)

Start the Clock
Step 1

Assuming that you've decided to go ahead and invest in your company retirement plan, check to see whether there are any decent investments in it. Focus on funds with reasonable costs, long-tenured management teams, and sensible, core-type strategies. (See Chapter 17 for details on how to select appropriate investments for your retirement plan.)

Keep an eye out for index funds, which frequently appear in company retirement plans and are almost always serviceable, even if they're not best of breed. These offerings track a given market benchmark rather than attempting to beat it, and they allow you to obtain broad market exposure at a reasonable cost. Even if the index funds in your plan aren't the best—say, your plan offers an S&P 500 fund from Dreyfus or Morgan Stanley rather than the ultracheap options from Vanguard and Fidelity—you're probably still better off going the index route than you are opting for a lackluster active fund. True, the active manager—even the one with a subpar past record—has a shot at beating his or her benchmark, at least in theory. In practice, however, the active fund's expenses—as well as transaction costs that aren't reflected in its expense ratio—weigh heavily on that manager's ability to beat the benchmark.

If your plan includes one or two respectable actively managed or index-tracking funds in the major asset classes—U.S. stock, foreign stock, and bond—you can split your contributions across these vehicles. (See Chapter 11 for guidance on finding the right stock/bond mix.) If not, move on to the next step.

Step 2

It's natural to want to craft a 401(k) portfolio that's diversified across all the major asset classes (bonds and U.S. and foreign stocks), but that might not be practical or prudent if your company plan doesn't offer viable options in all these areas. If you've identified just one or two standout funds in your plan—index or otherwise—you can load up on those and avoid the rest. You can use your IRA, your taxable accounts, or your spouse's retirement plan to delve into those asset classes and investment styles in which your own plan is lacking.

In other words, think of the overall portfolio working together. Each part doesn't have to be complete unto itself. For example, say the stock funds in your company plan are poor but the lineup does offer a top-quality core bond fund. Even though your overall asset-allocation plan calls for just 30 percent in bonds, you could sink a big share of your 401(k) portfolio into the bond fund and then go light on bonds in your other accounts.

The key to making this strategy work is to look at all the assets geared toward a particular goal or time horizon in aggregate. Morningstar's Instant X-Ray tool, available at www.morningstar.com/goto/30MinuteSolutions, can make easy work of this task. Just enter all your retirement-related holdings into the tool, then click Show Instant X-Ray to see your whole portfolio's asset-class breakdown. You can then compare that with your target allocations.

Step 3

If your plan doesn't include any worthwhile options, you can still make a save. Increasingly, 401(k) plans—particularly those from large employers—are offering so-called brokerage windows (also called self-directed accounts). If your plan offers such an option, you'll have the opportunity to delve into hundreds of other mutual funds, stocks, and even exchange-traded funds that aren't part of your 401(k) plan's preset menu.

Having the option to choose from such a wide array of securities might appear to be a godsend if your plan consists of pricey, mediocre funds. You'll likely be able to buy individual stocks, topnotch mutual funds, and even exchange-traded funds via the brokerage window.

But before you jump aboard, be sure to read the fine print. You may pay an extra fee (often levied annually) to participate in the brokerage window, and those extra costs can quickly erode the extra returns you might gain by venturing beyond your plan's preset menu. In addition, you may pay separate transaction costs to buy and sell securities that are part of the brokerage window. (That will almost certainly be the case when buying stocks and ETFs, so if you're going to go this route, it pays to do so by investing a single lump sum rather than making a lot of small purchases.) Finally, many brokerage windows don't allow you to put your investments on autopilot by investing every two weeks or month, as is the case with 401(k) contributions. So if you want to invest at regular intervals, you may have to manage it yourself.

And while the brokerage window might give you the opportunity to venture beyond the plain vanilla offerings that are often mainstays of company retirement plans, don't use the brokerage window as your license to load up on niche offerings with extreme risks. Even though the brokerage window might offer an array of sector funds, niche bond vehicles, and region-specific international offerings, large-cap stock funds and intermediate-term bond funds should still serve as the linchpins of your 401(k) portfolio.

Next Steps

▶ If your plan is truly lousy, you may be better off forgoing it altogether and investing in a combination of an IRA and your taxable accounts instead. In Part Six I have covered investing inside an IRA, whereas in Part Eight

I discuss how to limit Uncle Sam's cut when investing in your taxable accounts.

► Company retirement plans don't get better on their own. If you've researched your company plan and determined that it leaves a lot to be desired, communicate your specific findings to your company's human resources department, and urge your co-workers to do the same.

PART SIX

Invest in an IRA

BACK IN SEPTEMBER 2008, I attended the Vanguard Diehards conference with a couple of my Morningstar coworkers. As you may remember, stocks were dropping like a stone during that period, as it became clear that what we had been calling "the subprime crisis" was really a global economic catastrophe.

Amid the turmoil, the Diehards—who favor the low-cost, no-nonsense, index-fund investment strategy of Vanguard founder Jack Bogle—were the very picture of Zenlike calm. My colleague David Chung shot a video of me asking the Diehards how they were changing their portfolios in the wake of the crisis, and their responses went something like this:

Diehard 1:   "I'm staying the course, obviously."

Diehard 2:   "I'm not doing anything. I'm comfortable with what I've got."

Diehard 3:   "Staying the course."

Diehard 4:   "Just sticking with my plan."

After the 26th Diehard responded to my question with some version of "I'm staying the course," we decided that our video was too boring to run on Morningstar.com.

That experience illustrated that the Diehards have mastered one of the key tenets (perhaps *the* key tenet) of successful investing: Know what you can control and what you can safely tune out.

The direction of the economy, interest rates, inflation, and the dollar? Clearly in the "out of my hands so might as well tune it out" category.

By contrast, you have some or a lot of control over the securities that you select for your portfolio, the price that you pay for them, how much you trade, and how much you pay in investment-related taxes. Those are the topics that tend to occupy most of the Vanguard Diehards' time and conversation, both on their web site, bogleheads.org, and at their conference.

I know, you're probably thinking that taxes usually go in the "beyond my control" column; after all, death and taxes are usually called the only two certainties in life. But you might be surprised to learn that you can exert quite a lot of influence over your investment-related tax payments. One key is to take advantage of all of the tax-sheltered vehicles you can, including an IRA. Depending on the IRA type you choose, you can enjoy tax-deferred or tax-free withdrawals in retirement, and paying less to Uncle Sam on a year-to-year basis can result in an improved take-home return for you.

Believe it or not, prospective IRA holders are faced with even more "choice overload" than are those investing in 401(k) plans. For starters, there are two key types of IRAs in which you can invest, traditional and Roth. Deciding which type makes sense for you is the focus of Chapter 19. Once you've made that decision, you need to select what to put inside the IRA wrapper, and your options are virtually limitless. That's daunting, but it's also a good thing, because you can use your IRA to hold investments that aren't available to you in your company retirement plan and also take maximum advantage of the tax-sheltered nature of the IRA. In Chapter 20, I discuss how to select appropriate investments for your IRA.

If you have a traditional IRA but determine that a Roth is the better vehicle for you, the IRS lets you convert to a Roth, provided you pay the taxes on any deductible contributions or investment earnings at the time you make the conversion. As I write this in 2009, investors have a golden opportunity to do so: Not only are many IRA account values still way down due to the recent bear market, which reduces the tax costs of converting, but in calendar year 2010 the IRS has also eliminated the strictures about who can convert to a Roth. Making a conversion can help you obtain tax-free withdrawals, and, if you're one of the lucky ones and don't expect to need your IRA assets during retirement, the Roth can help you "stretch out" the tax benefit. Deciding whether an IRA conversion makes sense for you is the focus of Chapter 21.

Finally, the vast majority of the money sitting in IRAs now didn't get there because investors started IRAs from scratch; rather, that money is there because an IRA is usually the best place to put retirement assets if you've changed jobs and have taken money out of your previous employer's retirement plan. If you're in need of guidance on how to handle a so-called IRA rollover, Chapter 22 walks you through the steps for doing so.

19

Determine What Type of IRA Is Best for You

As with 401(k)s and other company retirement plans, would-be IRA holders confront a bewildering array of choices, and maybe that helps explain why so few investors fund an IRA on their own. (The vast majority of IRA assets are there because individuals rolled over their company retirement plans after they left their employers.) In addition to deciding what types of investments to put in the IRA (which I discuss in the next chapter), you also have to decide what type of IRA you want to save in. More choice overload.

There are two main IRA types: a traditional IRA and a Roth IRA. With a traditional IRA, you won't have to pay taxes on your IRA's investment earnings until you begin taking distributions from it during retirement; thus, your money enjoys the benefit of tax-deferred compounding. (That means that you'll have to pay taxes on your earnings when you begin withdrawing money from the kitty, but not as you go along.)

The Roth, however, has a couple of huge advantages over a traditional IRA. Whereas traditional IRAs carry restrictions governing when you have to begin taking distributions, the Roth carries no such restrictions; you won't be forced to take distributions at any age. And perhaps even more significantly, qualified distributions from a Roth will be *tax-free*, not tax-deferred as is the case with a traditional IRA.

With that information, the choice might seem clear: Roth IRA all the way. And while the Roth is generally going to be the better option for most investors, it's not a slam-dunk in every single situation. If your income falls below a certain threshold, you can make at least a partial contribution (and possibly a full one) to a traditional IRA and deduct that contribution from that year's income tax return. Individuals in higher income tax brackets can also contribute to a traditional IRA, whereas a Roth might not be available to them because they earn too much. Higher-income savers won't be able to deduct their contributions on that year's tax return, but they'll still enjoy tax-deferred compounding on their money. (And, in 2010, investors at all income levels will be able to convert a traditional IRA into a Roth—an option that was heretofore off-limits for those at higher income levels. If you earn too much to contribute to a Roth, this can be a good way to get into one. I discuss converting an IRA in Chapter 21.)

So, how do you add some rigor to the decision-making process about whether to invest in a Roth or traditional IRA? The following steps will help you decide.

To determine what type of IRA is right for you, you'll need:

▶ Anticipated income level for the current tax year
▶ Current income tax rate
▶ Morningstar's IRA Calculator (available at www.morningstar.com/goto/ 30MinuteSolutions)

Start the Clock

Step 1

Start by gauging which IRA type you're eligible to contribute to. As I noted above, you can't make a deductible contribution to a traditional IRA if your income comes in above a certain level. But raw income isn't the only factor that can affect which type of IRA you might be eligible for; you'll also have to factor in your tax-filing status and whether you're eligible to contribute to a company retirement plan.

To help simplify the task, go to Morningstar's IRA Calculator, available at www.morningstar.com/goto/30MinuteSolutions. On the Eligibility tab, plug in a few of these variables to see how much you can contribute to a traditional IRA (deductible and nondeductible contributions) and a Roth IRA each year.

Step 2

After you've input your information into the IRA Calculator, you may find that certain IRA types are automatically off-limits to you because of your income level. For example, if you're in one of the higher tax brackets, you'll find that you can't contribute to a Roth; your only IRA option is to make a nondeductible contribution to a traditional IRA.

But what if you establish that you're eligible to make more than one type of IRA contribution—for example, you can contribute to a Roth and make a deductible contribution to a traditional IRA? You may decide to split your contribution between both vehicles, or you could go back to the IRA Calculator for a more definitive answer. Click on the Comparison tab at the top of the calculator, then enter the data you're asked to provide. If you're not sure about your tax rate, refer to the IRS' web site, www.irs.gov. You'll also have to provide an estimate of your income and capital gains tax rates in retirement. If retirement is many years off and you have no idea, you can use your current rates or nudge them higher or lower depending on your outlook for future tax rates. The current capital gains tax rate is 15 percent for most investors, one of the lowest levels in history.

After you've entered all your information, click Submit. You'll see a comparison of how a contribution to each of these investment vehicles would have compounded, on an aftertax basis, by the time you're ready to retire. We also show you how an investment in a regular old taxable account would have fared.

For example, if you're eligible to make a deductible contribution to a traditional IRA and fund a Roth IRA, you may find that the traditional IRA contribution is your best bet because you'll be able to contribute that money without having to pay income taxes on it. Similarly, even if you're not eligible to make a deductible traditional IRA contribution or a Roth IRA contribution, you might find that a nondeductible contribution to a traditional IRA might still make sense for you because you'll enjoy tax-deferred compounding on your money—an option you wouldn't have if you saved in your taxable account.

Once you've gone through the process of selecting the right IRA type for you, you'll need to find the right investment(s) to put in it. (Remember, the IRA is just the "wrapper" for whatever investments you select, and your investment choices are virtually unlimited.)

Step 3

The IRA Calculator does a good job of quantifying whether you're better off investing in a Roth or traditional IRA. But also consider the following questions, which the calculator doesn't delve into.

▶ Have you amassed a lot of assets in a traditional 401(k)? If so, a Roth IRA will probably make sense for you because it will ensure that you won't have to pay taxes on at least some of your assets in retirement.
▶ Do you expect that you may not need your IRA assets for income during retirement? If so, the Roth is probably a good bet for you. Unlike a traditional IRA, you're not required to take distributions from a Roth IRA once you're age $70^1/_2$. That allows you to stretch out the tax benefits of the IRA for a longer period of time, giving your assets more time to grow.

Next Steps

▶ If you already have a traditional IRA and have decided the Roth is a better vehicle for you, you may find it beneficial to convert to a Roth. In Chapter 21 I discuss how to decide whether to convert to a Roth IRA from a traditional one.
▶ If it turns out that you're eligible to invest only in a traditional nondeductible IRA, you don't have to embrace this route. A good tax-managed mutual fund will mimic the tax treatment of a traditional IRA—you're not likely to have to pay taxes from year to year, though your contributions will be taxed as will your withdrawals. As an added benefit, tax-managed funds don't require minimum distributions when you're $70^1/_2$, unlike a traditional IRA.

20

Identify the Best Investments for Your IRA

"The lord works in mysterious ways."

Uh-oh, I thought, as I read the first line of a letter from a Morningstar reader, who proceeded to regale me with an investment-related tale worthy of an O. Henry story.

A fifty-something computer programmer, he was devastated when he lost his job in the financial services industry back in mid-2008. With a mortgage and two kids hurtling toward college, the layoff obviously brought worries about what the future would bring.

At the time of his layoff, he was also panicked about his 401(k) portfolio, which included a healthy dose of stock funds as well as many shares of his employer's stock, which was quickly going from bad to worse.

Here's where the plot twist comes in: Shortly after the layoff, he had rolled over his 401(k)—the bulk of his retirement savings—into an IRA. Paralyzed by indecision over where to invest the money, he had left the assets sitting in an ultra-low-yielding, but ultra-safe money market fund. In so doing, his retirement portfolio was cushioned during the late 2008-early 2009 market sell-off, the worst since the Great Depression, which saw the S&P 500 dropping by 50 percent. Even more fortuitously, he had also dumped his company stock at an opportune time. Soon after he sold the stock and rolled his money into the IRA, shares of his former company skidded from $25 a share down to about $3. He hadn't yet found a new job at the time he wrote to me, but he noted that his inaction toward his retirement portfolio had saved him far more money than he had lost in income from his job.

Yet, he didn't want to look a gift horse in the mouth. He knew how lucky he had been in sidestepping the market's troubles, but he also knew that his conservative portfolio could be left in the dust if the market rebounded. And indeed, when he wrote to me in the spring of 2009, the major stock indexes were scoring huge gains each day. He wanted guidance, posthaste, on getting his portfolio invested for good.

It's easy to see why this programmer, as well as a lot of other would-be IRA investors, suffer from "analysis paralysis." Once you decide whether to invest in a traditional or Roth IRA, you then have to sort among an overwhelming array of options. You can put almost anything inside an IRA wrapper: individual stocks and bonds, money market funds, CDs, or mutual funds. Life insurance policies and investments made on margin—that is, those funded with borrowed money—are among the few mainstream asset types that can't go inside an IRA.

However, because IRAs offer either tax-free (Roth IRA) or tax-deferred (traditional IRA) compounding, it's usually a mistake to put any sort of investment that itself has tax benefits inside an IRA wrapper. Municipal bonds are a great example: You don't typically pay federal taxes on the income from municipal bonds or bond funds, but in exchange you usually have to accept a lower level of income than you'd have from a taxable bond or bond fund. For that reason, you're better off holding tax-advantaged investments like municipal bonds and variable annuities (to the extent that you own them) in your taxable accounts, and only after you've funded your IRA and company retirement plan.

To identify the best investments for your IRA, you'll need:

► Statements for all your retirement holdings: 401(k)s, 457s, 403(b)s, and other IRAs

▶ Morningstar's Instant X-Ray tool (available at www.morningstar.com/
goto/30MinuteSolutions)

 Start the Clock

Step 1

The first step in selecting investments for your IRA is to think about what
role your IRA will play in your retirement portfolio. Will it take up a big
share—either because you're just starting out and plan to make many more
IRA investments in the future or because you've rolled over a large sum of
money from your company retirement plan? If so, move on to Step 2.

If you consider your IRA to be more of a supporting player because the
bulk of your retirement assets are elsewhere, either in your company retirement
plan or your taxable account, go to Step 3.

Step 2

If you already have a large sum of money stashed in an IRA—or expect that
your IRA will grow to be a large share of your overall retirement portfolio in
the future—you'll want your IRA to be well-diversified and populated with
core investment types like large-cap stock mutual funds and high-quality
bond funds.

If you have other assets earmarked for retirement, in addition to the money
that you're putting into an IRA, be sure to take those holdings into account
when deciding what to put in your IRA. Morningstar's Instant X-Ray tool,
available at www.morningstar.com/goto/30MinuteSolutions, can help you size
up your existing portfolio's stock/bond/cash composition and also shows you
how well it's diversified across various investment styles. (The Morningstar
Style Box™ provides a visual depiction of a portfolio's investment-style mix.)
Simply enter the tickers for each of your holdings into the X-Ray tool, then
click Show Instant X-Ray.

Compare the current allocations of your existing retirement portfolio with
the sample allocations shown in Figure 11.1. Once you've determined where
you need to add, you can select the specific investments. I've included some
of Morningstar's favorite core funds for an IRA in Table 20.1.

Table 20.1   Morningstar's Favorite Core Picks for an IRA

Name	Ticker	Category	IRA Investment Minimum ($)
U.S. Stock Funds			
Dodge & Cox Stock	DODGX	Large Value	1,000
Fairholme	FAIRX	Large Blend	2,500
Fidelity Contrafund	FCNTX	Large Blend	2,500
iShares S&P 500 (ETF)	IVV	Large Blend	N/A
Oakmark	OAKMX	Large Blend	1,000
Oakmark Select	OAKLX	Large Blend	1,000
Schwab S&P 500	SWPPX	Large Blend	100
Schwab Total Stock Market Index	SWTIX	Large Blend	100
Sequoia	SEQUX	Large Blend	2,500
Sound Shore	SSHFX	Large Value	2,000
T. Rowe Price Equity Income	PRFDX	Large Value	1,000
T. Rowe Price New America Growth	PRWAX	Large Growth	1,000
Vanguard Dividend Appreciation (ETF)	VIG	Large Blend	N/A
Vanguard 500 Index	VFINX	Large Blend	3,000
Vanguard Total Stock Market Index	VTSMX	Large Blend	3,000
Foreign-Stock Funds			
Artio International Equity II	JETAX	Foreign Large Blend	100
Artisan International	ARTIX	Foreign Large Growth	1,000
Dodge & Cox Global Stock	DODWX	World Stock	1,000
Dodge & Cox International	DODFX	Foreign Large Value	1,000
Harbor International	HIINX	Foreign Large Value	1,000
Harbor International Growth	HIIGX	Foreign Large Growth	1,000
Masters' Select International	MSILX	Foreign Large Blend	1,000
Oakmark Global	OAKGX	World Stock	1,000
T. Rowe Price Global Stock	PRGSX	World Stock	1,000
Vanguard All-World ex-US (ETF)	VEU	Foreign Large Blend	N/A
Vanguard Total Int'l Stock Market Index	VGTSX	Foreign Large Blend	3,000

Table 20.1   Morningstar's Favorite Core Picks for an IRA (*Continued*)

Name	Ticker	Category	IRA Investment Minimum ($)
Bond Funds			
Dodge & Cox Income	DODIX	Intermediate-Term Bond	1,000
Fidelity Total Bond	FTBFX	Intermediate-Term Bond	2,500
Harbor Bond	HABDX	Intermediate-Term Bond	1,000
Metropolitan West Total Return Bond	MWTRX	Intermediate-Term Bond	1,000
T. Rowe Price Spectrum Income	RPSIX	Multisector Bond	1,000
Vanguard Total Bond Market Index	VBMFX	Intermediate-Term Bond	3,000
Combination Stock/Bond Funds			
Dodge & Cox Balanced	DODBX	Moderate Allocation	1,000
T. Rowe Price Personal Strategy Income	PRSIX	Conservative Allocation	1,000
Vanguard Wellesley Income	VWINX	Conservative Allocation	3,000
Vanguard STAR	VGSTX	Moderate Allocation	1,000

These broadly diversified funds would serve as solid linchpins for an IRA portfolio.

Step 3

Are you opening an IRA to augment retirement monies that you hold elsewhere? If so, you, too, can hold core-type investments in your IRA, and Chapters 11 and 14 can help you both identify an appropriate asset allocation and find solid core investments.

But you can also use the IRA to fill holes in your company retirement plan. (Chapter 15 includes a discussion of how to evaluate the quality of your 401(k) plan.) For example, say your plan includes adequate stock funds but its bond funds charge more than 1 percent per year in annual expenses—a princely sum that's sure to take a big cut of your long-term return. If that's the case, you can fill up your company retirement plan with the decent stock funds and leave the bond portion of your portfolio to an IRA. Again, Morningstar's Instant X-Ray tool can help you see where you've got holes in your existing asset mix.

And because the world is your oyster when funding an IRA, you can also include investment types not commonly found in company retirement plans, including funds dedicated to real estate investments, commodities, or Treasury Inflation-Protected Securities. All these investment types do a good

Table 20.2   Morningstar's Favorite "Supporting Player" Picks for an IRA

Name	Ticker	Category	IRA Investment Minimum ($)
U.S. Stock Funds			
Ariel Appreciation	CAAPX	Mid Blend	250
Artisan Mid Cap Value	ARTQX	Mid Value	1,000
Bridgeway Small-Cap Growth	BRSGX	Small Growth	2,000
Bridgeway Small-Cap Value	BRSVX	Small Blend	2,000
Buffalo Mid Cap	BUFMX	Mid Growth	250
Clipper	CFIMX	Large Blend	4,000
Masters' Select Smaller Companies	MSSFX	Small Blend	1,000
Perkins Mid Cap Value	JMCVX	Mid Value	1,000
Royce Special Equity	RYSEX	Small Value	1,000
Royce Total Return	RYTRX	Small Value	1,000
T. Rowe Price Mid-Cap Growth	RPMGX	Mid Growth	1,000
T. Rowe Price Mid-Cap Value	TRMCX	Mid Value	1,000
T. Rowe Price Real Estate	TRREX	Real Estate	1,000
Third Avenue Small-Cap Value	TASCX	Small Blend	2,500
Turner Midcap Growth	TMGFX	Mid Growth	2,000
Vanguard Explorer	VEXPX	Small Growth	3,000
Vanguard Mid Cap Index	VIMSX	Mid Blend	3,000
Wasatch Small Cap Growth	WAAEX	Small Growth	1,000
Foreign-Stock Funds			
Artisan International Small Cap	ARTJX	Foreign Small/Mid-Value	1,000
T. Rowe Price Emerging Markets Stock	PRMSX	Emerging-Markets Stock	1,000
Third Avenue International Value	TAVIX	Foreign Small/Mid-Value	2,500
Third Avenue Real Estate Value	TAREX	Global Real Estate	2,500
Third Avenue Value	TAVFX	World Stock	2,500
Vanguard Emerging Markets Stock (ETF)	VWO	Diversified Emerging Markets	N/A

Table 20.2   Morningstar's Favorite "Supporting Player" Picks for an IRA (*Continued*)

Name	Ticker	Category	IRA Investment Minimum ($)
Bond Funds			
Fidelity High Income	SPHIX	High-Yield Bond	2,500
Fidelity New Markets Income	FNMIX	Emerging Markets Bond	2,500
Fidelity Strategic Income	FSICX	Multisector Bond	2,500
Harbor Real Return	HARRX	Inflation-Protected Bond	1,000
iShares Barclays TIPS Bond (ETF)	TIP	Inflation-Protected Bond	N/A
SPDR Barclays Capital High Yield (ETF)	JNK	High-Yield Bond	N/A
T. Rowe Price High-Yield	PRHYX	High-Yield Bond	1,000
T. Rowe Price International Bond	RPIBX	World Bond	1,000
Vanguard High-Yield Corporate	VWEHX	High-Yield Bond	3,000
Vanguard Inflation-Protected Securities	VIPSX	Inflation-Protected Bond	3,000
Other Funds			
ELEMENTS S&P CTI (ETN)	LSC	Commodity	N/A
Harbor Commodity Real Return	HACMX	Commodity	1,000
iPath Dow Jones-AIG Commodity (ETF)	DJP	Commodity	N/A

If you've already built out the core of your retirement portfolio, these funds may work well as supplementary holdings. Many of them are tax-inefficient, making them a good fit within an IRA wrapper.

job of diversifying a portfolio that's composed primarily of stocks and bonds. They also can be a headache when held outside a tax-sheltered account, because they generate a lot of taxable income, so they're ideal holdings for an IRA.

I've included some of my favorite "Supporting Player" IRA investment ideas in Table 20.2.

Next Steps

▶ To the extent that you hold bonds in your portfolio, it generally makes sense to hold them within tax-protected accounts like your IRA or company retirement plan. That's because bonds tend to generate a lot of income, which is taxed at rates as high as 35 percent. Stocks, meanwhile, typically crank out less income. Also, the tax rate on capital gains and stock dividends is currently much lower than is the case for bond income, though that treatment is set to expire at the end of 2010.

► I tend not to be a big fan of mutual funds with high turnover rates, meaning that the manager makes frequent changes to his or her investment portfolio. However, to the extent that you're attracted to such a fund type, it makes sense to shelter it within the confines of an IRA, where you won't owe taxes on your holdings from year to year. That's because high-turnover funds often generate short-term capital gains, which are taxed at your relatively high ordinary income tax rate. (Long-term capital gains receive much more favorable tax treatment.)

21

Determine Whether to Convert Your IRA

"Go run around the block," was my mom's advice to me when I was little and pestering her for something to do. She knew it would get me out of her hair, for at least a few minutes, and it might also help me burn off some energy.

I began to feel a little like my mother during the bear market of 2008. Investors were clamoring to do something, anything, and could you blame them? At a certain point, telling them to "stay the course" just didn't cut it, even though the sentiment was generally correct.

I wrote many columns about productive ways to use your time and energy when the market—and your portfolio—are going down, including shopping for investment bargains, rebalancing, and tax-loss selling. While I didn't specifically advise running around the block, I also urged investors to do whatever they could to burn off their nervous energy, including playing tennis and getting together with friends—anything that might get their minds off their portfolios.

And, as the market grew worse, one additional strategy became very easy to recommend: converting a traditional IRA to a Roth IRA. Yes, you'll have to pay tax on any investment earnings, plus any pretax contributions, when you make a conversion. In exchange, however, you'll be able to make tax-free withdrawals in retirement. Withdrawals from a traditional IRA, in contrast, are fully taxable.

So, why did making a conversion start to look like a better and better bet as the bear market wore on? The key reason is that as the market slumped, fewer and fewer investors had investment gains in their IRAs; the securities in their portfolios were trading at prices below where they bought them. That lessened—or in some cases totally negated—the tax hit that they would take when they made the conversion.

The economic slump also made an IRA conversion look more attractive. That's because increased government spending, while intended to pull the economy out of the doldrums, also has the potential to result in higher taxes down the line. If higher taxes do ensue, you'll want to take advantage of every means that you can to pay taxes now—as a Roth conversion enables you to do—rather than waiting until later, as you'll have to do if you leave your assets in a traditional IRA.

A Roth IRA also gives you more flexibility than you'll have with a traditional IRA. Notably, you won't be required to take mandatory distributions from a Roth at age $70^{1}/_{2}$, as is the case with traditional IRA assets. That's a huge boon if you don't expect to need your IRA assets during retirement; you can allow those investments to grow and pass on a greater amount to your heirs.

To determine whether to convert your IRA, you'll need:

► IRA account statements, including information about the purchase price of the securities in your portfolio as well as the amount of deductible versus nondeductible contributions
► Expected income level in the current year
► Morningstar's IRA Calculator (available at www.morningstar.com/goto/30MinuteSolutions)
► IRA Conversion Worksheet (Worksheet 21.1, available at www.morningstar.com/goto/30MinuteSolutions)

Worksheet 21.1

IRA Conversion Worksheet

PREPARED FOR: _____ DATE: _____ / _____ / _____

In 2010, anyone will be able to convert from a traditional IRA to a Roth IRA, regardless of income level. The key differences between these two vehicles are as follows:

Traditional IRA
- Contributions may or may not be tax-deductible
- Tax-deferred compounding
- Taxed upon withdrawal in retirement

Roth IRA
- After-tax contributions
- Tax-free compounding
- Tax-free withdrawals

You'll Need:
- IRA account statements, including information about the purchase price of the securities in your portfolio as well as the amount of deductible versus nondeductible contributions
- Expected income level in the current year

DETERMINE WHETHER A CONVERSION IS BENEFICIAL

	Beneficial for Conversion	Not Beneficial for Conversion
Have past contributions been deductible or nondeductible?	○ Nondeductible	○ Deductible
How many years do you have until you retire?	○ 10 or more	○ Fewer than 10
Do you expect to tap your IRA assets for living expenses in retirement?	○ No	○ Yes
Is your income lower now than it normally is?	○ Yes	○ No
Is your income higher now than it normally is?	○ No	○ Yes
Is there a chance you will need to tap your IRA assets prior to retirement?	○ Yes	○ No
Is the bulk of your retirement portfolio stashed in a traditional (non-Roth) 401(k)?	○ Yes	○ No
Do you expect your income to be higher or lower in retirement than it is now?	○ Higher	○ Lower
Has your IRA account suffered significant losses over the past several years?	○ Yes	○ No

RESULTS

- If most of your answers fell under the Beneficial for Conversion column, that's likely the better option for you.
- If most of your answers fell under the Not Beneficial for Conversion column, you may be better off sticking with a traditional IRA than switching to a Roth.

TO HELP QUANTIFY WHETHER A CONVERSION IS BENEFICIAL:

- Use the Conversion tab of the IRA Calculator, available at www.morningstar.com/goto/30MinuteSolutions. Plug in the requested information, then click Submit for an estimate of your at-retirement IRA balance.

Print your worksheet at: www.morningstar.com/goto/30MinuteSolutions

Start the Clock

Step 1

Your first step is to determine whether you're *eligible* to convert your IRA.

If you're considering a conversion in 2010, you're in luck: For 2010 (and 2010 alone), anyone—regardless of income level—can convert their traditional IRA to a Roth. (Prior to 2010, your adjusted gross income had to be $100,000 or less for you to be able to convert, whether you filed your tax return as a single or were part of a married couple filing jointly.) You'll also get some help with paying the tax if you convert in 2010. You'll still have to pay ordinary income taxes on any deductible contributions and investment earnings when you convert from a traditional IRA to Roth; that part isn't going away. But if you make the conversion in 2010, you'll be able to spread the tax hit over the subsequent two years, 2011 and 2012.

If it's 2011 or beyond, check IRS Publication 590 for details on the income limits that apply to conversions. If you earn too much, a conversion will be off-limits to you.

Step 2

If it turns out that you're eligible to make a conversion, your next step is to determine whether it would be beneficial to you. Morningstar's IRA Calculator, available at www.morningstar.com/goto/30MinuteSolutions, can help you quantify your decision.

As you use the calculator, bear in mind that your results—your estimated IRA balance at the time of conversion—will only be as good as the data you put in. If you're confident in the information you put in, particularly your expected tax bracket during retirement, you can feel confident about what the tool is telling you. If your income—and in turn your tax bracket—will be substantially lower than what it is now, you're not likely to be better off converting your IRA than you are standing pat with your traditional IRA. If, on the other hand, you expect that your tax bracket will stay the same or go higher in retirement, you're apt to be better off by making the conversion.

If you're a long way away from retirement, however, it will be extremely difficult to estimate your tax bracket. But you can still use the calculator to experiment with the variables.

Step 3

If the IRA Calculator didn't yield conclusive results—or if you weren't sure about some of the data you put into it—use the IRA Conversion Worksheet (Worksheet 21.1) to help you decide. Here are some details on the questions and why they're relevant to the decision about whether to convert your traditional IRA to a Roth.

1. **Have past contributions been deductible or nondeductible?**

   You're a good candidate for a Roth conversion if you've primarily made nondeductible contributions in the past, because you won't owe taxes on those nondeductible contributions when you convert—only your investment earnings and deductible contributions will be taxed at the time of conversion. Deductible contributions will result in an increased tax bill when you convert.

2. **How many years do you have until you retire?**

   In general, the younger you are, the more beneficial a conversion will be. That's because you'll have more years to recoup the tax hit. That's not to say a conversion should automatically be off the table if you're nearing or even in retirement, though. If it's fairly early in your retirement, longevity runs in your family, and you won't need to put your hands on your IRA assets for five years or even more, a conversion may well be worth it because you'll have a good shot at recouping the tax hit you'll take when you convert.

3. **Do you expect to tap your IRA assets for living expenses in retirement?**

   The larger your total portfolio, the better a candidate you're apt to be for a conversion. The Roth doesn't require mandatory distributions, thereby allowing your assets to compound and increasing the amount you can pass to your spouse or heirs. The second key reason relates to estate tax. Because you've already paid tax on Roth assets, the overall nest egg that you pass to your heirs will be smaller under the estate tax system, and therefore could help to reduce your estate tax liability. The traditional IRA assets, by contrast, will be included in your estate tax liability. Your heirs will have to pay taxes on those assets.

4. **Is your income lower than it normally is?**

If you're unemployed or your income is currently appreciably lower than it normally is, it can also be advantageous to convert your IRA. Provided you have the cash to pay the tax bill, your taxes related to the conversion will be lower than they would be if your income were higher. On the flip side, be careful if it looks like your conversion will push you into a higher tax bracket in the year in which you convert. You could disqualify yourself for tax benefits, such as credits and deductions, for which you would otherwise be eligible. (Check with an accountant if you have concerns about this.)

5. **Do you have the money to pay the taxes due upon conversion?**

When you convert your IRA, you'll owe taxes on any pretax contributions you made, as well as any investment earnings. If you don't have the money to pay the tax associated with the conversion (that is, you'll need to sell part of your IRA assets to convert), that's a big strike against converting. If you're younger than $59\frac{1}{2}$ and your only option is to use part of the traditional IRA assets to pay the tax, you'll pay a 10 percent early distribution penalty on any assets you don't roll directly into the Roth. Plus, you'll have less money at work for your retirement.

6. **Is there a chance you will need to tap your IRA assets prior to retirement age?**

While it's never ideal to tap your retirement savings prior to retiring, the Roth is a much better option than a traditional IRA should you need to do so. If you convert to a Roth and five years have elapsed since you made the conversion, you can withdraw the converted amount, plus any additional contributions, prior to age $59\frac{1}{2}$ and you won't have to pay taxes or penalties.

Step 4

If you've circled the majority of the items under the Beneficial for Conversion column, you're likely to be a good candidate for a conversion. If you circled mostly items in the Not Beneficial for Conversion column, a conversion is apt to be less profitable.

Step 5

If you determine you want to move forward with a conversion, it pays to double-check with a financial advisor or tax specialist to make sure you're thinking through all the variables. And when you do convert, make sure you mind your Ps and Qs. IRS Publication 590 (Individual Retirement Arrangements) includes all the nitty-gritty details. Your investment provider should be able to walk you through the forms you need to fill out for the conversion; some investment providers now allow you to make the conversion using online tools.

Next Steps

▶ Be aware that you needn't convert all your IRA in one fell swoop. Partial conversions are also permissible. However, you can't pick and choose which IRA assets to convert—for example, you can't convert all your nondeductible IRAs and leave your deductible IRAs intact, although that would be advantageous. Instead, each dollar you convert will receive exactly the same tax treatment based on your aggregate IRA's breakdown between deductible contributions/investment earnings and nondeductible contributions.

▶ If you convert your IRA from a traditional to a Roth, you needn't change your investments—you're changing the tax treatment of those investments, not the investments themselves. Finally, be mindful of the deadlines related to conversions. Whereas you have until April 15 of the following year to make an IRA contribution, the conversion will need to be done by December 31 to count for that tax year.

22

Roll Over Your Retirement Plan into an IRA

My husband and i have both worked at the same companies for more than 15 years. While we can pat ourselves on the backs for being loyal employees, our longevity within our respective firms makes us dinosaurs relative to the rest of the population. Unlike our parents' generation, most people don't stay put in one job for years and years. In fact, the typical U.S. worker holds 11 jobs in his or her lifetime.

What does that mean? Besides the new responsibilities, higher salary (one hopes), quality-of-life issues (how long your commute is, how nice your coworkers are, how good the coffee is), and other considerations that normally accompany job changes, you'll also have to make some important decisions about your benefits package. Key among them: how much to invest in your company retirement plan as well as what to do with your money from the plan that you're leaving behind.

That last question leaves many people paralyzed with indecision. You really have four main options for your company retirement plan when you leave your employer:

Option 1: Take the money and run. Cashing out of a former employer's 401(k) plan altogether is apt to have particular appeal for those who have lost their jobs and are feeling cash-strapped. But tapping your 401(k) prematurely means you'll get hit with taxes and penalties that can wipe out close to half of your account's value. Even more important, by eating into your retirement savings now, you'll be depriving yourself of the growth of those assets had they remained invested. That means less dough for your later years, which is a risky road to take. Pursue this option only if not doing so means you'll have to take on additional debt or you're already behind on debts you owe.

Option 2: Roll it into your new employer's plan. You could also roll the money into your new employer's plan; Chapter 15 gives you tips for evaluating whether a 401(k) plan measures up. The key advantage of taking this route is that you'll have fewer accounts to oversee and it will be easier to keep tabs on your stock/bond mix. But if you do your homework and find out that the new plan is subpar, you'll probably want to pursue other options for your 401(k) proceeds.

Option 3: Let it be. Another option is to do nothing, which has obvious appeal for the lazy and/or time-pressed. In fact, leaving your money in your former employer's company retirement plan also makes sense if that plan is a particularly good one. You can't contribute any additional monies to the old plan, but at least you'll feel confident in the quality of your holdings.

The key downside to maintaining your balance in your former employer's 401(k) plan is that you may be paying extra administrative costs for the plan. (Your plan's Summary Plan Description—which should be available on request through your HR department—should spell out the other, non-investment-related costs.) Also, you'll still have to monitor that old account, including rebalancing to keep your stock/bond mix on track, checking up on performance, and monitoring management changes. Considering that you'll probably have to keep tabs on other retirement assets—such as your new employer's 401(k) plan or an IRA—in addition to the old plan, you may be on the hook for more research and oversight than you bargained for.

Option 4: Roll it into an IRA. This option will be most desirable for the broadest group of investors. Doing this will give you more choices than you would have available through your old 401(k) plan; you can invest in almost any kind of stock, bond, or mutual fund through an IRA. It also eliminates the layer of expenses that you'll find in many 401(k) plans. (The one caveat: If you ever get sued, your investment assets will tend to be safer in a company retirement plan than in an IRA. If this isn't a concern, don't let it hamstring you.)

Rolling over an IRA isn't complicated, and it shouldn't result in paying any extra fees or taxes, provided that you follow the proper steps.

To roll over your retirement plan into an IRA, you'll need:

► Latest 401(k) statement
► Any information that your company provides about what to do with your 401(k) assets when you leave the company
► Morningstar's IRA Calculator (available at www.morningstar.com/goto/ 30MinuteSolutions)

 Start the Clock

Step 1

Spend a few moments determining what type of IRA you want to set up. You can roll your assets into a traditional IRA or a Roth IRA. Chapter 19 coaches you on that decision, and the IRA Calculator available at www.morningstar.com/goto/30MinuteSolutions can also help.

I generally think that the Roth IRA is preferable to a traditional IRA for investors at most life stages: You'll be able to make tax-free withdrawals from the account and you won't be required to take minimum distributions at age $70^1/_2$. If you do decide to opt for a Roth IRA, however, you'll owe taxes on any pretax contributions you made to your company retirement plan, as well as any investment gains. (Chapter 21 focuses on IRA conversions; the main considerations that I outline in that chapter—including taxes—apply to this decision as well.) If you don't have the money in hand to pay the tax bill right now, you may be better off rolling your company retirement plan balance into a traditional IRA until you have the money to pay the taxes that will be due upon conversion to a Roth.

Step 2

Next, identify where you want to invest the assets you're pulling from your company retirement plan. Whereas your retirement plan menu might have limited you to a fixed number of choices, you can put almost anything inside an IRA wrapper: mutual funds, individual stocks, you name it. That can be overwhelming, but Chapter 20 coaches you on some things to think about and also provides some of Morningstar's favorite IRA picks (Tables 20.1 and 20.2).

If you're rolling over a large sum of money or you plan to make additional contributions, you'll want to choose a mutual fund company or brokerage firm that offers you solid stock and bond investments. T. Rowe Price and Vanguard rank among Morningstar's favorite one-stop firms because both do a solid job across asset classes; a fund supermarket—like those from Vanguard, Schwab, Fidelity, and T. Rowe Price—can also be a good option.

Bear in mind that you can roll over your retirement plan assets into an already existing IRA; reducing your number of separate IRA accounts will also make it easy to keep tabs on your investments and help tame the paperwork coming into your house.

Be careful, however, if you may eventually roll the assets from your former employer's plan into another company retirement plan. If that's the case, it's important not to commingle those assets with other IRA assets; you'll want to segregate them in a separate IRA if there's a possibility you will roll them into another 401(k) plan down the road.

Step 3

Once you've determined what firm you'll use for your IRA, fill out an application. Be sure to specify whether you're establishing a traditional IRA or Roth, and clarify that you're doing a direct rollover. If you have any questions, call the firm where you're setting up the IRA. (They should be more than happy to help, because you're giving them your money to manage.)

Step 4

Once you've identified the firm where you'll hold your IRA assets, contact your company's human resources department to obtain a form to do a "direct rollover." That simply means that your former retirement plan provider and your new IRA provider are dealing with one another on this transaction; you're not putting your hands on the money. Your company will then either transfer the funds electronically to your IRA account or send you a check made payable to the new custodian (that is, to the new fund company, brokerage firm, or supermarket); the funds, in turn, can be deposited into your IRA account.

If you don't go the direct route—that is, you obtain a check from your retirement plan—you'll pay a 20 percent withholding penalty; you get that 20 percent back only when you file your taxes and prove that you've followed the rules about rolling your money into another retirement plan. You'll have 60 days to complete the rollover to another IRA. If you don't complete the rollover within the 60-day window, you'll owe income taxes plus a 10 percent penalty on the withdrawal. Because not following the proper steps can result in dire consequences, go the direct route if at all possible.

Next Steps

▶ Although this chapter has focused largely on rolling assets from a company retirement plan into an IRA, you can also roll over assets from an already existing IRA to a new IRA with another firm. If you're doing this, it also pays to do a direct rollover rather than acting as the middleman.

▶ If you've left your employer and are considering pocketing the proceeds from your 401(k), first calculate what you'll actually receive when you cash out. That balance may look tantalizing, but it will shrink considerably once you factor in your tax hit as well as the 10 percent early withdrawal penalty.

PART SEVEN

Invest for College

WHILE HELPING A YOUNG couple make over their finances in early 2009 I suggested that they start using 529 college savings plans to begin saving for their two young daughters' educations. I went on to note that the plans offer valuable flexibility: If their oldest child doesn't end up going to college, their younger girl could use the funds for her education.

As I was talking, I could see them shaking their heads. Was there something about the 529 idea that they found disagreeable? No, that wasn't the problem. Rather, they had a visceral—and negative—response to my offhanded mention of the chance that either of their kids might not go to college. "It's just not an option," the mother responded.

As is almost always the case, this young couple had an emotional stake in making sure their kids earn their degrees. Their parents had paid for their college educations, and they wanted to pay back the favor by doing the same for their children. Their goal of educating their children was also rooted in economic reality. College graduates, on average, earn twice as much during their lifetimes as those who have completed high school only, according to U.S. Census data.

Yet, just as earning a college degree has become more important than ever, so has the demand for college degrees skyrocketed, and, so, in turn, have the costs. Tuition and fees at a public university averaged $7,000 in 2008, and private school fees and tuition rang in at an average of $25,000. With college tabs rising nearly twice as fast as the general inflation rate, it's more essential than ever that college savers have a plan.

As is the case with saving and investing for retirement, those socking it away for college have a bewildering array of options from which to choose, including 529 plans, Coverdells, UGMA/UTMA accounts, prepaid college savings plans, Roth IRAs, and taxable accounts. Helping you home in on the vehicle (or vehicles) with the right combination of tax-saving features and flexibility is the focus of Chapter 23.

Because of their generous contribution limits and favorable tax treatment, Section 529 college savings plans have emerged as the college funding vehicle of choice for many households. Yet, if you've decided to save in one, your next step is to decide which 529 plan to use. You may receive a tax break for staying in-state, but the investment options may be better if you opt for an out-of-state plan. (The quality varies widely among these plans.) Chapter 24 discusses the factors that should go into your decision-making process and also features Morningstar's most recent listing of the best and worst 529 plans.

Once you've determined what kind of wrapper you'll use for college savings, the next step is to decide what type of investments to put inside it. As with retirement savings, your time horizon for the money—in this case, your child's matriculation date—is the key determinant of what stock/bond mix to use for your college savings. It's also essential that your child's asset mix become extra conservative as he or she nears college age. Helping you arrive at an appropriate mix of investments for your college savings plan is the focus of Chapter 25.

23

Find the Right College Savings Vehicle

WE'VE ALL HEARD TALES OF COMPETITIVE, well-heeled young parents applying for elite preschools when their children are infants or even still in the womb. But one of my friends upped the ante by saving for her child's college education *before* she was expecting a baby or even dating her husband. That may sound strange, but her logic was straightforward. She knew that she wanted to have a child no matter what the future held, so she figured that getting started on college savings would help her baby's college fund fully benefit from the power of compounding. Ten years and three little ones later, she and her husband feel grateful for her foresight.

The more I've talked to parents and would-be parents, the more I've realized how rare my friend's preparedness is. Most will tell you that their children went from onesies to "Can I borrow the car keys?" in the blink of an eye, giving them little time to devote to building a college fund. Parents also have to juggle saving for college alongside competing financial priorities, including squirreling away money for their own retirements. (Part Three provides guidance on how to sort through competing financial priorities, but the short answer is that retirement savings should always trump saving for college. The reason is simple: You can't get a loan to pay for your retirement, but your child will probably be able to borrow money to pay for college.)

It would also be hard to blame would-be college savers for being put off by the magnitude of the task at hand: Not only are college costs sky-high and rising fast, but college savers also have to sort through an alphabet soup of options: 529 plans, Coverdell accounts, and UGMA/UTMA accounts, to name some of the most commonly used vehicles. College savers also have to consider how financial aid fits into the mix and whether any of these vehicles jeopardize their eligibility for it.

I can't help you find time or money to kick-start your child's college savings program, but identifying the right vehicle for college funding doesn't have to be a horribly cumbersome process. Table 23.1 provides the basic details of the major college funding vehicles, as well as the pros and cons of each.

Bear in mind that there may not be one right answer for you. Most families pay for college with a combination of savings, loans, and financial aid, and they may also use multiple savings vehicles, such as a 529 plan for the tax savings and a taxable account.

To find the right college savings vehicle, you'll need:

▶ Most recent income tax return, as well as an estimate of your earnings for the current tax year
▶ An estimate of how much you plan to save for a child's education in the current tax year and in total

Start the Clock

Step 1

It's gut check time. Use the College Cost Calculator, available at www.morningstar.com/goto/30MinuteSolutions, to determine how much college will cost by the time your child is ready to begin. The calculator allows you to see average, inflation-adjusted costs for tuition plus room and board at a private college as well as at a public university, both in-state and out-of-state. Of course, the school your child selects may be more or less costly than the averages provided. (If you completed the Goal Planning Worksheet [Worksheet 3.1], you'll already have completed this step.)

Don't be put off by the size of these numbers. In an ideal world, you'd be able to cover four years' worth of tuition and you'd have that money in hand during your child's senior year of high school. In reality, however, only a small fraction of families have that luxury. Instead, most children and their families pay for college using a combination of savings, loans, work-study, out-of-pocket payments, and financial aid. The point of looking at these numbers isn't to scare you to death but rather to show you what you're aiming for. This step will also help you set expectations with your child. If your child needs to revisit his or her preferences about college because of financial constraints, it's better to start that discussion sooner rather than later.

Step 2

Next, think about the following six questions.

1. **How much do you plan to contribute to college savings per year until your child goes to college?**

    If you plan to amass a lot of assets in a college savings fund, none of these vehicles are automatically off-limits, but you may have to use them in conjunction with another vehicle. For example, the Coverdell Education Savings Account has a contribution limit of $2,000 per year currently (and the limit may go even lower, to $500 per year, in 2011 unless Congress takes action). If you were planning to tap your Roth IRA to pay for college, that vehicle allows contributions of only $5,000 per year ($6,000 if you're over 50). If you'd like to contribute to just one type of college funding vehicle, a 529 plan or taxable account will allow you to amass the most assets; you can obviously save an unlimited amount in your taxable account as well, but you won't receive any tax breaks if you do so.

    Table 23.1 provides an overview of the pros and cons of the various college funding options and also shows the contribution limits for each.

2. **Which vehicles are you eligible to contribute to?**

    In addition to limits on contributions, some of the college funding vehicles won't let you contribute if your income is over a certain threshold. Thus, the next step is to determine which of them you're eligible to contribute to. The Coverdell Education Savings Account and Roth IRA both carry income limits, and you can't make tax-free withdrawals from

Table 23.1 Which College Funding Vehicle Is Right for You?

Vehicle	Tax Benefits	Annual Contribution Limits
529 College Savings Plan	Qualified withdrawals tax-free; possible state tax breaks	Vary by state; generally high
529 Prepaid Tuition Plan	Qualified withdrawals tax-free; possible state tax breaks	Vary by state; lower than 529 college savings plans
Coverdell Education Savings Account	Qualified withdrawals tax-free	$2,000 per beneficiary
UGMA/UTMA	Income taxed at child's rate; kiddie tax may apply	No limit, but gift tax may apply
Roth IRA	Withdrawals of contributions are tax-free	$5,000 if under 50; $6,000 if over 50
Taxable Account	None	None
Series I or EE Savings Bonds	Income tax-free if used for college	$30,000 per owner
Home Equity Loan/Line of Credit	Interest paid may be tax-deductible	N/A

Vehicle	Income Limits	Available Investments
529 College Savings Plan	None	Limited to plan's menu of choices
529 Prepaid Tuition Plan	None	Low-risk investments; participant does not oversee
Coverdell Education Savings Account	$110,000 (individuals); $220,000 for marrieds filing jointly in 2009	Wide variety, though not all mutual funds offer
UGMA/UTMA	None	Nearly anything
Roth IRA	$120,000 (singles); $176,000 (joint filers) in 2009	Nearly anything
Taxable Account	None	Unlimited
Series I or EE Savings Bonds	$82,100 (singles); $130,650 (joint filers) in 2009	Series I or EE Savings Bonds
Home Equity Loan/Line of Credit	None	N/A

Vehicle	Financial Aid Impact	Best For
529 College Savings Plan	Limited to moderate	High-income individuals looking to sock a lot away for college
529 Prepaid Tuition Plan	Limited to moderate	Conservative savers looking to keep up with rising college costs
Coverdell Education Savings Account	Limited to moderate	Those investing relatively small sums
UGMA/UTMA	High	Not recommended
Roth IRA	Can be significant	Those saving for college and retirement simultaneously
Taxable Account	Limited to moderate	Those who may need the money for other goals
Series I or EE Savings Bonds	Limited to moderate	Very conservative types
Home Equity Loan/Line of Credit	Limited to moderate	Those with substantial home equity, limited college assets

Vehicle	Key Drawbacks
529 College Savings Plan	Extra layers of costs, choices may be limited
529 Prepaid Tuition Plan	You may be able to earn a better return on your own
Coverdell Education Savings Account	Contribution caps
UGMA/UTMA	Assets are property of child and don't have to be used for college; financial aid impact
Roth IRA	Cuts into retirement nest egg
Taxable Account	No tax benefits
Series I or EE Savings Bonds	Skimpy current yields
Home Equity Loan/Line of Credit	Interest could be higher than student loan

Series I or EE savings bonds if your income comes in above a certain level. So, if your income level disqualifies you from any of these vehicles, you can cross it off your list.

Table 23.1 shows the income limitations for various types of college savings vehicles.

3. **How much flexibility do you need? Are you determined to save for college and confident that you'll never need the money for another use?**

If so, you can feel free to consider dedicated college savings vehicles such as a 529 plan or Coverdell Education Savings Account.

If, on the other hand, you're looking for a college savings vehicle that will allow you to multitask—perhaps saving for retirement or shorter-term goals at the same time that you're saving for college—you'll want to shy away from 529 plans or Coverdells. That's because those vehicles require you to pay taxes and/or penalties if you need to withdraw the money prematurely or for another purpose. Instead, you should focus on a more versatile vehicle for college savings, such as Roth IRAs or taxable accounts. You can withdraw your Roth contributions at any time and for any reason (though it's rarely a good idea to rob your retirement account to pay for college). Saving and investing in a taxable account offers you the most ready access to your money, though you will have to pay taxes on any investment appreciation when you withdraw your money.

Table 23.1 shows the rules regarding non-college-related withdrawals for various college funding vehicles.

4. **Do you expect that you'll need to rely on financial aid to fund your child's education?**

If so, bear in mind that assets held in the child's name are generally less advantageous than assets in the parents' names when it comes to qualifying for financial aid. Coverdell accounts and 529 plans held by the parents have less effect on financial aid eligibility. UGMA/UTMA accounts, on the other hand, are considered to be assets of the child and therefore are less desirable if you expect that you'll be applying for financial aid.

Table 23.1 depicts the financial aid impact of various types of college savings vehicles.

5. **Does your state offer a generous tax deduction for contributions in its 529 college savings plan? Do you live in a state with a particularly high tax rate?**

Currently, 32 states (out of 44 states that levy state tax) offer state tax deductions if you invest in your home state's 529 plan. If your state offers a large deduction and you live in a high tax state, that provides a strong incentive to prioritize a 529 plan over other types of college savings vehicles. Go to www.morningstar.com/goto/30MinuteSolutions for a link to a tool that will show you whether your state offers a tax deduction linked to its 529 plan and, if so, how much. (There are a few exceptions, but you generally won't be able to receive a state tax deduction if you buy a 529 plan offered by another state.)

6. **How much control would you like to exercise over your investments?**

You can put almost anything inside Coverdell Education Savings Accounts, Roth IRAs, taxable accounts, and UGMA/UTMA accounts, whereas 529 plans limit you to a fixed menu of choices.

Step 3

Once you've answered the preceding questions, you should have a clearer view of the vehicle(s) that will work best for you. If you've decided to invest in a Coverdell, UGMA/UTMA, Roth IRA, or in your own taxable account, you can set that up by contacting the investment provider directly; Chapter 25 provides tips for identifying the right investments for your college savings program.

If you've decided to opt for a 529 plan, Chapter 24 helps you determine whether you're better off sticking with your home state's plan or investing in another state's plan.

Next Steps

▶ At the risk of stating the obvious, start early. If you invested $2,000 in a college savings fund at the time of your child's birth, put in $100 per month every month thereafter, and earned a 6 percent rate of return, you would have more than $45,000 saved by the time your child was 18. You'd amass less than half as much if you waited until your child was 7 years old to begin investing and made identical contributions and earned an identical rate of return.

▶ Although the provision in the tax code that allows for tax-free withdrawals from 529 plans was due to expire (or, in tax parlance, "sunset") at the end of 2010, Congress took action in 2006 to maintain 529s' beneficial tax treatment. That means that you can safely invest in 529 plans without worrying that the currently beneficial tax treatment could go away.

24

Find the Right 529 Plan

BURIED AMID NEWS OF THE ECONOMIC CRISIS in early 2009 was a curious factoid: The Obama daughters' college savings, invested in Illinois broker-sold Bright Directions College Savings Program, were estimated to have lost roughly 30 percent in 2008.

Of course, the first daughters have plenty of time to recoup their losses: Malia has roughly six more years until college, and Sasha has about nine. And in any case, I'm not going to lose any sleep over the Obamas' ability to pony up for tuition when the time comes. Barack and Michelle Obama contributed $240,000 to the girls' 529 plans in 2007 (the maximum they could contribute that year without having to pay gift tax), putting their daughters' college funds light years ahead of most other kids' in their age range.

Nonetheless, their losses point out the difficulty of navigating the crowded 529 landscape. Participants first have to decide whether they should stick with their states' own plans—as the Obamas did—or opt for an out-of-state plan and forgo the tax deduction that they may receive on in-state contributions. That judgment rests on an assessment of the quality of the in-state plans, as well as quantifying the savings associated with the tax deduction.

And if 529 investors choose to go out of state, they then have to sift through nearly 100 separate programs, comparing fund choices, layers of fees, and asset allocations. To make matters worse, official 529 documents can be opaque. It's no wonder parents struggle with the decision about what to do, or put off investing in a 529 plan altogether, despite the plans' generous contribution limits and favored tax treatment.

To help 529 plan participants find their way across this rocky terrain, Morningstar began analyzing 529 plans back in 2005. We also began producing an annual list of the best and worst 529 plans, which has become one of our most popular features on Morningstar.com. This list can help you see if your state's plans are subpar or some of the elite, and it can also help you find your way if you need to go out of state in order to find a better 529 program.

To help find the right 529 college savings plan, you'll need:

▶ An estimate of how much you intend to contribute to a 529 plan

▶ 529 State-Tax Calculator (available at www.morningstar.com/goto/ 30MinuteSolutions)

 Start the Clock

Step 1

Check to see whether your home state's plan is on Morningstar's list of the best 529 plans (Table 24.1). If so, your work is almost done. Even if you receive a limited tax deduction, or none at all, for investing in a home-state plan, it's probably worth investing in. Not only is your plan a good one, but the tax treatment could improve in the future.

Step 2

If your state's plans don't appear on our "best" list, you'll need to investigate how much you'll save on taxes by opting for an in-state plan. Start by considering how much you plan to invest in the plan per year. If grandparents or other relatives also plan to contribute to the plan, consider their prospective contributions as well.

Step 3

If you're not planning to save a lot in a 529, the tax deduction you receive by sticking with one of your home state's plans may not amount to much. If, on

Table 24.1   Morningstar's Best and Worst 529 College Savings Plans

Plan	Manager	Direct or Broker-Sold
The Best 529 College Savings Plans		
Ohio CollegeAdvantage 529 Savings Plan	Multiple	Direct
Comment: Reasonable costs, multimanager setup are pluses.		
Indiana CollegeChoice 529 Direct Savings Plan	Multiple	Direct
Comment: Flexibility, sensible age-based options, low costs.		
Utah Educational Savings Plan Trust	Vanguard	Direct
Comment: Longtime Morningstar favorite boasts ultralow costs.		
Virginia Educational Savings Plan Trust	Multiple	Direct
Comment: Plenty of diversification across multiple fund shops.		
Virginia CollegeAmerica 529 Savings Plan	Multiple	Broker-Sold
Comment: Topnotch plan mainly features American Funds.		
The Worst 529 College Savings Plans		
Nebraska State Farm College Savings Plan	Oppenheimer	Broker-Sold
Comment: Age-based options performed abysmally in 2008.		
New Jersey Best 529 College Savings Plan	Franklin Templeton	Broker-Sold
Comment: Plan is costly and has limited flexibility.		
Montana Pacific Life Funds 529	Pacific Life	Direct
Comment: High costs, no individual-fund options.		
Ohio Putnam CollegeAdvantage	Putnam	Broker-Sold
Comment: Putnam has had performance troubles, manager turnover.		
Nebraska AIM College Savings Plan	Invesco/AIM	Broker-Sold
Comment: Costly plan lacks individual-fund options.		

In assembling our annual list of the best and worst 529 plans, we look at a host of factors, including costs, quality of the investment manager, flexibility (ability to invest in single fund or age-based options), and whether the age-based options use sensible asset allocations.

the other hand, you plan to contribute a lot and your plans offer a generous tax deduction, those savings may supersede other considerations, such as the quality of your state's plans.

To help quantify your decision making, go to www.morningstar.com/goto/30MinuteSolutions for a link to a calculator that can help you determine how much you'll save by opting for one of your home state's 529 plans. Enter how much you plan to save per year, as well as your state of residence. The calculator will then factor in your state tax rate as well as the 529 contribution amount that's deductible.

After you've entered your information, you'll see the per-year tax savings that you'll receive if you invest in one of your home state's plans.

If it turns out that investing in a home-state plan will save you a good chunk of change—and that's subjective—move on to Step 4.

If investing in a home-state plan won't save you much, however, you're free to look elsewhere. Again, turn to Morningstar's "Best 529" list (Figure 24.1) for guidance on the top plans outside your state.

Step 4

If you've determined that opting for an in-state plan will save you some money, it's time to conduct due diligence on the plan. Even if the plan doesn't appear on our "Worst" list, if it's a poor and/or costly plan, those negatives can quickly erode your state tax deduction.

To check up on the quality of your state's plans, hop on Morningstar.com and click on the Personal Finance tab. Once there, click on 529 Data Center. You'll see a listing of each state's 529 plans, organized alphabetically.

Click on each link to read our analyst's summary of your state plans' pros and cons. That will provide you with a good indication of whether your state's plans are worthwhile or not. If you have the time, you can also dig into the data provided about your plans. As you read the Analyst Reports and/or survey the data, focus on the following:

► **Costs:** As with any investment, costs are a big determinant of how good a 529 plan is: 529 investors have to contend with underlying fund expenses as well as administrative and management fees, and they may also have to pay a sales charge if they invest through a broker. Our analysts characterize the all-in costs of some plans as high; in such cases, the tax savings you gain by deducting your contribution can be eroded. As with our fund analyses, costs will be a big factor in whether our analyst gives a plan thumbs-up or thumbs-down. (The 529 plans on Morningstar's "Best" list are usually a bargain, whereas those on our ignominious "Worst" list are generally pricey.)

▶ **Quality of provider:** Next, check out who's managing the investments. Some plans stick with a single provider, while others include investments from several different firms. If your plan has investments run by various managers, such as T. Rowe Price and Royce, that's often a good sign that the plan administrator has tried to find managers who are specialists in a specific investment style. If, on the other hand, your plan is managed by a single firm, that company had better be a decent multitasker. You'll want to make sure that it does a good job of managing stock investments, which will feature prominently in your 529 plan if your child is young, as well as bond investments, which will consume the lion's share of your 529 investments as your child gets closer to college age. Among Morningstar's favorite "one-stop shops" are Vanguard, T. Rowe Price, and American Funds.

▶ **Asset allocation:** Most 529 plans offer what are called "age-based" options, meaning the investments in the plan gradually become more conservative as a child gets closer to college age. These options can be attractive for those looking to create a simplified, one-stop 529 plan, but some of these age-based options may be overly conservative or aggressive. If you're interested in an age-based plan and would like a read on whether its asset allocation is appropriate, compare its stock/bond mix with those of the pie charts provided in Figure 25.1 in the following chapter. Minor variations are not a deal-breaker. But if an age-based plan's asset allocation is radically more conservative or aggressive than those provided in Figure 25.1, that's a red flag.

▶ **Diversification:** In addition to costs, quality of investment management, and asset allocation in age-based plans, check to see how much diversification a plan offers. Does it offer the opportunity to invest in small-company stocks as well as asset classes like Treasury Inflation-Protected Securities or real estate? If so, the opportunity to diversify may be attractive, particularly if you plan to invest a lot in a 529.

However, I'd put this criterion in the "nice to have" rather than the "must-have" category. If a 529 plan checks out on the first three criteria, it's not a disaster if it doesn't offer more-specialized investments.

Next Steps

▶ Morningstar updates its analyses of the best and worst 529 plans each year. Go to www.morningstar.com/goto/30MinuteSolutions to see if we've updated our list recently.

▶ In general, the 529 landscape has greatly improved over the past decade, with firms working to one-up one another in terms of investment management, costs, and tax breaks. If your home state's plans are subpar, review the details on a periodic basis: They may have improved.

▶ Once you've homed in on a specific 529 plan in which to invest, you'll have to determine how to allocate your assets within that plan. Chapter 25 covers that terrain.

▶ Conducting due diligence on a 529 plan is important. But if it turns out that you've made a mistake in your selection, you're allowed to change to a new 529 plan once a year. Just be sure to follow the proper procedure and read the fine print before rolling over 529 assets from one plan to another. Some states charge a fee for rolling over assets from their plan into another, and if you've received a state tax deduction on your contributions, your state may "recapture" those tax savings.

25

Select the Right Investments for Your College Savings Plan

"I CAN'T UNDERSTAND THIS. We've tried to do everything right from the day she was born."

So lamented a friend, right after telling me that the college fund of her daughter, a senior in high school, had dropped by nearly 50 percent in 2008. My friend and her husband were facing a tough choice: They could either tell their daughter to look at cheaper schools or they could try to finance tuition at a more costly college by dipping into their retirement savings or asking their daughter to take out loans.

Ultimately, their daughter opted to go to a public university that cost thousands less than some of the private schools she was originally eyeing. That's not a calamity—in fact, she was happy with her decision and the school she chose is highly rated. However, this family's predicament is a common one. Not only have many families not been able to save for college at all, but even some of those who have been saving assiduously have had to confront a shortfall in their college funds at precisely the wrong time.

In the previous two chapters, I discussed how to select the right "shell" for your college investments. But once you have done so, it's crucial to choose the right investments to go inside that vehicle. You want your assets to grow, of course; given the soaring costs of college, it's hard to imagine saving enough without a little help from the market. But it's equally important to adjust your college portfolio to become more conservative as your child nears college age. That, unfortunately, is the part of the equation that tripped up my friend and many other college savers in 2008. By holding too much in stocks too long, their college portfolios dropped sharply just as high school graduation was drawing near. Some 529 college savings plans also featured poorly performing investments that were supposed to be conservative but in reality were anything but, including bond funds that were loaded with risky derivative securities.

When it comes to selecting specific investments for a college portfolio, asset allocation is every bit as crucial as—if not more so than—it is for retirement savers. Retirement dates can be a little squishy: Although they may not do so happily, retirees can delay retirement or work part-time longer than they had originally planned if their retirement portfolios come up short. Most young people want to go to college right after high school, making the target date for a college fund much more specific than is the case for a retirement portfolio. Moreover, because retirement may be 25 or 30 years long, retiree portfolios have time to make up lost ground if they lose money early on in retirement. But because it takes most students only four to five years to get through college, a college fund's drop in value during the high school or early college years can be catastrophic.

Paying due attention to risk when selecting individual investments for your college savings plan is therefore essential. If your child or grandchild is young or if you're starting late and want to make up for lost time, you may be tempted to invest in something that's risky but has great long-term potential: an individual stock, perhaps, or an emerging markets or sector mutual fund or ETF. But my advice is to err on the side of caution when it comes to selecting securities in a college savings plan. Stick with well-diversified, plain vanilla mutual funds, such as index funds or conservatively managed active funds. All-in-one age-based options, as are available in most 529 plans, can also make sense. Of course, these can lose money, too, as 2008's bear market amply illustrated. But presuming that you've spent time arriving at the right asset allocation for you, buying a well-diversified fund can help limit your college portfolio's exposure to company- or sector-specific problems.

To select the right investments for your college savings plan, you'll need:

▶ An idea of what type of vehicle you plan to use for college savings. Chapter 23 discusses how to select the right college savings plan, and Chapter 24 gives advice for selecting among different 529 college savings plans.

Start the Clock

Step 1

Your first job when building or managing a college portfolio is to identify an appropriate stock/bond/cash mix given your child's age. I've provided asset-allocation pie charts for five different age groups in Figure 25.1. If your child's

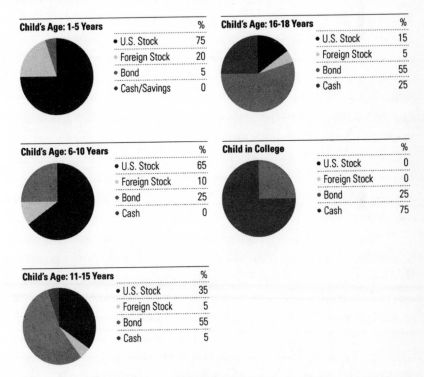

Child's Age: 1-5 Years	%
● U.S. Stock	75
● Foreign Stock	20
● Bond	5
● Cash/Savings	0

Child's Age: 16-18 Years	%
● U.S. Stock	15
● Foreign Stock	5
● Bond	55
● Cash	25

Child's Age: 6-10 Years	%
● U.S. Stock	65
● Foreign Stock	10
● Bond	25
● Cash	0

Child in College	%
● U.S. Stock	0
● Foreign Stock	0
● Bond	25
● Cash	75

Child's Age: 11-15 Years	%
● U.S. Stock	35
● Foreign Stock	5
● Bond	55
● Cash	5

How much you have saved, as well as your own risk tolerance, should determine whether your portfolio is more stock- or bond-heavy than those depicted here. The most essential thing to remember is to begin dramatically scaling back the portfolio's equity weighting when the child is in his or her early teens.

Figure 25.1   Sample Asset Allocations for Five Time Horizons

age is somewhere between the age bands I've identified, select asset allocations that fall between the two.

You'll notice that my recommended allocations for children who are in their teens and in college are very conservative—predominantly bonds and cash. That means that your college fund won't grow much once your child is in that age range, but it will not suffer a big drop, either. If you're just beginning to build a college fund for a child who's within five or six years of college, it's wise to stick with safe investments and know that you'll have to make up any shortfalls in your college portfolio by saving more, obtaining financial aid, or taking out loans. By all means, avoid building a more stock-heavy portfolio in an effort to make up for lost time; the risks of doing so are simply too great.

On the flip side, if you're one of the rare individuals who has socked away enough to cover four years of expenses at the school of your child's choice, there's no need to lose it by holding stocks in your child's college fund.

Step 2

Once you've arrived at an appropriate asset allocation, you can populate that asset mix with individual investments.

If you're using a 529 plan, most offer age-based options that are calibrated to suit children of various ages. These age-based options can vary dramatically, and some suffered big losses in 2008, owing to their too-heavy stock weightings as well as their reliance on a single firm's (sometimes subpar) lineup of investments. Those losses were especially injurious for those plans geared toward students getting close to college age, and age-based options in 529 plans are receiving some overdue scrutiny in the wake of this debacle.

Still, that shouldn't lead you to dismiss these all-in-one vehicles out of hand, because they can be great tools for those looking for straightforward, one-stop solutions. If you do opt for such a program, compare its asset allocation with the ones that I've provided in Figure 25.1. There are varying schools of thought about asset allocations for college savers, but if your 529 plan's age-based options are dramatically out of whack with the targets shown, that's a red flag to look to another 529 plan or to create your own age-appropriate portfolio using individual funds.

If you're investing outside a 529 plan or would like to select your own investments within the 529 framework, it's fairly simple to create a portfolio with an appropriate target allocation. I've included some of my favorite college savings building blocks in Table 25.1.

For your core equity holding, look to a broadly diversified fund that gives your portfolio exposure to stocks small and large, value and growth in a single shot. You might also consider a fund that provides you with some international exposure; you can add a dedicated international fund or consider a global fund for your core-stock exposure. When looking for bond and short-term/cash options, focus on low costs, because expenses are an especially important determinant of returns for lower-returning asset classes like these. I've provided some sample portfolios for five different time horizons in Figure 25.2.

Step 3

If you're creating your own college savings portfolio rather than relying on a prepackaged solution like an age-based 529 plan, double-check that its asset allocation jibes with the one you're targeting. Enter each of your holdings into Morningstar's Instant X-Ray tool (available at www.morningstar.com/goto/30MinuteSolutions), then click Show Instant X-Ray. Your percentages needn't match those of your target precisely; in fact, if you're using actively managed mutual funds, there's a very good chance that you'll wind up with more cash in your portfolio than you're targeting. Nonetheless, divergences of more than 5 or 10 percentage points should send you back to the drawing board.

Step 4

Making your college fund more conservative as your child gets closer to college age is an essential part of the process, and it's particularly important once a child is nearing or in high school. For that reason, I'd recommend doing a full checkup on your college savings program every year. At that time, you can determine whether you need to adjust your asset allocation because your child is getting closer to needing the money.

Make a date on your calendar to check back in on your college savings program within the next 12 months or so. I discuss how to conduct a checkup of your portfolio, including your college assets, in Chapter 32.

Table 25.1   Top Building Blocks for College Savings

Name	Ticker	Category	Investment Minimum ($)	Coverdell Available?	Coverdell Minimum ($)
U.S. Stock Funds					
Dodge & Cox Stock	DODGX	Large Value	2,500	No	—
Fairholme	FAIRX	Large Blend	2,500	Yes	2,000
Fidelity Contrafund	FCNTX	Large Blend	2,500	No	—
Fidelity Spartan 500 Index	FSMKX	Large Blend	10,000	No	—
Fidelity Spartan Total Market	FSTMX	Large Blend	10,000	No	—
iShares S&P 500 (ETF)	IVV	Large Blend	N/A	Yes	N/A
Oakmark	OAKMX	Large Blend	1,000	Yes	500
Oakmark Select	OAKLX	Large Blend	1,000	Yes	500
Schwab S&P 500	SWPPX	Large Blend	100	Yes	100
Schwab Total Stock Market Index	SWTIX	Large Blend	100	Yes	100
Selected American	SLADX	Large Blend	10,000	Yes	1,000
T. Rowe Price Equity Income	PRFDX	Large Value	2,500	Yes	1,000
T. Rowe Price New America Growth	PRWAX	Large Growth	2,500	Yes	1,000
Vanguard 500 Index	VFINX	Large Blend	3,000	Yes	2,000
Vanguard Dividend Appreciation (ETF)	VIG	Large Blend	N/A	Yes	N/A
Vanguard Total Stock Market Index	VTSMX	Large Blend	3,000	Yes	2,000
Foreign-Stock Funds					
Artio International Equity II	JETAX	Foreign Lrg Blend	1,000	Yes	100
Artisan International	ARTIX	Foreign Lrg Gr	1,000	Yes	1,000
Dodge & Cox Global Stock	DODWX	World Stock	2,500	No	—
Dodge & Cox International	DODFX	Foreign Lrg Value	2,500	No	—
Fidelity Spartan International Index	FSIIX	Foreign Lrg Blend	10,000	No	—
Harbor International	HIINX	Foreign Lrg Value	2,500	No	—
Harbor International Growth	HAIGX	Foreign Lrg Gr	2,500	No	—
Masters' Select International	MSILX	Foreign Lrg Blend	10,000	No	—
Oakmark Global	OAKGX	World Stock	1,000	Yes	1,000
T. Rowe Price Global Stock	PRGSX	World Stock	2,500	Yes	1,000
Vanguard All-World ex-US (ETF)	VEU	Foreign Lrg Blend	N/A	Yes	N/A
Vanguard Total Intl Stock Market Index	VGTSX	Foreign Lrg Blend	3,000	Yes	2,000

Table 25.1   Top Building Blocks for College Savings (*Continued*)

Name	Ticker	Category	Investment Minimum ($)	Coverdell Available?	Coverdell Minimum ($)
Bond Funds					
Dodge & Cox Income	DODIX	Int-Term Bond	2,500	No	—
Fidelity Total Bond	FTBFX	Int-Term Bond	2,500	No	—
Harbor Bond	HABDX	Int-Term Bond	1,000	No	—
Metropolitan West Total Return Bond	MWTRX	Int-Term Bond	5,000	No	—
T. Rowe Price Spectrum Income	RPSIX	Multisector Bond	2,500	Yes	1,000
Vanguard Total Bond Market Index	VBMFX	Int-Term Bond	3,000	Yes	2,000
Vanguard Short-Term Bond Index	VBISX	Short-Term Bond	3,000	Yes	2,000
Combination Stock/Bond Funds					
Dodge & Cox Balanced	DODBX	Moderate Alloc	1,000	No	2,500
T. Rowe Price Personal Strategy Income	PRSIX	Conserv Alloc	1,000	Yes	1,000
T. Rowe Price Spectrum Growth	PRSGX	Large Growth	1,000	Yes	1,000
Vanguard Balanced Index	VBINX	Moderate Alloc	3,000	Yes	2,000
Vanguard LifeStrategy Conservative Gr	VSCGX	Conserv Alloc	3,000	Yes	2,000
Vanguard LifeStrategy Growth	VASGX	Moderate Alloc	3,000	Yes	2,000
Vanguard LifeStrategy Income	VASIX	Conserv Alloc	3,000	Yes	2,000
Vanguard LifeStrategy Moderate Gr	VSMGX	Moderate Alloc	3,000	Yes	2,000
Vanguard Wellington	VWELX	Moderate Alloc	10,000	Yes	10,000
Vanguard Wellesley Income	VWINX	Conserv Alloc	3,000	Yes	2,000
Vanguard STAR	VGSTX	Moderate Alloc	1,000	Yes	1,000
Vanguard Tax-Managed Balanced	VTMFX	Conserv Alloc	10,000	No	—

These funds are all good options for those investing for college outside the confines of a 529 plan.

Next Steps

▶ You'll notice that the following portfolios don't include any exchange-traded funds. I have nothing against these investments. In fact, they can be great core building blocks for any type of portfolio, because they are often broadly diversified, extremely inexpensive, and tax-efficient. However, you'll have to pay a brokerage commission each time you buy and sell shares in an ETF. If you're investing a lump sum and letting it ride, paying the commission isn't a big deal. But if you're investing in a college

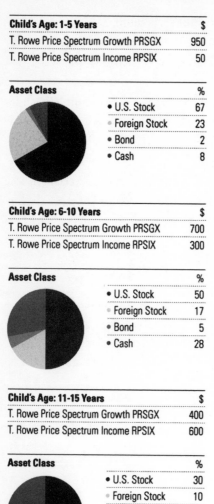

Child's Age: 1-5 Years	**$**
T. Rowe Price Spectrum Growth PRSGX	950
T. Rowe Price Spectrum Income RPSIX	50

Asset Class	**%**
• U.S. Stock	67
• Foreign Stock	23
• Bond	2
• Cash	8

Child's Age: 6-10 Years	**$**
T. Rowe Price Spectrum Growth PRSGX	700
T. Rowe Price Spectrum Income RPSIX	300

Asset Class	**%**
• U.S. Stock	50
• Foreign Stock	17
• Bond	5
• Cash	28

Child's Age: 11-15 Years	**$**
T. Rowe Price Spectrum Growth PRSGX	400
T. Rowe Price Spectrum Income RPSIX	600

Asset Class	**%**
• U.S. Stock	30
• Foreign Stock	10
• Bond	9
• Cash	51

Child's Age: 16-18 Years	**$**
T. Rowe Price Spectrum Growth PRSGX	250
T. Rowe Price Spectrum Income RPSIX	500
Cash	250

Asset Class	**%**
• U.S. Stock	19
• Foreign Stock	6
• Bond	8
• Cash	67

Child in College	**$**
T. Rowe Price Spectrum Growth PRSGX	0
T. Rowe Price Spectrum Income RPSIX	0
Cash	1,000

Asset Class	**%**
• U.S. Stock	0
• Foreign Stock	0
• Bond	0
• Cash	100

It's possible to create effective college portfolios with two (or even fewer) funds. These portfolios assume the investor is committing to ongoing investments of $25 or more per fund per month.

Figure 25.2   Model College Portfolios for Five Time Horizons, Starting with $1,000 or Less

fund on an ongoing basis, all those brokerage commissions will take a big bite out of your take-home returns. For that reason, I'd recommend no-load mutual funds for most people building their own portfolios for college savings.

► Everyone's thinking globally these days, and you may well want to include some foreign-stock exposure in your college fund. However, if you buy a foreign-stock mutual fund, bear in mind that it may be subject to currency fluctuations. If the dollar is weak versus the foreign currencies in which your fund's securities are denominated, your fund may appreciate; if it's strong versus foreign currencies, your fund may go down. The potential for currency fluctuations—and the fact that you simply can't predict whether they'll work for you or against you—argues for scaling back your college fund's foreign-stock exposure as your child gets closer to college.

PART EIGHT

Invest in Your Taxable Account

My colleague russ kinnel once observed that most people could much more readily tell you how much they pay for cable TV each year than they could estimate what they pay in investment management fees, even though the latter bill could be several times as much as the former.

I would say the same thing about investment-related taxes. It's not that investors are dumb or that they knowingly choose to ignore costs that can add up to thousands of dollars a year. Rather, it's that most investors don't write a check for investment management expenses or investment-related taxes. That means that they never see, in dollars and cents, exactly how much they're paying. Investment management expenses are often subtracted directly from the investor's account. And while you do write a check if you owe the IRS, the taxes you pay on your investments get lumped together with all of the other taxes that you're on the hook for in a given year. Because those costs are never clearly depicted, most investors tend not to be too attuned to them.

That's a shame, because these costs are fairly easy to control if you put your mind to it. And controlling them can have a meaningful impact on your bottom-line return.

Limiting the effect of taxes on your investment return is the focus of this section. To the extent that you hold investments in your taxable accounts—and you'll have to if you've maxed out your tax-sheltered investments and/or need ready access to your cash—you'll want to make sure that the investments you hold are as tax-friendly as they can be. Helping you identify the best investments for your taxable account is the focus of Chapter 26. I provide you with broad guidelines as well as share some of Morningstar's best ideas for tax-efficient investments.

Taking care to select tax-efficient investments is only half the battle, however. You also have to practice tax-sensitive techniques when it comes to managing your portfolio. That means limiting the trading that you do in your taxable account to avoid taxable capital gains, as well as taking full advantage of all the tax-sheltered options available to you—401(k)s, IRAs, and various college savings vehicles. It also makes sense to put your least tax-efficient investments into those tax-sheltered accounts and to actively manage your portfolio to limit taxes. I discuss these and other tax-limiting strategies in Chapter 27.

One of the best strategies for reducing your tax bill is to actively sell losers when you have them; you can then use those losses to offset income or capital gains. Tax-loss selling can be psychologically difficult, but it's one way to ensure that something good comes of an investment you're holding at a loss. Chapter 28 focuses on the ins and outs of tax-loss selling.

26

Identify the Best Investments for Taxable Accounts

ALTHOUGH IT CAN BE A HUMBLING EXPERIENCE FOR AN AUTHOR, seeing how many page views various articles receive on Morningstar.com provides some great insights into investor psychology. Any headline with "all-weather" or "sleep easy" (as in "these all-weather funds let you sleep easy") always resonates, particularly in a tough market like 2008. And any article with a number in the headline, as in "Five Stocks to Buy and Hold," offers the promise of instant gratification and therefore is also a click magnet. Surveying our most-trafficked articles always gives me a good idea of what's on investors' minds.

And what's not. If clicks are a guide to investor sentiment, some topics are almost always guaranteed to draw a yawn from our readers. On the short list, particularly lately, is anything tax-related. Given that U.S. stocks had only slight gains over that stretch, most investors weren't overly concerned with investment-related taxes.

Even in a flat or declining market, however, investment-related taxes can take a toll. The typical domestic-equity fund in Morningstar's database gained an average of 1.4 percent per year in the decade through mid-2009, yet taxes gobbled up more than 1 percentage point of that return. In an up market, taxes may take an even bigger bite out of investors' returns. And no matter what the market climate, you're probably going to keep some of your taxable account in bonds or cash; income from these securities is taxed at your ordinary income tax rate (usually higher than the capital gains rate).

I'll concede that you shouldn't prioritize tax avoidance over generating strong returns—that's putting the cart before the horse. Yet careful decisions about what types of investments you put into your taxable portfolio can greatly reduce the investment-related taxes that you'll owe later on.

To identify the best investments for taxable accounts, you'll need:

▶ Morningstar's Bond Calculator (available at www.morningstar.com/goto/ 30MinuteSolutions)

 Start the Clock

Step 1

Before you begin selecting investments for your taxable account, take a step back and think about what you're trying to achieve there. If you're like many people, your taxable holdings address a grab bag of different financial needs: funds for unanticipated expenses like car or home repairs, savings for intermediate-term financial goals like a new car or a new patio, and possibly even longer-term investments like college or retirement savings. Your goals for that money, in turn, will determine whether you invest it in stocks, bonds, or ultrasafe investments like money market accounts or CDs.

If you've got money socked away for your emergency fund or other very short-term needs, that cash should be parked in an ultrasafe investment like a CD or money market fund. For intermediate-term financial needs and goals, consider a short- or intermediate-term bond fund. Chapter 13 discusses the best investments for goals that are close at hand.

If you have assets earmarked for retirement or other long-term goals in your taxable account as well as your retirement account, start by creating an overarching asset allocation. (Chapter 11 helps you do that.)

Step 2

To the extent that your asset mix calls for bonds or cash, be careful: Income from bonds and short-term securities like money market accounts, CDs, and even a good old passbook savings account, while nice to have, is going to cost you from a tax standpoint. Those payouts are taxed at your ordinary income tax rate, which for most investors is substantially higher than the capital gains rate. (You pay capital gains tax when you sell a stock, bond, or fund for more than you paid for it.)

One way to circumvent those taxes is to hold municipal bonds rather than taxable bonds in your taxable portfolio. These bonds are typically free of federal tax and, if the municipality that issued the bond is in your state, the muni bond's income may be free of state tax, too. Because of their tax advantages, municipal bond yields are usually lower than taxable bond yields, but investors in higher tax brackets often come out ahead with munis once their tax rate is factored in.

To help determine whether a municipal bond fund is a better bet for your taxable account than is a taxable bond fund, find the yields for both the muni and taxable funds you're considering. (On Morningstar.com, you can see a fund's yield over the past 12 months on the main page for each mutual fund; for the most current yield figures, look for a fund's "SEC yield" on the fund company's web site.) After you've found the yields, enter them into Morningstar's Bond Calculator, available at www.morningstar.com/goto/30MinuteSolutions. Then enter your tax rate and click Calculate. You'll see the municipal bond fund's yield with its tax benefits factored in, which you can then compare with the taxable fund's yield.

For example, say a municipal bond fund has a 5 percent yield and a taxable fund has a 6 percent yield, and assume that you're in the 25 percent tax bracket. Owing to the tax savings, you pick up an additional 1.25 percent in yield by owning the muni fund (5% × 0.25%), making it a better bet than the taxable bond fund. (5% + 1.25% = a 6.25% yield for the muni fund, once the effect of taxes is factored in.)

It's possible to buy municipal securities at every maturity range, from very short-term securities suitable for an emergency fund to intermediate- and long-term muni bonds, and munis also vary in their credit quality. For

Table 26.1   Morningstar's Top Municipal Bond Fund Picks

Name	Ticker	Category	Investment Minimum ($)
Funds for Short Time Horizons			
Fidelity Short-Intermediate Muni Income	FSTFX	Muni Short	10,000
T. Rowe Price Tax-Free Short-Intermediate	PRFSX	Muni Short	2,500
Vanguard Limited-Term Tax-Exempt	VMLTX	Muni Short	3,000
Vanguard Short-Term Tax-Exempt	VWSTX	Muni Short	3,000
Funds for Intermediate and Long Time Horizons			
Fidelity Intermediate Muni Income	FLTMX	Muni Intermediate	10,000
Vanguard Intermediate-Term Tax-Exempt	VWITX	Muni Intermediate	3,000
Fidelity Municipal Income	FHIGX	Muni Long	10,000
Vanguard Long-Term Tax-Exempt	VWLTX	Muni Long	3,000

Thanks to their low costs, these funds have been able to deliver strong long-term returns relative to other municipal bond funds without taking on a lot of risk. All of them invest in bonds issued by municipalities throughout the United States.

most types of bonds, including municipal bonds, I prefer a high-quality mutual fund to individual bonds because you get built-in diversification and professional management; that helps mitigate the risk that any one municipality will have trouble paying back its bondholders. When selecting bond funds, focus on those with very low costs and risk-conscious management teams; muni funds from Fidelity and Vanguard are among Morningstar's favorites. I've included lists of Morningstar's favorite municipal bond funds in Table 26.1.

Income from municipal bonds or funds dedicated to your home state is usually free of state taxes, too. However, unless you live in an ultra-high-tax state, carefully weigh whether the tax break that you're getting is worth the loss of diversification. Considering the financial straits of many states these days, you may be better off spreading the risk around by investing in bonds issued by municipalities across the United States—not just those in one state.

If you're a muni investor, it also pays to bear in mind whether you're subject to the Alternative Minimum Tax, an alternate tax system that was designed to ensure that the ultrarich didn't dodge taxes altogether. Today, however, many upper-middle-class taxpayers have to pay AMT. If you find that you're in the AMT bucket, avoid private-activity bonds or mutual funds

Table 26.2   Morningstar's Top AMT-Lite Picks

Name	Ticker	Category	Investment Minimum ($)
Fidelity Tax-Free Bond	FTABX	Muni Long	25,000
T. Rowe Price Tax-Free Short-Intermediate	PRFSX	Muni Short	2,500
T. Rowe Price Tax-Free Income	PRTAX	Muni Long	2,500

These municipal bond funds avoid private-activity bonds, which are subject to the Alternative Minimum Tax. In the past, AMT was primarily an issue for high-net-worth households, but more and more upper-middle-income individuals have fallen into the AMT zone over the past decade.

that own them. Municipal bond funds without AMT-subject bonds will have "AMT-free" or "tax-free" in their names. I've included a few of my favorites in Table 26.2.

Step 3

Will your taxable portfolio include stock funds or individual stocks? If so, there are a few different ways to limit taxes without sacrificing return potential.

Good—Index funds: Index mutual funds that own a broad basket of stocks, such as those that track the S&P 500 or Dow Jones Wilshire 5000 Index, tend to be naturally tax-efficient. Their underlying holdings don't change a lot, meaning that management doesn't have to sell appreciated securities and realize capital gains. Not all index funds are tax-efficient, however. If an index provider makes frequent and/or substantial changes to an index—and this can be an issue if an index hews to a specific size or type of investment—or if the fund sees big redemptions and has to sell stocks or bonds to pay off departing shareholders, the fund may generate taxable capital gains.

Better—Individual stocks: Because they have to pay out any capital gains on their books each year, mutual funds can sock shareholders with a tax bill even when those investors haven't sold any shares. Owners of individual stocks face no such issues, however. Instead, they'll owe taxes only when the companies that they own pay a dividend or they sell their stocks and realize a capital gain. That gives individual stockholders a level of control that fundholders don't have. Of course, owning individual stocks is

Table 26.3   Morningstar's Favorite Core Exchange-Traded Funds

Name	Ticker	Asset Class	Category
Vanguard Total Stock Market ETF	VTI	Domestic Stock	Large Blend
iShares S&P 500 Index	IVV	Domestic Stock	Large Blend
Vanguard Dividend Appreciation	VIG	Domestic Stock	Large Blend
Vanguard FTSE All-World ex-US	VEU	Foreign Stock	Foreign Lrg Blend
Vanguard Total World Stock Index	VT	Foreign Stock	World Stock

Because investors buy and sell exchange-traded funds among themselves rather than turning their shares into the fund company for redemptions, ETFs tend to make few, if any, capital gains distributions from year to year.

tax-friendly only if you maintain a very long-term mind-set and keep trading to a minimum. Furthermore, monitoring a portfolio of individual stocks requires more work than monitoring a fund, so you have to decide if that's a worthwhile trade-off for you.

Best (tie)—Exchange-traded funds: Like traditional index mutual funds, nearly all ETFs passively track market benchmarks, meaning their holdings change infrequently. Plus, ETFs have a few other tax-limiting characteristics. For starters, they don't have to sell stocks to meet investor redemptions; instead, ETF buyers and sellers trade with one another rather than going through the fund company. Also, when large investors cash in their shares, they can receive shares of the stocks in the index; that allows the fund to flush out the shares with the biggest tax burden. As a result, ETFs have generally been quite tax-efficient. I've included some of Morningstar's favorite ETFs in Table 26.3.

Best (tie)—Tax-managed funds: Tax-managed funds have never really taken off in popularity, but they've done a phenomenal job of keeping Uncle Sam's cut of investors' returns to a minimum. While plenty of investments have been tax-efficient in the past, tax-managed funds aim to reduce taxes in the future, too. They use a variety of strategies, but most of them loosely track a market benchmark, such as the S&P 500, and employ techniques to avoid dividend and capital gains payouts. Most work to offset appreciated securities by selling losers. The best of these, such as Vanguard's lineup of tax-managed funds, have a record of never making

Table 26.4   Morningstar's Favorite Tax-Managed Funds

Name	Ticker	Asset Class	Category	Investment Minimum ($)
Fidelity Tax-Managed Stock	FTXMX	U.S. Stock	Large Blend	10,000
Vanguard Tax-Managed Capital Appreciation	VMCAX	U.S. Stock	Large Blend	10,000
Vanguard Tax-Managed Growth & Income	VTGIX	U.S. Stock	Large Blend	10,000
Vanguard Tax-Managed Small Cap	VTMSX	U.S. Stock	Small Blend	10,000
Vanguard Tax-Managed International	VTMGX	Foreign Stock	Foreign Lrg Blend	10,000
Vanguard Tax-Managed Balanced	VTMFX	Stock/Bond	Cons. Allocation	10,000

Tax-managed funds have waned in popularity over the past several years, as many funds have had capital losses, not gains. In a strong up market, however, these tax-efficient funds should do a good job of limiting capital gains distributions.

capital gains distributions, though they may pay dividends. I've included some of my favorite tax-managed funds in Table 26.4.

Next Steps

▶ Choosing tax-efficient investments is one way to reduce the amount of taxes that you'll owe on your investments. The other key way is to manage your own holdings with tax efficiency in mind, by trading infrequently (and not running the risk of generating taxable capital gains) and knowing which investments to play in your tax-sheltered accounts. I discuss these and other strategies in Chapters 27 and 28.

▶ Although the opportunity may not be available for long, many mutual funds have large tax-loss carryforwards on their books—losses that they can use to offset gains in the future. That means that they could generate strong gains in the future but investors in them may not owe any capital gains taxes. Some of the funds with the biggest tax-loss carryforwards have been mismanaged, but others are decent funds that have since had management changes or operate in hard-hit market sectors. Among the funds that currently fit the bill are Clipper CFIMX, Royce Opportunity RYPNX, and Thornburg Value TVAFX.

27

Manage Your Portfolio for Tax Efficiency

SOME THINGS IN LIFE ADD INSULT TO INJURY.

That's precisely what my friend experienced when he purchased a China-focused mutual fund, Matthews China MCHFX, in early 2008. Although Matthews is a fine firm that specializes in investing in Asia, I tried to dissuade him. I didn't have any special premonition about China or its prospects, but I suggested that he'd be better off with a diversified emerging markets fund with the latitude to invest in China as well as the ability to get out if the going got tough.

Lo and behold, his fund dropped 50 percent in 2008. And because Matthews China saw a rash of investors yanking out their shares in the wake of the losses, the fund's assets dropped by more than two thirds, forcing management to sell some of its long-held positions. As a result, the fund ended up making a capital gains distribution. In the end, my friend ended up owing taxes on his investment, even though his account shriveled from $10,000 to $5,000 over the course of a year and even though he still owned it.

The moral of the story is that taxes can cost you, and that's true not just in good markets but in bad ones, too. That may sound like a "heads they win, tails you lose" situation, but it doesn't have to be. In fact, taxes are one of the few factors in investing over which you can actually exert some control. While the market is unpredictable and its direction is ultimately out of your control, working to limit taxes in your portfolio, by selling your losers or using other tax management strategies, is one way to put yourself in the driver's seat.

A good starting point is to make sure that you understand the basic rules of investment-related taxation.

The easiest to get your head around is how the government treats income: If you own a bond or bond fund that pays you income, or if you earn interest on a CD or checking account, you need to pay taxes on that income at your regular income tax rate. (Currently, the highest tax rate is 35 percent.)

If you receive income from a stock—called dividend income—you'll also pay taxes, but the rate is currently lower than your ordinary income tax rate—just 15 percent for most investors through 2010.

If you're an investor you may also have to pay capital gains tax—a tax on the difference between your purchase price and the price at which you sold the security. For example, say you bought a stock at $25 and it's now selling at $35. If you were to sell, you'd owe capital gains taxes on that $10 worth of appreciation. The government wants to encourage long-term investing over short-term trading, so you'll pay a higher tax rate—your regular income tax rate—if you sell appreciated securities within one year of purchasing them. If you sell stocks that you've held for more than one year, the rate is more favorable: currently 15 percent for most investors. (That rate is scheduled to go up in 2011, however.)

Due to a wrinkle in the tax law, mutual fund investors may also have to pay capital gains tax on funds they haven't sold—and that's exactly what happened to my Matthews China–owning friend. Fund managers generate capital gains for their shareholders when they sell appreciated shares of stocks or bonds, and those gains get paid out to all shareholders each year. In turn, shareholders who own those funds in taxable accounts have to pay capital gains tax, even though they may not have sold a share of the fund or even made any money in it.

That's not to say that you have to take all those taxes lying down, however. By employing the strategies that follow—and yes, admitting you were wrong on occasion—you can greatly reduce your investment-related taxes.

To limit the tax collector's cut of your returns, you'll need:

► Most recent account statements
► A target stock/bond mix for your portfolio

 Start the Clock
Step 1

The preceding may have made it sound like the IRS really has it in for investors. However, employing tax-sheltered investments like 401(k)s, IRAs, and 529 college savings plans allows you to minimize or even avoid paying taxes on your investments. With all these vehicles, you won't ever owe taxes on the buying and selling of shares in any one calendar year; nor will you owe taxes if one of your holdings makes a capital gains distribution or a dividend or income payment. (You won't be able to pocket the distribution either; you'll have to reinvest it into the security that made the payout, or else you'll be on the hook for taxes and penalties.) You'll owe taxes when you begin taking income out of your 401(k) plan and traditional IRA during retirement, but holders of Roth IRAs, Roth 401(k)s, Coverdell Education Savings Accounts, and 529 plans won't owe any taxes on qualified distributions.

Table 27.1 illustrates how much you can contribute to some of the major tax-sheltering vehicles, as well as whether your income level qualifies you to make contributions.

Look at your current statements to determine how much you're saving in those vehicles during the current tax year. If you're not currently contributing the maximum, prioritize investing within those vehicles before you invest in your taxable accounts. The one exception is your emergency fund, which I discussed in Chapter 10. Because you'll need to gain access to that cash in a pinch, your emergency fund should reside in your taxable account rather than in a tax-sheltered vehicle.

Table 27.1   Are You Maxed Out? Contribution and Income Limits for Key Tax-Sheltered Vehicles

Vehicle	Primary Purpose	Annual Contribution Limit (under 50)($)	Annual Contribution Limit (over 50)($)	Income Limit/ Singles ($)	Income Limit/ Married Filing Jointly ($)
Roth IRA	Retirement Savings	5,000	6,000	120,000	176,000
Traditional IRA (deductible)	Retirement Savings	5,000	6,000	63,000	120,000
Traditional IRA (nondeductible)	Retirement Savings	5,000	6,000	None	None
401(k)	Retirement Savings	16,500	22,000	None*	N/A
403(b)	Retirement Savings	16,500	22,000	None*	N/A
457	Retirement Savings	16,500	22,000	None*	N/A
Coverdell Ed. Savings Account	College Savings	2,000/child	2,000/child	110,000	220,000
529 Plan	College Savings	Vary by state	Vary by state	None	None

*Rules regarding highly compensated employees may affect ability to contribute.

One of the best ways to reduce Uncle Sam's cut of your investment returns is to take advantage of all the tax-sheltered vehicles available to you. The income and contribution limits listed here are for 2009; after 2009, these amounts will be indexed to the inflation rate.

Step 2

If you have assets in your taxable accounts as well as in tax-sheltered vehicles, take a look at what types of assets you have stashed where and consider whether your asset *location* is optimal.

Ultimately, the decision is personal and depends on your asset allocation and the amount of assets you hold in your tax-sheltered and taxable accounts. In general, however, you're better off holding stocks in your taxable accounts and bonds in your tax-sheltered vehicles. There are two key reasons. The first is that the tax rate for bond income is currently nearly twice (or even more than) that of the dividend or capital gains tax rates. The second reason is that stock investors have more control over their tax burdens than do bond investors. A bond or bond fund usually pays a yield no matter what, and there's no way to dodge the taxes from bond income earned in a taxable account (unless you opt for municipal bonds, which are free of federal and in some cases state taxes). Investors holding stocks in taxable accounts, by contrast, have many more opportunities to avoid taxes from year to year: They can hold individual stocks, exchange-traded funds, or tax-managed funds, all of which provide the opportunity to avoid taxable capital gains. Chapter 26 covered how to select tax-efficient investments for your taxable account.

Step 3

While the type of assets that you put into your tax-sheltered and taxable accounts can have a big impact on how good your after-tax returns are, so can your own trading activity.

Take a moment to consider how much you trade. Are you hands-off or do you find yourself buying and selling frequently?

I'll say flat-out that I'm not a big believer in frequent trading—patient, buy-and-hold investing usually leads to a better outcome for investors. In fact, research compiled by University of California professors Brad Barber and Terrance Odean showed that households with the most trading activity systematically earned lower returns than the average household did.

That said, if you trade frequently with at least part of your portfolio and realize capital gains from time to time, you're better off doing so in your IRA or company retirement plan than in your taxable account. There are usually no tax implications from trading in your company retirement plan—assuming you don't actually take money out of your account. You can also trade within an IRA and even shift IRA assets among different investment firms without having to pay taxes, assuming that you follow the rules for doing so. By contrast, you'll owe capital gains tax if you sell a security that has appreciated within your taxable account; if you've held the appreciated security for less than a year, the tax is levied at your ordinary income tax rate.

Next Step

▶ Another key way to reduce investment-related taxes is to engage in a practice called tax-loss selling, which involves pruning your losers in an effort to offset income and capital gains. I discuss tax-loss selling in Chapter 28.

28

Harvest Tax Losses

ONE OF MY RELATIVES CALLED me in late 2008, seeking advice about what to do with her flagging portfolio. Like everyone else, she was panicked and wanted to take action, even though she has a good 10 to 15 years until retirement. She wanted to stop the losses by selling her many poorly performing stocks and stock funds.

I told her that she was absolutely right and agreed that she should sell at least some of her holdings—especially the ones that had performed the worst.

There was silence on the other end of the line. "But I thought you would tell me to sit tight, like you always do," she said, clearly puzzled.

This time was different, at least in one sense. I didn't recommend getting out of stocks altogether. Doing so would ensure that her portfolio would bear the brunt of the sell-off—even more than it had already—and would also fail to participate in any subsequent recovery.

However, completely sitting tight didn't make sense at that point, either. I suggested that she sell the biggest losers from her taxable brokerage account and then buy other, similar investments in their place. In so doing, she'd be able to use those losses to reduce her tax bill, not just for 2008 but potentially for future years, too. She may even be able to upgrade the quality of holdings along the way. Amid the calamitous market environment of 2008, many long-closed and highly desirable mutual funds flung open their doors for new business, and many high-quality companies were trading at very attractive prices.

Tax-loss selling is one of the most effective ways to seize control in a volatile market environment. It not only provides a much-needed feeling that you are taking definitive action, but it also allows you to make sure that you have a lot of conviction in your remaining holdings. It can help you save on taxes, too. By selling losers in your portfolio, you can use those losses to offset capital gains from other holdings, and you can also use your tax losses to offset as much as $3,000 in ordinary income in a single year. You can use unused losses to offset income or capital gains in future years.

You don't have to wait for a terrible bear market to engage in tax-loss selling, either. Even in a robust bull market, you may find that some of your holdings are selling at prices well below what you paid for them. In fact, selling your losers can be particularly valuable in a market like that, when your other investments are riding high and generating big gains.

Chapter 27 covered some of the key ways to limit the effects of taxes on the investments that you hold in your taxable account, including maxing out your tax-sheltered options and being careful about asset location—where you hold which types of investments. Tax-loss selling is another such technique, but it's one that many investors don't take enough advantage of (unless their accountants or financial advisors egg them on). Many investors view tax-loss selling as tantamount to admitting a mistake, and if their portfolios have suffered big losses they might not be inclined to look at their holdings at all.

Bear in mind that tax-loss selling is primarily appropriate for your taxable account. While it's also possible to take a loss in a Roth or traditional nondeductible IRA, the rules are more complicated and the strategy is generally less advantageous than is harvesting losses from a taxable account.

To harvest tax losses, you'll need:

▶ Most recent investment statements, indicating the current prices of your investments as well as the prices you paid for them. If your statements don't include information on the prices you paid for your shares (your cost basis) and you no longer have the transaction records, your fund company or brokerage firm may be able to supply you with a record. Over the past few years, financial services firms have begun to provide increasingly sophisticated cost-basis tracking to their clients.

Start the Clock
Step 1

Your first step in the tax-loss harvesting process is to identify possible sale candidates; the Tax-Loss Worksheet (Worksheet 28.1), available at www.morningstar.com/goto/30MinuteSolutions, can help you keep track.

Not everything that's down should be on the chopping block, because some of your hardest hit holdings could have the greatest rebound potential. Instead, start by scouting around for stocks and funds where you misjudged the basic attributes, as well as securities that were simply a poor fit for you to begin with. For example, perhaps you underestimated the risks inherent in a bank with a lot of mortgage-related exposure or you've decided that you didn't really need a health care–specific exchange-traded fund because your portfolio already has plenty of health care stocks.

Also be on the lookout for investments where there's a viable alternative in the same category or industry. For example, say you want to take a loss on a fund like Dodge & Cox Stock DODGX but you don't want to give up on the value style of investing altogether; you could buy another value-oriented fund, such as Sound Shore SSHFX. As long as you don't replace that stock or fund within 30 days with what the IRS calls a *substantially identical security*, you can claim a loss on your tax return but still retain exposure to that part of the market. Be careful that you're not chasing performance, though. If a fund you're buying has had substantially better performance than one you're selling, there's a chance that its luck could run out or it could make a taxable capital gains distribution in the future.

Step 2

Next, quantify how big your loss is. Central to this process is getting your arms around what you paid for your shares, also known as your *cost basis*. Cost basis is your original purchase price plus any reinvested dividends or capital gains.

Worksheet 28.1

Tax-Loss Worksheet

PREPARED FOR: _____   DATE: /   / _____

You'll Need:
■ Most recent investment statements, indicating the current prices of your investments as well as the prices you paid for them. If your statements don't include information on the prices you paid for your shares (your cost basis) and you no longer have the transaction records, your fund companies or brokerages may be able to supply you with a record.

COST BASIS CALCULATION

Stock/Fund Name	Category/Industry	# of Shares	Cost ($)	Current Price/NAV ($)	Possible Loss ($)

Print your worksheet at: www.morningstar.com/goto/30MinuteSolutions

If you made a one-time purchase of a stock or fund, haven't made additional purchases, and are not reinvesting capital gains and dividends, arriving at your cost basis is easy. It's simply the price you paid for your first and only set of shares. For example, if you bought 1,200 shares of a non-dividend-paying stock for $10 apiece two years ago and they're now trading at $7, your cost basis is a straightforward $10. You're holding all those shares at a loss, and they could be likely candidates for pruning.

If you made purchases on multiple occasions and/or are reinvesting dividends and capital gains, there are several different methods for calculating cost basis. By finding the right one, you'll be able to make tax-loss selling particularly advantageous.

▶ **Specific share identification:** With this method you identify shares that you'd like to sell, and sell only those that are advantageous to you from a tax standpoint. For example, say you bought some shares of a stock at $12 and some more at $7, and the stock is now at $8.50. You can sell the number of shares you bought at $12 and realize the loss, but hang on to the number of shares you bought at $7. This method can make a lot of sense if you think a stock is apt to rebound but still want to get the tax benefit. This method allows you to exert the highest level of control over your taxes but is also the most labor-intensive.

▶ **Averaging:** Another method of calculating cost basis involves averaging your purchase prices. There are two different methods. In the first, you add up all your purchases of the security, including reinvested dividends and capital gains, and divide by the total number of shares you own. To determine whether your gains/losses are short-term or long-term, you assume that the oldest shares are sold first. Once you use this method to calculate the cost basis of shares you've sold, you must continue to use this method for the rest of the shares you sell in the future.

A less common method of averaging is to sort your shares into two categories: those in which your gains and losses are short-term and those in which you have a long-term gain or loss. Then you add up the purchases in each category and divide by the number of shares in each category. (This method of calculating cost basis isn't for Sunday drivers; it's obviously a lot more complicated than the averaging method I discussed in the previous paragraph.)

▶ **First in, first out:** Finally, you could calculate your cost basis by using the "first in, first out" method that the IRS uses as a default if you don't specify—essentially, you'd sell the shares that you purchased first. That method can work out just fine if you've purchased a security that has subsequently gone down in price, but you generally wouldn't want to go this route if you own a security that has appreciated steadily since you bought it.

Step 3

Once you've identified some potential sale candidates and determined the method of calculating cost basis, your next step is to find out where your whole portfolio stands with regard to realized and unrealized gains and losses. "Realized" gains and losses relate to any selling you've already done so far this year; for example, if you purchased a stock at $25 per share in March and sold it for $40 per share in July, you have a realized gain. Unrealized gains or losses mean that a security in your portfolio has changed in value since you bought it but you still hold it. In the example above, if you purchased a stock at $25, it's now trading at $40, and you're still hanging on, you have an unrealized gain.

In tax parlance, you "net" those gains and losses against one another. If you have sold a security that you held for longer than one year, you'll have realized either a long-term capital gain (if you sold it for more than you paid for it) or a long-term capital loss (if you sold it for less than you paid for it). If you held the security for less than a year, you'll have short-term gains or losses.

If you look at where your portfolio stands right now and find that you have realized gains but not realized losses, you may want to realize losses to offset your gains. If your realized losses outweigh your realized gains, you can use those losses to offset income and reduce your tax hit.

Step 4

The final step in the tax-loss selling process is to identify viable candidates to replace what you've sold, assuming you'd still like your portfolio to retain exposure to that part of the market. Chapters 13 and 14 feature many of Morningstar's favorite funds in a cross-section of categories.

Again, be careful not to trigger the wash-sale rule by buying two investments that are overly similar to one another. For example, the IRS would likely frown on replacing one S&P 500 Index fund with another, but you can readily replace an actively managed large-cap blend fund with an S&P 500 Index fund.

And if it's near year-end, also be careful about replacing your losing mutual fund with another fund that's poised to make a big capital gains distribution. (Mutual funds have to distribute any gains they have realized during the year to their shareholders by year-end.) Most funds make distributions in the fourth quarter, usually during the month of December. So, before you buy a new fund to replace the one you're selling, call the fund company or hop on its web site to check on impending distributions.

Next Steps

▶ If you've completed the preceding steps and have found yourself frustrated because you couldn't find good information on your cost basis, plan to keep better records in the future. Saving all trade confirmations is a good start, but you can take your record keeping a step further by maintaining a spreadsheet with all your purchase prices and the number of shares you bought. This is particularly advantageous if you're using the specific share identification method of calculating cost basis.

▶ If you don't have losses in your taxable account but do in your IRA, bear in mind that the rules for claiming a loss are more stringent, and those IRA losses may not be as valuable to you as are losses from your taxable accounts. You can deduct a loss on an IRA only if you withdraw all your assets from that IRA type, whether Roth or traditional, and your cost basis in all those accounts is above the accounts' current values. If you've accumulated a sizable balance in a Roth or traditional IRA, that should be a big deterrent against selling, because future contributions will be subject to calendar-year contribution limits. And in contrast with losses from taxable investments, which can be deducted directly from your ordinary income on your income tax form, IRA losses are part of the miscellaneous itemized deductions that you claim on Schedule A of your Form 1040. These deductions must amount to 2 percent of your adjusted gross income or they won't be usable. You must also use these losses in the year in which you generate them. That stands in contrast with losses from taxable accounts, which can be carried forward from year to year if you don't use them.

PART NINE

Invest during Retirement

"I WILL SAY THAT not one of my clients' retirements looked the way they thought it was going to look. They lived longer than they thought, they lived shorter than they thought, they were healthier than they thought, they were less healthy than they thought they would be."

Financial planner Ross Levin made that point to me in a 2009 interview, and I think he neatly summed up the challenges of planning for retirement.

Financial planning for life events such as college or a home purchase is straightforward: It's not all that difficult to determine when you'll need the money, how much you'll need, and how long you'll need it.

But planning for retirement is different, because all three of those variables are up in the air. It may not be that difficult to determine when you *want* to start retirement, but when you *should* start retirement is another matter; no one wants to be in the position of retiring early but running out of money later in life. And longevity and health—two enormous unknowables—affect how much money you'll need during your retirement years and how long you'll need it.

The fact that retirees are so different, too, makes it tough to give one-size-fits-all advice.

Despite the jokes about shuffleboard and early-bird specials, retirees are not a monolith. The needs of a 60-year-old retiree who has a $3 million portfolio and has just sold his business are very different from the person who's retiring at 81 with health problems and $125,000 in retirement savings.

Nonetheless, that doesn't mean that you can't plan for retirement based on what you do know. It's still possible to put some rigor behind the decision-making process about when to retire and how much you'll be able to spend without depleting your assets. The starting point for this process is to give serious thought to what you hope your retirement will look like and what your spending needs will be. In the past, financial planners suggested that retirees should expect to spend at a rate of 80 percent of their pre-retirement income. But the reality is that some retirees have spent just as much—if not more—in retirement than they did during their working years.

Whether the amount you want to spend is realistic, however, is another matter. How much you *should* spend in retirement—your withdrawal rate—given the size of your portfolio, its stock/bond/cash mix, your income from other sources, and the number of years you expect to be retired—is the focus of Chapter 29. No one wants to run out of money during retirement, but the good news is that it may be possible for you to adjust some of these variables to ensure that your nest egg lasts.

How to position your retirement portfolio to deliver the income you need, without depleting your assets early or taking on excessive risk, is the focus of Chapter 30. I discuss balancing income with growth potential and risk control, and I also provide some sample portfolios for retirees at various stages in their lives.

Chapter 31, the last one in this section, covers a topic that hasn't received a lot of attention over the years: the sequence in which you should tap your assets during retirement—IRAs, your company retirement plan, and taxable assets. Getting these decisions right can help you save on taxes over the duration of your retirement, which in turn will help your retirement portfolio last longer. In addition, knowing which pool of money you'll dip into first—and last—can help ensure that you match each portfolio's asset allocation to your time horizon for it.

29

Determine Your Portfolio Withdrawal Rate

"CAN WE AFFORD TO RETIRE?"

That's a common question, and it's one that a subscriber to my newsletter, *Morningstar PracticalFinance,* posed to me in a request for a Portfolio Makeover in mid-2009.

A former community college administrator, this 59-year-old reader had already retired, but her husband, 58, was still working in a position in state government. His commute took roughly three hours a day, cutting into this couple's leisure time and prompting them to consider whether full-time retirement was a possibility for both of them.

They had diligently saved and lived frugally; they also would be able to draw on pensions in retirement. That helps explain why they were able to consider retiring at a much younger age than most of us can contemplate. However, their retirement portfolio had taken a big hit during the bear market, and this couple had also invested in two real estate properties in 2006, near the peak of the bubble. They had hoped to use one of the properties as a vacation home and sell the other to help fund retirement, but the tanking markets for property had called that plan into question.

Determining the feasibility of an early retirement for this couple depended on a combination of factors, some of them knowable, some of them not. In the (at least somewhat) knowable column was how much they intended to spend in retirement as well as the income they could expect from sources other than their investment and real estate portfolios—in this couple's case, both Social Security and their pensions. In the unknowable category were two biggies: what kind of investment return they could expect as well as how long they would each live. We also had to evaluate some factors that were specific to their situation, such as whether (and when) they wanted to sell their investment properties and whether they wanted to leave a legacy for their loved ones.

In the end, we determined that they could retire sooner rather than later, in part because their two pensions fulfilled more than half of their income needs. When they began taking Social Security payments, they would be even closer to meeting their income needs without having to aggressively draw on their investment portfolio. And if this couple wanted to further ensure that their assets would last throughout their retirement years, I recommended that one or both of them consider working part-time (closer to home, of course) and that they delay the receipt of Social Security benefits until they're in their mid-sixties rather than taking them as soon as they're eligible.

As this couple's story illustrates, determining when you can retire and how much you can safely withdraw from your investments when you do is a complicated exercise. And unfortunately, the numbers won't always tell you what you want to hear. However, the advantage of checking up on when and how you might be able to retire is that it can help you determine whether changes are in order while there's still time to make them. You can work longer, save more, or spend less; you can also recalibrate your planned spending during retirement or make changes to your investments in an effort to optimize your returns.

To determine how much you can spend during retirement, you'll need:

▶ Most recent investment statements with current account balances
▶ Morningstar's Instant X-Ray tool, available at www.morningstar.com/goto/30MinuteSolutions
▶ Retirement Income Worksheet (Worksheet 29.1, available at www.morningstar.com/goto/30MinuteSolutions)

Worksheet 29.1

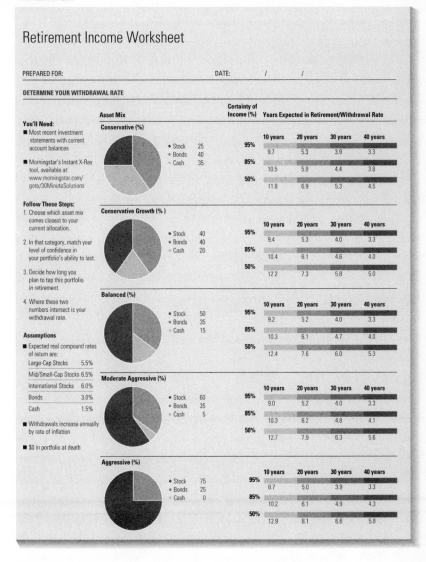

Retirement Income Worksheet

PREPARED FOR: DATE: /   /

DETERMINE YOUR WITHDRAWAL RATE

You'll Need:
- Most recent investment statements with current account balances
- Morningstar's Instant X-Ray tool, available at: www.morningstar.com/goto/30MinuteSolutions

Follow These Steps:
1. Choose which asset mix comes closest to your current allocation.
2. In that category, match your level of confidence in your portfolio's ability to last.
3. Decide how long you plan to tap this portfolio in retirement.
4. Where these two numbers intersect is your withdrawal rate.

Assumptions
- Expected real compound rates of return are:

Large-Cap Stocks	5.5%
Mid/Small-Cap Stocks	6.5%
International Stocks	6.0%
Bonds	3.0%
Cash	1.5%

- Withdrawals increase annually by rate of inflation
- $0 in portfolio at death

Asset Mix

Conservative (%)
- Stock 25
- Bonds 40
- Cash 35

Certainty of Income (%)	Years Expected in Retirement/Withdrawal Rate			
	10 years	20 years	30 years	40 years
95%	9.7	5.3	3.9	3.3
85%	10.5	5.9	4.4	3.8
50%	11.8	6.9	5.3	4.5

Conservative Growth (%)
- Stock 40
- Bonds 40
- Cash 20

Certainty of Income (%)	10 years	20 years	30 years	40 years
95%	9.4	5.3	4.0	3.3
85%	10.4	6.1	4.6	4.0
50%	12.2	7.3	5.8	5.0

Balanced (%)
- Stock 50
- Bonds 35
- Cash 15

Certainty of Income (%)	10 years	20 years	30 years	40 years
95%	9.2	5.2	4.0	3.3
85%	10.3	6.1	4.7	4.0
50%	12.4	7.6	6.0	5.3

Moderate Aggressive (%)
- Stock 60
- Bonds 35
- Cash 5

Certainty of Income (%)	10 years	20 years	30 years	40 years
95%	9.0	5.2	4.0	3.3
85%	10.3	6.2	4.8	4.1
50%	12.7	7.9	6.3	5.6

Aggressive (%)
- Stock 75
- Bonds 25
- Cash 0

Certainty of Income (%)	10 years	20 years	30 years	40 years
95%	8.7	5.0	3.9	3.3
85%	10.2	6.1	4.9	4.3
50%	12.9	8.1	6.6	5.8

Print your worksheet at: www.morningstar.com/goto/30MinuteSolutions

Start the Clock

Step 1

Start by finding your portfolio's current asset allocation—how your investment assets are apportioned among stocks, bonds, and cash.

If you don't know yours, Morningstar's Instant X-Ray tool, available at www.morningstar.com/goto/30MinuteSolutions, can help you determine it. Enter each of your holdings into the tool and then click Show Instant X-Ray. (If your current asset allocation is different from what you expect it to be when you're close to retirement, Chapter 11 can help you identify an appropriate asset allocation for your retirement years.)

On the Retirement Income Worksheet (Worksheet 29.1, downloadable at www.morningstar.com/goto/30MinuteSolutions), circle the portfolio mix that most closely matches your own.

Step 2

Next, circle the number of years that you expect to be retired. Go to www.ssa.gov/OACT/STATS/table4c6.html to determine your life expectancy. If you're married, use the female partner's life expectancy because it's longer. If you and/or your spouse are in good health, add a few years or more.

Step 3

How much certainty do you need in your life? Are you a "live for today" sort of person, willing to spend now even if it could result in a shortfall in your income later in life? Or are you someone who would rather spend less during retirement if it means a greater degree of certainty that your money won't run out?

The answer to this question will determine the percentage that you mark in the Certainty of Income column. If you'd like a high degree of certainty that your money will last throughout your retirement years, circle 85 percent or 95 percent. If you're willing to tolerate the possibility of a shortfall in exchange for more spending power early in your retirement years, circle 50 percent.

Step 4

To help determine your optimal portfolio withdrawal rate given the specifics you've just outlined, find the point where Asset Mix, Certainty of Income, and Years Expected in Retirement intersect. For example, someone with a

Moderate Aggressive portfolio seeking an 85 percent degree of income certainty who expects to be retired 30 years would target a 4.8 percent withdrawal rate. That's the percentage of your portfolio that you can withdraw per year without running out.

Note that these withdrawal rates assume that your withdrawals will step up annually to keep pace with inflation. They also assume that you'll completely deplete your assets during retirement. Thus, if you're hoping to leave assets to your heirs, you'll need to shrink your withdrawal rate, switch to a more aggressive asset allocation, save more, or plan to retire later.

Step 5

To help determine whether that amount is enough to cover your spending needs in retirement, look at the second page of the worksheet. Start by totaling up your investment assets, including taxable accounts as well as any company retirement plan assets.

Step 6

Next, multiply that amount by the percentage withdrawal amount that you came up with in Step 4. That's the actual amount that you can withdraw from your portfolio during the first year of retirement. (Divide by 12 to arrive at a monthly withdrawal amount.)

If you're retiring and won't have income from other sources—for example, if you don't have a pension and aren't yet eligible for Social Security—decide whether that income—plus an annual inflation adjustment—is enough to sustain you during your retirement years.

If you're expecting retirement income from other sources during retirement, move on to Step 7.

Step 7

After you've figured out how much help you'll get from your portfolio during retirement, take stock of other expected sources of income during retirement—excluding any withdrawals or income from your investment portfolio. Include income from part-time work, pensions, and any annuity income you're expecting. Also estimate your Social Security benefits using one of these calculators: www.ssa.gov/planners/calculators.htm.

Step 8

Add together the amounts that you arrived at in Steps 6 and 7. That's the amount of income that you can expect during your first year of retirement.

Step 9

Finally, adjust your income for taxes. The quick and dirty way to do this is to multiply the income amount by your tax rate. In reality, however, your tax burden may be higher or lower.

Next Steps

▶ Will your expected income cover your spending needs during retirement? If not, spend some time tinkering with the variables. For example, switching to a more aggressive asset-allocation mix could improve your portfolio's return potential (but it could also increase its risk level). And if you're willing to work longer, you could reduce the number of years that you'll spend in retirement (and, in turn, the need for income from your investment portfolio).

▶ The questions of how much you'll need to retire—and how much you'll be able to withdraw from your investments when you do—are crucial ones, so it's helpful to seek a variety of opinions. Morningstar's Asset Allocator tool can help you determine whether your current portfolio—both in terms of its size and asset mix—is sufficient relative to your income needs. (Asset Allocator is a Premium tool on Morningstar.com, meaning that you have to be a paying member of our site.) T. Rowe Price's free Retirement Income Calculator www3.troweprice.com/ric/ric/public/ric.do can provide yet another read on whether your current investments are enough to provide you with the income you seek.

▶ Although we've discussed a fixed withdrawal rate (with an inflation adjustment) in this exercise, you of course will be able to withdraw more or less as circumstances dictate. In fact, a 2008 study from T. Rowe Price showed that the best strategy for retirees who encountered a bear market early on in retirement was to reduce their withdrawal rates. Doing so would help them avoid turning paper portfolio losses into real ones by having to sell out of their long-term investments at an inopportune time.

30

Build an In-Retirement Portfolio

THE E-MAILS POURED IN throughout 2008 and continued into 2009. During the economic crisis and the worst bear market since the Great Depression, retirees were seeking hand-holding and guidance about what to do next.

There was Oscar, who was concerned about what would happen if his pension—which he had counted on for income during retirement—failed. How could he check up on the health of his pension, and would his retirement savings cover the shortfall in his income if his pension plan did run into problems?

I also heard from Diane—and other grown children of aging parents. An overly high stock weighting had reduced her 85-year-old mom's portfolio down to a dangerously low level, and she was trying to make sure the assets would last throughout her mother's lifetime.

And then there were Bob and Janet. Bob had moved most of the couple's assets into cash late in the bear market. That had helped them avoid a further drubbing when the market continued to sell off in early 2009, but with stocks roaring back, they found themselves in a quandary: Was it time to get back in? And if not now, when?

No doubt about it, the recent bear market tested the portfolio strategies (and nerves) of nearly all retirees, even those who were in relatively good shape at the outset and especially those who weren't.

It also demonstrated how much more challenging today's retirement landscape is than it was a few decades ago. Not only did many individuals retire with the luxury of a pension, but interest rates were substantially higher than they are today; in the 1970s, you could earn a double-digit yield with very limited risk. Now, however, most individuals are in charge of building and managing part or all of their retirement portfolios, and they're confronting wimpy yields to boot. Many retirees still cling to the notion of being able to live solely off the yield generated by their portfolios, but that's become unrealistic except for the very well-off. Whereas not invading their principal may have been a key challenge for affluent retirees a few decades ago, the key challenge for most retirees today is to not deplete their nest eggs.

So, where do you begin to create an in-retirement portfolio that will provide you with the right combination of income, stability, and growth—one that will help you navigate varying market conditions without prompting you to change course midstream? Ideally, your in-retirement portfolio will not only be effective and suit your needs, it will also be low-stress and low-maintenance. Those are important attributes for your investment portfolio whatever your life stage, but especially so during retirement, when you've no doubt got better things to do than fret about your investment results.

Chapter 29 covered the first steps in the retirement portfolio planning process: determining whether you have enough assets to retire and how much you can safely take out each month and each year without running out of money. Worksheet 29.1 also examined the impact that different asset allocations would have on withdrawal rates and the potential for asset depletion.

Once you've culled that information, you can then turn your attention to the nitty-gritty of selecting specific investments for your in-retirement portfolio.

To create an in-retirement portfolio, you'll need:

▶ An estimate of your income from all sources (other than your investment portfolio) during retirement. (If you completed Worksheet 29.1, you should have this information handy.)

► An estimate of your in-retirement spending needs
► Morningstar's Instant X-Ray tool, available at www.morningstar.com/
goto/30MinuteSolutions

Start the Clock

Step 1

First, make sure you have an adequate cash cushion in place. Every retiree should have two to five years' worth of living expenses set aside in highly liquid (that is, checking, savings, money market, CD) investments at all times.

If you're receiving income from other certain sources—such as Social Security—you can reduce the amount accordingly. For example, say your annual living expenses are $60,000 a year but you bring in half of that in income: $24,000 in Social Security and another $6,000 from a small pension. If that's the case, the amount of assets you should keep in cash should range between $60,000 ($30,000 × two years) and $150,000 ($30,000 × five years).

In general, if you're confident in your portfolio's ability to last throughout your retirement, you can keep closer to five years' worth of living expenses in these highly liquid accounts. (After all, you shouldn't take risks if you don't need to.) If you're less confident and can't afford to keep such a big chunk of your portfolio tied up in low-returning investments, your cash holdings may stay at the low end of this range.

Step 2

The next step is to arrive at an appropriate asset allocation. There aren't any one-size-fits-all solutions for retirees. Age and the number of years you expect to be retired are big swing factors, of course: Generally speaking, having a longer time horizon will make you better-equipped to tolerate, and regroup from, stock market losses. The size of your portfolio and what other sources of income you'll be able to rely on during retirement also play roles in whether your retirement portfolio tilts toward equities or bonds, or balances the two. For example, an individual whose pension covers most of his living expenses and is mainly investing to leave money behind for his children and grandchildren can hold a lot more in stocks than one who's entirely reliant on his portfolio for income.

Worksheet 29.1 helped you view asset allocation through the lens of your own situation: your optimal withdrawal rate, the number of years you expect to be retired, and your willingness to tolerate the possibility of falling short. You can tinker with each of these factors to help identify an appropriate asset allocation given your own inputs.

I've also provided some sample in-retirement portfolios in Figure 30.1. You'll notice that all of them include at least some stock exposure—including

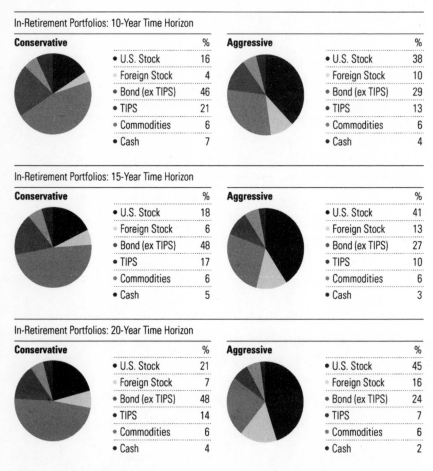

In-Retirement Portfolios: 10-Year Time Horizon

Conservative	%		Aggressive	%
• U.S. Stock	16		• U.S. Stock	38
• Foreign Stock	4		• Foreign Stock	10
• Bond (ex TIPS)	46		• Bond (ex TIPS)	29
• TIPS	21		• TIPS	13
• Commodities	6		• Commodities	6
• Cash	7		• Cash	4

In-Retirement Portfolios: 15-Year Time Horizon

Conservative	%		Aggressive	%
• U.S. Stock	18		• U.S. Stock	41
• Foreign Stock	6		• Foreign Stock	13
• Bond (ex TIPS)	48		• Bond (ex TIPS)	27
• TIPS	17		• TIPS	10
• Commodities	6		• Commodities	6
• Cash	5		• Cash	3

In-Retirement Portfolios: 20-Year Time Horizon

Conservative	%		Aggressive	%
• U.S. Stock	21		• U.S. Stock	45
• Foreign Stock	7		• Foreign Stock	16
• Bond (ex TIPS)	48		• Bond (ex TIPS)	24
• TIPS	14		• TIPS	7
• Commodities	6		• Commodities	6
• Cash	4		• Cash	2

Sample allocations for three different in-retirement time horizons. If your risk tolerance is moderate, you'll want your portfolio to fall between the extremes for a given time horizon.

Figure 30.1   Model Portfolio Allocations for Retirees

foreign stocks. Long gone are the days when retirees could get by with all-bond portfolios: Long life spans and paltry bond yields mean that even conservative retirees need the appreciation potential of stocks in their portfolios. But don't go overboard. If you have stocks in your portfolio, you'll need at least a 10-year time horizon for that money. For example, say you have a $1 million retirement portfolio and $350,000 (35 percent) of that pool is in stocks. The remaining $650,000 in bonds and cash should be enough to cover your living expenses over the next 10 years.

Step 3

Once you've found an appropriate asset allocation, take a look at your current stock/bond/cash mix to determine where you need to make changes in your existing mix—if at all. If you don't know your current asset allocation, use Morningstar's Instant X-Ray tool, available at www.morningstar.com/goto/30MinuteSolutions, to help you find it. Simply enter the tickers for each of your holdings, then click Show Instant X-Ray. Compare that asset allocation with the target you identified in the preceding step.

Step 4

Once you've determined the asset classes you'll be adding to and subtracting from, it's time to select individual securities for the job. Choosing individual holdings for an in-retirement portfolio isn't radically different from selecting securities for a pre-retirement portfolio. You'll want to make sure you have a good balance of investment styles, such as small and large stocks and bonds of varying credit qualities and maturities.

The portfolios in Figure 30.1 include some of Morningstar's favorite in-retirement mutual fund holdings, both stock and bond. Most of these funds have somewhat conservative personalities—for growth-stock exposure, for example, I prefer a mild, high-quality-oriented fund like Jensen Portfolio JENSX over a more aggressively positioned growth fund like Fidelity Growth Company FDGRX.

You'll also notice that all the portfolios include inflation-fighting investments. That's because as you add fixed-rate investments like bonds and bond funds to your portfolio, inflation will gobble up more and more of your purchasing power.

Step 5

As you craft your retirement portfolio, look for opportunities to streamline. It's easier to monitor a compact portfolio. By taking care to reduce your number of holdings early in your retirement years, you'll greatly reduce your oversight responsibilities.

If you have multiple IRAs, for example, consider consolidating them into a single account. And while many retired individuals buy individual stocks and bonds, mutual funds and exchange-traded funds allow for less ongoing oversight, which can be particularly valuable later in your retirement years. You may also consider anchoring your portfolio with broadly diversified broad-market index funds and ETFs; these investments give you a lot of diversification in a single shot.

Step 6

Once you've set a course for your in-retirement portfolio, revise your investment policy statement to reflect your current goals, asset-allocation policy, individual investment parameters, and monitoring criteria. (Chapter 12 discussed the ins and outs of investment policy statements.) Doing so will provide you with a template for managing your in-retirement portfolio on an ongoing basis and help ensure that you won't make changes to your portfolio that you'll later regret. Be sure that your investment policy statement specifies guidelines that your portfolio should have two to five years' worth of living expenses in highly liquid assets at all times.

Next Steps

▶ The portfolios provided in Figure 30.1 feature plain vanilla bond and stock mutual funds because they tend to be the most cost-effective building blocks for retiree portfolios. However, retirees often look to other securities—notably annuities—for their in-retirement portfolios. Single-premium immediate annuities can be a cost-effective way to make sure you receive a steady paycheck, but your payout will tend to ebb and flow based on prevailing interest rates. With current rates exceptionally low, it may pay to wait until rates head back up before committing to an annuity.

▶ If your retirement portfolio has taken a big hit over the past few years, don't try to make up lost ground by using an asset allocation that's too aggressive given your age and life stage. It's reasonable to modestly increase your stock weighting relative to the targets that you've identified, but do so judiciously. For example, you might hold 45 percent in stocks even though your target is 40 percent, but you shouldn't nudge your equity weighting as high as 60 percent.

Find the Right Sequence of In-Retirement Withdrawals

WHEN JACK AND CATHERINE E-MAILED ME IN 2009, they were seeking direction on how to invest during their impending retirement. Both were in the process of stepping back from demanding careers—Jack as an executive at a large pharmaceutical firm and Catherine as a hospital administrator. Although they had amassed more than enough money to retire—their combined portfolio totaled more than $2.5 million—their portfolio was, in Jack's words, "a mess."

Jack, who had been in charge of the couple's investments for most of their lives, used the "all-you-can-eat buffet" approach to portfolio management, meaning that their investment accounts consisted of a little bit of this and a little bit of that. He had sought the advice of advisors for portions of their portfolio and used the DIY method for other accounts. In all, this couple had more than 80 separate holdings, both individual stocks and bonds as well as traditional mutual funds and a few exchange-traded funds thrown in for good measure.

And because both partners had logged busy careers with multiple employers, the couple's portfolio was a crazy quilt of multiple brokerage accounts, IRAs (both traditional and Roth), and company retirement plans.

Their question wasn't whether they could retire—they clearly could. Instead, they were wondering *how* to retire. Before they said farewell to the working world, they had to position their portfolio for withdrawals during retirement, determining which accounts they would draw on first and which they would tap later in retirement (or perhaps not at all).

But, you may be wondering, why does it even matter? After all, money is money, and a $1,000 withdrawal to cover monthly expenses during retirement is still $1,000, right?

Not exactly. In fact, by sequencing your withdrawals properly, you can help make your overall retirement nest egg last longer.

Taxes are a key reason why. To the extent that a retiree has both taxable and tax-sheltered assets like IRAs and company retirement plans, it's best to hold on to the assets with the most generous tax treatment the longest, thereby "stretching out" the tax benefit.

There isn't a one-size-fits-all sequence of withdrawals; your age and your tax rate when you take withdrawals also play a role. But assuming that you have more than one pool of assets to draw on during retirement, the following sequence makes sense for many retirees:

1. If you're over age 70½, your withdrawals should come from those accounts that carry required minimum distributions, or RMDs, such as traditional IRAs and company retirement plans. (You'll pay penalties if you don't take these distributions on time.)
2. If you're not required to take RMDs or you've taken your RMDs and still need cash, turn to your taxable assets. Start by selling assets with the highest cost basis first and then move on to those assets where your cost basis is lower (and your tax hit is higher). Relative to tax-deferred or tax-free assets, these assets have the highest costs associated with them while you own them, so it makes sense to deplete those first.
3. Next, move on to any accounts funded with nondeductible contributions, such as traditional nondeductible IRAs.
4. After that, tap company retirement plan accounts.
5. Finally, tap Roth IRA assets.

The sequence in which you tap your accounts will, in turn, help you determine how to position each pool of money. The money that you'll draw upon first—to fund living expenses in the first years of retirement—should be invested in highly liquid securities like CDs, money markets, and short-term bonds. The reason is pretty commonsensical: Doing so helps ensure that you're taking money from your most stable pool of assets first, and therefore you won't have to withdraw from your higher-risk/higher-return accounts (for example, those that hold stocks or more-risky bonds) when your account is at a low ebb. That strategy also gives your stock assets, which have the potential for the highest long-term returns, more time to grow.

To find the right sequence of in-retirement withdrawals, you'll need:

▶ An estimate of your annual spending needs for the next three to five years
▶ Most recent statement for all retirement accounts

 Start the Clock

Step 1

Every retiree should have two to five years' worth of living expenses set aside in highly liquid (that is, checking, savings, money market, CD) investments at all times. (Step 1 in Chapter 30 discussed this topic in detail.)

Once you've arrived at the amount of cash that you need to have on hand, determine if your RMDs will cover your income needs for the next two to five years (if you're older than $70^1/_2$).

If you're not $70^1/_2$ and/or your RMDs won't cover your income needs, see if your taxable account will cover your income needs over the next two to five years.

If your taxable account doesn't cover two to five years' worth of living expenses, carve out any additional amount of living expenses from your IRA or company retirement plan assets using the sequence outlined above.

Step 2

Once you've set aside your cash position, put in place a plan to periodically refill your cash stake so that it always will cover two to five years' worth of living expenses.

Step 3

Next, determine a sequence of withdrawals for your longer-term assets, based on the guidelines provided above. The accounts you tap sooner should be in relatively more-liquid investments than those you tap later in retirement. (Chapter 30 discussed how to create an appropriate stock/bond mix for your in-retirement portfolio.) Your longest-term, riskiest assets should go in your Roth IRA or 401(k).

Next Steps

► The preceding has focused primarily on retirees who are older than age $59^1/_2$, the age at which you can begin tapping retirement accounts without penalty. However, if you're between 55 and $59^1/_2$ and you left your employer after you turned age 55, you can tap your 401(k) without penalty. (You will pay taxes, however, as with all 401(k) distributions.)

► While taxable assets usually go in the "sell early" bin, that's not true if you have highly appreciated assets and plan to leave money to your heirs. If, for example, you own stock that has appreciated significantly since you bought it (and you have no way of offsetting that gain with a loss elsewhere in your portfolio) you may be better off leaving that position intact and passing it to your heirs. The reason is that your heirs will receive what's called a "step up" in their cost basis, meaning that they'll be taxed only on any appreciation in the security after you pass away. If you have a lot of highly appreciated securities in your portfolio (lucky you!), an accountant can help you sort through your options.

PART TEN

Monitor Your Investments

LIKE EVERYONE, I've had both good and bad bosses in my life. The worst ones hovered, offering feedback and advice on the most straightforward of tasks. Others, meanwhile, were so hands-off that I was never quite sure where I stood.

The best bosses—and I'm lucky enough to have had a few of them—manage to find the right balance. They pay attention to what their employees are doing but don't swoop in and take over unless it's necessary. They allow their employees to learn from them but also give them room to develop their own styles. They're willing to let small mistakes go but take action if there's a problematic pattern.

You want to steer a similar middle course when managing your portfolio. Being hands-off is far better than being too hands-on, but you also want to pay enough attention to your portfolio that you can make corrections if you need to. Like a good boss, you want to judge an investment on the totality of its record, not on what it's done (or hasn't done) for you lately.

And just as a good manager will be disciplined about reviewing your performance and telling you where you stand, it's also important to be disciplined about checking up on your portfolio's performance, and—even more important—its fundamentals: whether your mutual funds have had manager or strategy changes, for example. Because it's easy to get emotional and make rash investment decisions when the market is gyrating wildly, you should plan to monitor and make changes at predetermined intervals based on preset criteria. That's what this section is designed to help you do.

In Chapter 32 I discuss how to conduct a checkup of your portfolio: what you should look for to ensure that your portfolio is in good shape as well as what to tune out. If you created an investment policy statement for your portfolio (Chapter 12), reviewing your portfolio should be fairly quick and straightforward. But even if you haven't, this chapter shows you how to conduct a quick and thorough checkup.

You should make changes to your portfolio even less frequently than you review it. Because your stock/bond mix is such a big determinant of how your portfolio will perform—both on the upside and the downside—big divergences from your target weightings should be the main trigger for making changes. The process of restoring your stock/bond/cash mix back to your targets—called rebalancing—is one of the very best things you can do to improve your portfolio's risk/reward profile. In Chapter 33, I coach you on the nitty-gritty of rebalancing.

32

Conduct a Portfolio Checkup

"I'M JUST NOT OPENING MY STATEMENT."

I wish I had a dime for every investor who said that to me during the depths of the bear market. And I'll confess, that was my strategy, too, for at least part of the downturn. Although I had a general idea how much my husband and I had lost, I knew that seeing the number in black and white was just going to make us feel bad.

Moreover, many people who weren't opening their statements were doing so for a savvy reason. They knew that if they saw how much they had lost, they might be inclined to make changes that they would later regret.

In good markets and bad, it's always important to strike a balance between being too hands-off and too hands-on. If you're checking in on your portfolio holdings every day—or worse yet, throughout the day—you may be tempted to trade more than you need to. In turn, you may run up high tax and transaction costs. You're also more likely to chase hot-performing stocks and funds in the hope that they'll continue to outperform. If the market has gone down a lot, you might be inclined to switch to overly conservative investments at what could turn out to be an inopportune time.

But while a policy of benign neglect invariably beats overzealous portfolio oversight, you can't tune out your portfolio altogether. Even if you've taken care to assemble a simple, streamlined portfolio, you still need to check in periodically to make sure that your stock/bond mix is still in line with your targets, that you're adequately diversified, and that nothing is seriously amiss with any one of your holdings.

I'm a big proponent of conducting a portfolio review on an infrequent basis—annually, semiannually, or quarterly at the most. The purpose of this portfolio checkup is to systematically troubleshoot problem spots and identify changes you may want to make as part of your rebalancing program. (You should plan to rebalance your portfolio—remove money from those investments that have performed well and plow it into your portfolio's underachievers—if you find your asset allocation has veered meaningfully from the ranges you set out in your investment policy statement [Chapter 12]. In Chapter 33 I discuss how to rebalance your portfolio, as well as why you might want to move money out of investments that are performing well and put it into your portfolio's underachievers.)

To conduct a portfolio checkup, you'll need:

► Most recent investment account statements
► Investment Policy Statement Worksheet (optional) (Worksheet 12.1, available at www.morningstar.com/goto/30MinuteSolutions)
► Morningstar's Instant X-Ray tool

Start the Clock
Step 1

Calculating your portfolio's stock/bond/cash mix should be the starting point for your portfolio checkup. If you have pools of money dedicated to different goals—for example, one pool geared toward retirement and another geared toward college savings—it's best to size up your asset allocation for each separate pool.

Morningstar's Instant X-Ray tool, available at www.morningstar.com/goto/30MinuteSolutions, provides a quick way to view your portfolio's asset allocation. Simply gather up all your holdings' tickers and the amount you have in each stock or fund, and then enter this data into the tool.

You may hit a snag if you own securities that don't have tickers and therefore won't fit into Instant X-Ray. For example, Morningstar's portfolio tools don't accommodate individual bond holdings, guaranteed investment contracts, stable-value funds (found in defined contribution plans like 401(k) plans), collective investment trusts, or separately managed accounts.

There aren't perfect mutual fund proxies for individual bond holdings. But if you know the maturity and credit quality of a bond that you own, you can use a bond index mutual fund or exchange-traded fund that occupies the same square of the Morningstar Style Box to approximate your portfolio's exposure.

Guaranteed investment contracts and stable-value funds are trickier because there's no close analog in the mutual fund or exchange-traded fund realm. These funds invest in short-term, usually high-quality bonds and then buy an insurance "wrapper" to guarantee the principal and accumulated interest even if the bonds decline in value. Thus, they usually yield a few percentage points more than money market funds with only slightly more volatility. As with individual bond holdings, there are no perfect proxies for stable-value funds, though a short-term bond index fund such as Vanguard Short-Term Bond Index VBISX is as close as you're apt to come.

Company retirement plans are increasingly offering non–mutual fund investments such as separately managed accounts and collective investment trusts in their menu of choices. Such funds aren't necessarily worse than mutual funds, and in fact may be quite strong and inexpensive, but they don't have to provide the same level of disclosure that mutual funds do. If you're able to find out who's running the fund, you may be able to do a little bit of sleuthing to identify a mutual fund that's a near-clone of the investment in your plan—for example, if you find out that a firm like Dodge & Cox is running a fund called Core Stock for your company, it's a good bet that the fund is nearly identical to Dodge & Cox Stock.

Use any other information you have—such as manager names, return histories, or top 10 holdings—to corroborate that the mutual fund is a good proxy for the investment in your plan.

Step 2

Once you've calculated your current stock/bond/cash mix, compare your current asset allocation with your target allocations. (What if you don't know what your asset allocation should be? Chapter 11 provides guidance on this topic.)

I recommend rebalancing only if your allocation to an asset class has veered at least 5 percentage points out of your target range. For example, if you set a range for your equity allocation of between 40 percent and 50 percent, you'd rebalance if your equity stake dropped below 35 percent. Chapter 33 provides step-by-step guidance on rebalancing.

Step 3

In addition to checking up on your stock/bond/cash mix, also take note of how much you have in cash, in dollars and cents. There are no one-size-fits-all requirements, but most retirees and those who are within a few years of retirement should aim to hold two to five years' worth of living expenses in highly liquid investments like CDs, money market accounts, and checking and savings accounts. If you build such a cash cushion and periodically replenish it, you won't have to disrupt your longer-term investments to raise cash for living expenses. Bear in mind that if you have other sources of income—such as Social Security or a pension—your cash cushion need cover only those living expenses that aren't covered by your other income.

Those who have 10 or more years until retirement should have at least six months'—and preferably one year's—worth of living expenses in cash or cashlike investments; this cash will serve as your emergency fund. (Chapter 10 provides guidance on building your emergency fund.)

To check up on your portfolio's cash position, look at the dollar amount you have invested explicitly in these types of assets rather than the cash position generated by Instant X-Ray. X-Ray's cash statistic might be useful from the standpoint of asset-allocation monitoring, but it encompasses straight cash holdings like CDs as well as any residual cash in stock and bond mutual funds that you own. Thus, it may not provide a true depiction of the liquid investments you could tap in a pinch.

Step 4

If you've used Instant X-Ray to check up on your portfolio's asset allocation, you'll also be able to see how your stock and bond holdings are positioned by investment style and sector. Within Instant X-Ray, you can see stock and bond Morningstar Style Boxes (two nine-square grids in the upper right corner of the X-Ray page) that depict the investment styles of your holdings.

While you shouldn't expect to see an even distribution of holdings in each of the nine squares—and most diversified equity indexes will hold the bulk of their assets in large companies, represented by the top row of the style box—you do want to take note if the majority of your holdings are huddled in one or two regions of the style box. You also want to pay attention to where the big holes are; if you're planning to add new holdings, you can concentrate your efforts there. If you've specified sub-asset-class percentages in your investment policy statement—for example, if your investment policy statement calls for 80 percent of your equity exposure to be in large caps, 15 percent in mid-caps, and the remainder in small caps—the style box will show you whether your portfolio is currently in the right ballpark.

Instant X-Ray also shows you how your stock holdings are dispersed across various market sectors, as well as how that positioning compares with the S&P 500 Index's sector weightings. As with style-box positioning, you shouldn't get too worked up about some divergences, but you do want to take note of very big bets—sectors where your weighting is more than twice that of the index, for example.

To help you compare your portfolio to that of the broad market, Figure 32.1 shows the current style-box breakdown for the Dow Jones Wilshire 5000 Index, a proxy for the broad market. Figure 32.2 shows its sector breakdown.

Step 5

Next, examine performance. It's a big mistake to focus too much attention on short-term performance, but your portfolio review should include a quick assessment of which of your holdings are providing the biggest boost to or drag on your portfolio's overall return. It's fine to glance at year-to-date performance, but focus most of your attention on the longer-term numbers—each holding's return over the past three and five years relative to that of other offerings within that same category. Also take note of absolute

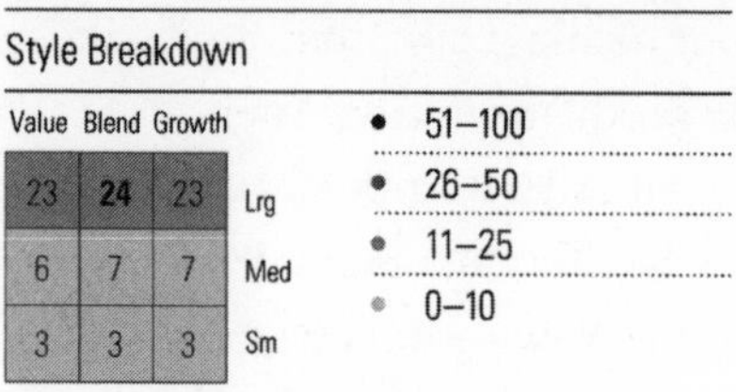

Style Breakdown

Value	Blend	Growth	
23	**24**	23	Lrg
6	7	7	Med
3	3	3	Sm

- 51–100
- 26–50
- 11–25
- 0–10

As part of your portfolio checkup, compare your portfolio's style-box positioning with that of the Dow Jones Wilshire 5000 Index, shown above. Don't worry if your portfolio isn't in sync with the index, but know that concentrating heavily in one style will subject your portfolio to greater swings than a more diversified portfolio would have.

Figure 32.1   Style Box Breakdown for Dow Jones Wilshire 5000 Index

☞ **Information Supersector**	**23.38 (%)**
🔲 Software	4.66
🖥 Hardware	9.68
📺 Media	2.13
📱 Telecom	6.91

☞ **Service Supersector**	**39.65 (%)**
✚ Healthcare	13.36
🗄 Consumer Srvcs	9.27
📋 Business Srvcs	4.69
💲 Financial Srvcs	12.33

🏭 **Manufacturing Supersector**	**36.96 (%)**
🛒 Consumer Goods	10.9
⚙ Industrial Mtls	10.5
🛢 Energy	11.95
💡 Utilities	4.35

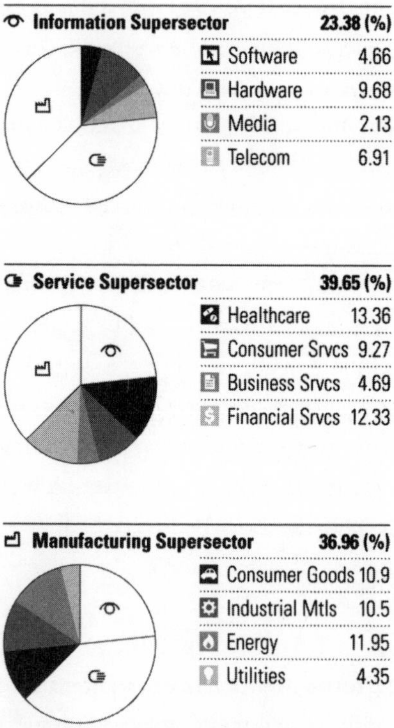

Here's how the Dow Jones Wilshire 5000 Index, a broad-market index that mirrors the total U.S. stock market, is positioned across various market sectors. Comparing your portfolio's sector positioning with that of the index can tell you if your portfolio is skewing heavily toward one or two sectors.

Figure 32.2   Sector Breakdown for Dow Jones Wilshire 5000 Index

returns. Which of your holdings have contributed the most to—or detracted the most from—your portfolio's bottom line?

Investments that have underperformed their peer groups or have generated weak absolute returns shouldn't automatically go on your sell list, however. In fact, that can be a recipe for disastrous investment returns, as funds that have been in a performance slump may in fact be poised to deliver strong returns in the future. But if you have an investment that both underperformed during the bear market and didn't snap back during the market recovery in 2009, you'll want to be sure to check up on whether there have been any substantive changes that have undermined that holding's attractiveness.

Step 6

Once you've checked out your aggregate portfolio's positioning and performance, it's time to conduct a quick checkup on each of your individual holdings. If you've prepared an investment policy statement in which you've spelled out what you're looking for from each of your investments, you can use that as a checklist as you evaluate each stock or fund.

If you haven't prepared an investment policy statement, here are some of the key fundamental questions to ask:

► Have there been any changes to the fund management team?
► Has investment style changed? (Don't be alarmed if your fund has shifted style boxes, as that's a frequent outcome if a manager is using a truly active approach. More concerning are signs of true strategy shift—for example, if a once fully invested mutual fund now holds a sizable cash position.)
► Has the expense ratio gone up?
► Has the fund company changed hands?

Next Steps

► After you've reviewed your portfolio's current status, it's time to plan your next move. It's not likely that you'll uncover a portfolio problem that you need to address right away, but you should make sure to schedule a time to rebalance your portfolio. Conventional financial planning wisdom holds that the best time to rebalance is at year-end, with an eye toward harvesting any losses to offset capital gains elsewhere in your portfolio. But if you'll have more time to focus at some other time of the year—say, earlier in the fourth quarter—by all means do so.

▶ If you have some extra time, set up a benchmark portfolio to determine whether your individual stock and fund selections have improved on or detracted from your portfolio's return with security selection. Would you have been better off with a passively managed portfolio of index funds or exchange-traded funds? To answer that question, start by finding your current asset allocation. Then use Morningstar's Instant X-Ray tool to enter an index fund portfolio that mirrors your own portfolio's asset allocation: Use Vanguard Total Stock Market Index VTSMX for the U.S. stock component, Vanguard Total Bond Market Index VBMFX for the bond portion, Vanguard Total International Stock Index VGTSX for the foreign-stock portion, and CASH$ for your cash holdings. Creating this kind of custom, blended benchmark will enable you to see how your portfolio is performing on an ongoing basis.

▶ The previous exercise discusses how to conduct a checkup of a portfolio that's composed primarily or exclusively of mutual funds or exchange-traded funds. If you own individual stocks, you already know that you'll need to exercise more hands-on oversight than is the case with mutual funds.

33

Rebalance Your Portfolio

WHEN JASMINE AND RONALDO WROTE TO ME requesting a Portfolio Makeover in mid-2009, they were still reeling from the shock of the bear market. Having watched the value of their retirement portfolio drop by more than a third, the couple, both in their early forties, were having a crisis of confidence. They had only just begun investing in earnest for retirement, and they had used multiple sources of information to help them select an asset mix that was appropriate for their time horizon. Following the downturn, their stock holdings were just a shadow of their former selves, but the couple hadn't taken steps to add to them—or made any changes at all—in the wake of the decline. Jasmine put it succinctly when she said: "We're worried about throwing good money after bad."

This couple's hesitation is common. If an investment type has inflicted big losses on your portfolio, it's natural to question the wisdom of holding it at all, let alone adding to it. But that's what rebalancing—the process of putting your portfolio's allocations back in line with your targets—requires you to do. Given how counterintuitive and psychologically difficult rebalancing is, it's really no wonder so many investors forgo it altogether.

That's a shame, because employing a rebalancing program is one of the best ways to improve your portfolio's return and lower its risk level.

Let's say that you put $10,000 in Dodge & Cox Income DODIX (a bond fund) and $10,000 in Dodge & Cox Stock DODGX in late 1999. By the end of 2007, your initial $20,000 investment would have more than doubled. Credit a lot of that success to the stock fund. It racked up a 12 percent average return per year, while Dodge & Cox Income gained a more sedate 6 percent per year. As a result of that outperformance, Dodge & Cox Stock soared to 60 percent of your portfolio in early 2008.

By late 2008, however, your portfolio would be down to about $30,000, a loss of nearly 25 percent in a one-year period. The culprit? Dodge & Cox Stock's 43 percent loss in 2008's bear market. The Income fund, on the other hand, stayed basically flat during 2008.

If, however, you had rebalanced your portfolio at the beginning of 2008, re-establishing equal positions in the funds, you wouldn't have lost half as much during that year. Rebalancing would have protected a sizable chunk of the gains you made with Dodge & Cox Stock.

Of course, that's a best-case scenario for rebalancing: Depending on when you do it, rebalancing may not look all that smart. For example, during the bull market of the 1990s, rebalancing out of stocks mainly hindered a portfolio's return, rather than helped, though it did reduce its risk level.

Even investors who are sold on the merits of rebalancing struggle with how often to do it. Some studies have pointed to the benefits of frequent rebalancing. For example, David Swensen, the manager of Yale's endowment, has said he rebalances the Yale portfolio daily, adding to the previous day's laggards and scaling back the winners. But while such tactics might work for big financial institutions and pension plans, which have minuscule transaction costs and don't pay taxes when they buy and sell, they don't translate well to the individual investor world. Individual investors may have to pay taxes and transaction costs to rebalance, and such a rigorous rebalancing program would take up a ridiculous amount of time, too.

Rather than committing to rebalancing at specific intervals or a certain time of the year, you're best off rebalancing when your stakes in stocks, bonds, or cash are 5 or 10 percentage points out of whack with your target ranges. At the same time you rebalance to bring your stock/bond/cash mix back in line with your targets, you can also address any dramatic investment-style shifts that have occurred in your portfolio—for example, if growth stocks or funds are crowding out the value-oriented stocks in your portfolio. That way you're not trading—and potentially racking up additional tax costs or brokerage commissions—just to alter your asset mix by a few percentage points.

To rebalance your portfolio you'll need:

▶ Most recent account statements
▶ Investment Policy Statement Worksheet (optional) (Worksheet 12.1, available at www.morningstar.com/goto/30MinuteSolutions)
▶ Morningstar's Instant X-Ray tool (available at www.morningstar.com/goto/30MinuteSolutions)

Start the Clock
Step 1

The starting point for the rebalancing process is to draw a bead on your current asset allocation.

If you've just completed a portfolio checkup (Chapter 32), you should have a clear—and current—read on your asset allocation, and you may have also identified any other imbalances you'd like to correct. If so, you can skip ahead to Step 4.

If you haven't looked at your portfolio's asset allocation recently, Morningstar's Instant X-Ray tool, available at www.morningstar.com/goto/30MinuteSolutions, provides a quick way to view your portfolio's asset allocation. Simply gather up all your holdings' tickers and the amount you have in each stock or fund, and then enter this data into the tool.

Step 2

Next, compare your current asset allocation with your targets. Chapter 11 coached you on how to arrive at an appropriate asset allocation. If you completed an investment policy statement (Chapter 12), you spelled out your asset-allocation parameters in terms of ranges.

Compare those ranges with the current allocation you noted in Step 1.

If you are outside your target range for any asset class by 5 or 10 percentage points, it's time to rebalance. Whether you tolerate divergences of

5 or 10 percentage points depends on your personality and your time horizon. If you're a laissez faire investor and you have a long time horizon for your money, you can choose to take action only if your asset allocations swing 10 percentage points above or below your targets. But if you like to be more hands-on or you're already retired, it's fine to rebalance when your allocation to any one asset class is 5 percentage points above your range.

Step 3

Bringing your portfolio's asset allocation in line with your targets is the main task when you rebalance. But it also pays to simultaneously check your portfolio's investment-style positioning, as depicted by the Morningstar Style Box in the Instant X-Ray tool. The style box shows you how your portfolio is dispersed across the U.S. stock universe. Having a decent distribution of investment styles in your portfolio will give your portfolio a shot at decent performance in varied market conditions. (There are no guarantees, though: In 2008, stocks of all types went down, and style-box diversification didn't get you very far. Only bonds—and high-quality bonds at that—managed a positive return.)

Stocks that land on the left-hand side of the style box are considered value; such stocks are often well-established, stable companies, but they may have lower growth prospects and are not accorded as high a price in the market as are stocks on the right-hand side of the style box. The horizontal bands of the style box show you how your portfolio is distributed among small-, mid-, and large-cap stocks.

When you look at your portfolio's style box in isolation, it can be hard to know whether any changes are in order. A good start is to compare your style box with the style box in Figure 32.1, which depicts how all U.S. stocks are distributed across the investment-style landscape. Your portfolio doesn't have to mimic the index exactly—if it does, you should ask yourself why you're not just holding a broad stock market index fund and calling it a day. But do take note of major tilts toward value or growth, small or large—for example, if 75 percent of your stock portfolio is in the value column of the style box but just 30 percent of the U.S. market index is. Figure 32.2 in the previous chapter shows the distribution of U.S. stocks across market sectors.

Step 4

If you've determined that you need to make changes to your portfolio—in terms of your asset allocation, investment-style mix, or both—it's time to scout around for likely candidates.

It's logical to look to your portfolio's biggest winners and losers—in absolute terms—as a starting point. If a few of your holdings have shot out the lights while a couple of others have stunk up the joint, you can subtract from the former and send that money to the latter.

Bear in mind, however, that selling appreciated securities could trigger a tax bill. So you should generally concentrate your rebalancing activities in your tax-sheltered accounts, where you can make changes—including selling some of your winners—without having to pay capital gains tax.

When it comes to deciding which securities to add, as well as how much to add to each, you'll probably find that the process of overhauling your portfolio is a matter of trial and error. Here again, I'd recommend Morningstar's Instant X-Ray tool to help you evaluate the impact of various holdings on your asset-allocation mix before you decide to buy. Also, pay attention to the impact that various holdings have on your style-box positioning. Your stock portfolio doesn't need to be an exact clone of the broad market, but you should at least be aware of whether your portfolio is skewing heavily to one style or sector.

In some cases, the alterations you need to make are obvious—if you're heavy on bonds, for example, adding to stocks should resolve the problem. Getting to the bottom of other bets might take a little more research. For example, if your portfolio has more cash than you want it to, that could be because one of your stock fund managers is holding a lot of cash. You could decide to live with it, and reduce your designated cash holdings accordingly, or else pare back your holdings in the cash-heavy stock fund.

If in Step 3 you took note of any investment-style biases—such as having a portfolio that's heavily tilted toward value stocks—address them at the same time you alter your stock/bond/cash mix. So, for example, if you've found that your portfolio is lighter on stocks than you'd like it to be, this step can help you figure out exactly what type of equity holdings you should begin adding.

If changes to your tax-sheltered portfolio are enough to bring your asset allocation and investment-style positioning back to where you want them to be, your work is done. But if you have a lot more assets in taxable accounts than you do in tax-sheltered, making changes to your tax-sheltered accounts may not be enough to move the needle. If that's the case, move on to the next step.

Step 5

If you need to rebalance in your taxable accounts, you'll have to exercise more care than is the case with rebalancing in tax-sheltered accounts. That's because selling your winners may result in a tax bill.

In an ideal world, you'd correct imbalances in your taxable accounts by putting new money to work: adding money to your losers rather than selling your winners. Alternatively, you could simply direct a large share of future contributions to your laggards and correct the imbalance over a period of months.

However, it's worth noting that the tax consequences of rebalancing right now may be lower than they've been in some time. You can obviously rack up a big tax bill when you sell stock holdings following a strong and prolonged bull market. But many investors are currently holding stocks at a lower price than what they paid, meaning the tax costs associated with selling could be limited. Bonds usually generate smaller capital gains than stocks, so if you determine you need to sell bond holdings, the tax implications aren't likely to be as great.

Next Step

▶ Rebalancing may also present some opportunities for tax-loss selling. To find out what tax-loss selling is and how you do it, see Chapter 28.

PART ELEVEN

Cover Your Bases on Estate Planning

THERE ARE THOSE OCCASIONAL MOMENTS IN LIFE when you think to yourself, "I guess I'm not a kid anymore." Like being called ma'am (or sir) for the first time. Concurring with your spouse that maybe a minivan is the best choice for your new vehicle. Saying, "Turn that noise down!" (or at least thinking it).

Creating an estate plan is yet another one of those times when you know that you're a grown-up. By taking steps to ensure that your wishes are carried out when your property is disposed of after you've died or become disabled, you're essentially admitting you won't be 25 forever, even if you still feel like you are.

Because pondering your own mortality is psychologically difficult, many people put off creating an estate plan. Others fail to do it because they assume that "estates" are only for the rich; when they hear "estate plan," they think of elaborate tax dodges designed for multimillionaires. Still others defer estate planning because they don't have children, or because they assume that the existing laws will take care of them just fine.

It's true that having a child or a lot of assets should prompt you to run, not walk, to your estate planning attorney's office. Ditto if you're divorced and have remarried. But creating an estate plan isn't just for the super-rich, those with heirs, or those with complicated family situations. And you most certainly don't want to wait until you're very old or in ill health to create one.

An estate plan will ensure that the most important decisions of your life—those involving the care of your children, your health care, and your financial assets—are carried out in accordance with your wishes when you die or become disabled. Without an estate plan in place, your estate would have to go through the long and costly probate process, and crucial decisions could be left up in the air.

While this book takes a DIY approach to most financial planning tasks, I have a one-word response to those inclined to go it alone for matters of estate planning: Don't. Estate planning is complicated and highly dependent on an individual's own situation. You're much better off seeking out a competent estate planning attorney rather than trying to tackle it on your own.

You'll still be very involved in the process, however. In Chapter 34 I coach you on the steps you need to take before, during, and after you meet with your attorney: gathering information and providing input as your attorney draws up crucial documents. This chapter also covers what you'll need in order to keep your estate planning documents up-to-date.

Even if you don't have a formal estate plan, chances are you've already put a portion of your plan in action by specifying beneficiaries for your various retirement accounts and life insurance policies. Designating beneficiaries might seem straightforward, but too often, individuals don't give them due attention. You have to make sure that your beneficiary designations are in sync with your estate plan—if you have one—and you also need to select your beneficiaries and word your designations so that there aren't unintended consequences. (Did you know, for example, that naming a minor child as a beneficiary would set off a tidal wave of legal expenses if you were to die before the child reached the age of majority?) Chapter 35 shows you how to make and update your beneficiary designations.

The final chapter of this book—Create a Personal Legacy—isn't financial at all—in fact, it's explicitly nonfinancial. But as you create a plan to dispose of your financial assets once you're gone, it's also a logical time to reflect on the intangibles that you'd like to leave with your loved ones: what you believe in, your important life experiences, and the people who have been most important to you. Creating such a legacy—often called an ethical will—is a completely open-ended project. Yours can be as long or short as you like it. It can be audio, video, or written, and you're in complete control over what you do with it. Chapter 36 helps you get started.

34

Get Started on Your Estate Plan

WHEN GINNIE AND ALAN WROTE TO ME in early 2009, they were feeling nervous about their portfolio's ability to last through what they hoped would be a long and fruitful retirement. But this couple wasn't thinking only about themselves. As parents of a daughter with special needs, they were seeking guidance on what to do to ensure that their child would be able to remain independent and have enough money to cover her needs. Their twenty-something daughter was employed and living on her own nearby, but she relied on them for ongoing financial support.

I gave them my ideas on how to improve their portfolio, and I also suggested that they consult an attorney about setting up a special-needs trust. But I stopped short of providing them with specific guidance on leaving a legacy for their daughter—even though I have a special-needs loved one in my life and feel knowledgeable about the topic.

While I strongly believe that you can tackle many aspects of financial planning on your own, without the assistance of a professional, estate planning—the process of distributing one's assets after death—isn't one of them. True, it's not hard to find do-it-yourself wills and other estate planning materials on the Internet. But the topic is extremely complicated and the right solution is specific to each individual. The tax laws related to estate planning have also undergone swift changes over the past several years. If you're creating or updating an estate plan, it's essential that you seek the advice of an attorney who's well-versed in the key issues. Not only can a professional ensure that your assets are distributed and that your health care proceeds in accordance with your wishes, but he or she can also do so with an eye toward reducing the tax burden on those assets.

Of course, any time you hear the word "attorney," it's natural to worry about the costs you'll rack up. You might be tempted to postpone creating an estate plan, assuming that you need to have a lot of assets to make the process worthwhile. Alternatively, many individuals wait until they have children to create an estate plan. But everyone—regardless of life stage or the size of their portfolio—should think about hiring an attorney to draft the basic estate planning documents: a will, a living will, and powers of attorney.

Before you hire an estate planning attorney to draft or update your estate plan, it's important to understand your role in the estate planning process. Your estate plan will be most effective if you spend some time at the outset finding the right attorney for your needs and thinking through what you're trying to achieve as well as whom you trust to see your wishes through.

To get started on your estate plan, you'll need:

▶ Most recent investment statements
▶ Most recent statements for any outstanding debts
▶ Net Worth Worksheet (Worksheet 1.1, optional; available at www. morningstar.com/goto/30MinuteSolutions)

 Start the Clock
Step 1

Begin the process of creating an estate plan by scouting around for a qualified attorney. Because your estate plan will likely need to be updated as the years go by and your personal circumstances change, it makes sense to find an attorney who practices in the community where you live. That way, you can meet with him or her on an ongoing basis if need be.

Start by asking friends and colleagues for referrals. If you have a specific situation that is likely to affect your estate plan—for example, if you're a small-business owner or if you have a special-needs child—it's ideal to seek referrals from other individuals who are in a similar situation. The web site for the American College of Trust and Estate Counsel, a nonprofit organization, allows you to search for highly qualified estate planning attorneys in your area: www.actec.org/public/roster/FindFellow.asp.

Before you select an attorney, it's perfectly reasonable to conduct a basic informational interview. (If the attorney is unwilling to answer these questions without charging you, that should be your cue to move on.)

Ask the following:

- How long have you been practicing law?
- How long have you been practicing this type of law?
- How many estates have you settled?
- What is the typical asset level for your clients?
- Do you have experience with situations like mine? (Blended/divorced family, business owner, special-needs child, child with chemical dependency, etc.)
- How do you charge for your services? What is an estimate of the charges for my estate plan?
- Do you have experience with tax planning? (This is particularly important for large estates.)

As you speak with a prospective estate planning attorney, also weigh the intangibles. Do you like this person, and would you be comfortable supplying him or her with personal information about your finances and family situation?

Step 2

Before you meet with your attorney, spend some time enumerating your assets and their value: your investment accounts as well as life insurance, personal assets such as your home, and your share of any businesses that you own. Also gather current information about any debts outstanding. (If you completed the Net Worth Worksheet [Worksheet 1.1], you'll have already amalgamated this information.) Your estate planning attorney is likely to provide you with a worksheet to document your assets and liabilities, but it's helpful to collect this information in advance.

Step 3
Another important aspect of estate planning is identifying the individuals you trust to ensure that your wishes are carried out once you're gone. You'll need individuals to fill the following key roles. (Note that the same individual can fulfill more than one role.)

▶ **Executor:** A person who gathers all your assets and makes sure that they are distributed as spelled out in your will. This person must be extremely detail-oriented and comfortable with numbers and should also be able to find the time to work on your estate. Many people call on family members to serve as executors, but it's also possible—and in some cases desirable—to hire a professional (such as a bank trust officer) to serve as your executor.

▶ **Durable (or financial) power of attorney:** A person you entrust with making financial decisions on your behalf if you should become disabled and unable to manage your own financial affairs. It's important that this person understand your general wishes, in this case about your financial affairs. Your durable power of attorney should also be detail-oriented and adept with financial matters.

▶ **Power of attorney for health care:** A person you entrust with making health care decisions on your behalf if you are disabled and unable to make them on your own. Ideally, this is a person who lives in close geographic proximity to you and who also understands your general wishes about your own health care.

▶ **Guardian:** A person who would look after your children if you and your spouse were to die when your children are minors. That's unlikely to happen, of course, but it's still important to give the decision due consideration. You want your children's guardian to share your and your spouse's values and views on parenting, and it's also important that the guardian you choose be willing to raise your kids if called on to do so. Financial wherewithal and acumen should also be considerations.

It's possible to designate two guardians—one to look after your children and another to look after your children's financial assets—although that's usually not desirable because the two guardians may disagree on various matters.

Step 4

When you meet with your estate planning attorney, he or she will make recommendations about your estate plan and that, in turn, will determine which documents you need. At a minimum, however, you should ask your attorney to draft the following:

- **Last will and testament:** A legal document that tells everyone—including your heirs—how you would like your assets distributed after you're gone.
- **Living will:** A document that tells your loved ones and your health care providers how you would like to be cared for if you should become terminally ill. It usually includes details about your views toward life-support equipment. (It is called a "medical directive" in some states.)
- **Medical power of attorney:** A document that gives an individual the power to make health care decisions on your behalf if you are unable to do so.
- **Durable (or financial) power of attorney:** A document that gives an individual the power to make financial decisions and execute financial transactions on your behalf if you are unable to do so.

Step 5

Once your estate planning documents are drafted, destroy any older versions of them. You must also keep the documents in a safe place, either in a home safe, in the top drawer of a secure file cabinet in your home, or in your safe-deposit box. The downside of storing these documents in a safe-deposit box is that third parties may have difficulty accessing them in the event of your death or incapacity.

Notify your executor of the whereabouts of your estate planning documents, and provide copies of the relevant documents to your executor, powers of attorney, and the guardian for your children. When you hand off these documents to your various agents, it's also a good time to discuss your wishes with them.

Step 6

Last but not least, plan to keep your estate plan current. One of the biggest estate planning pitfalls is drafting an estate plan but not bothering to keep it up to date. Plan to notify your estate planning attorney, and possibly revise your documents, if you experience any of the following:

- ▶ Change in marital or family status (for example, marriage, divorce, birth or adoption of child)
- ▶ Major change in assets—either sale or purchase
- ▶ Major change in financial status
- ▶ Death or ill health of one of your beneficiaries
- ▶ Death or ill health of executor, power of attorneys, guardian

Next Step

- ▶ With many assets—particularly company retirement plan and IRA assets—you're able to designate a beneficiary, and it's important that these designations are in sync with what's in your will. Chapter 35 covers the ins and outs of beneficiary designations.

35

Handle Beneficiary Designations

WHEN I SAT DOWN with my own estate planning attorney to do an interview for my newsletter, *Morningstar PracticalFinance,* I kicked off our discussion by asking her what she thought the most common estate planning pitfall was.

Without skipping a beat, she said, "Misunderstanding beneficiary designations."

The decision about how to designate beneficiaries for your company retirement plan, life insurance policies, and other assets might seem like a no-brainer. But naming beneficiaries is a more nuanced decision-making process than you might think, and it's one that may have significant repercussions for your loved ones. Your beneficiary designations may also change as your life does—for example, if you get married or have children.

You can typically name beneficiaries for a broad range of assets, including retirement plans, annuities, and life insurance policies. And you can name a broad range of beneficiaries, including individuals, charities, and trusts. (Children under the age of majority—age 18 or 21, depending on the state in which you live—cannot be named as beneficiaries of life insurance policies, retirement plans, or annuities, however.)

When you name a beneficiary, those assets can pass directly to whomever you designate; they won't have to go through probate, which can be a lengthy and costly process. In addition, bear in mind that your beneficiary designations will override bequests you've made in your will. For example, even though your will might state that you want your spouse to inherit all your assets, if you named your brother as the beneficiary of your company retirement plan and didn't bother to change it after you got married, he'll get that money.

For all these reasons, it's crucial that you give serious thought to whom you name on your beneficiary designation forms and keep these forms up to date as your life changes.

To handle beneficiary designations, you'll need:

► Estate planning documents, including your will
► Beneficiary designation forms for retirement plans, life insurance, or annuities

 Start the Clock

Step 1

The first step is to check up on your current beneficiary designations to make sure they reflect any life changes. Does your 401(k) beneficiary designation form name your sibling or parent as the beneficiary, even though you've gotten married since you filled out the form and would like your spouse to inherit your assets? Have you and your spouse created trusts but not yet updated your company retirement plan forms to reflect the specifics of those trusts?

The following types of beneficiary designations could be problematic and may need to be revised:

► Doesn't reflect your current life situation/wishes
► Doesn't reflect the fact that you have placed assets in trust
► Designates a minor child as beneficiary
► Designates a special-needs individual as beneficiary
► Designates a very wealthy person as beneficiary
► Designates a very elderly person as beneficiary
► Has multiple alternate beneficiaries

Step 2

If you have drafted estate planning documents, your next step is to call your attorney for coaching on how best to word your beneficiary designation forms so that they're simpatico with what you laid out in your estate plan. Be sure to alert your attorney if you've red-flagged any specific issues in the preceding step.

Step 3

If you don't have estate planning documents or an estate planning attorney, give some consideration to whom you would like to inherit your retirement plan, life insurance, or annuity assets. It may be as simple as naming your spouse or another relative on the beneficiary designation form; you can also name a charity as a beneficiary if you like.

Be aware, though, that minor children cannot own assets outright, so it's a mistake to name them as beneficiaries. Instead, the best way to pass assets to minor children is to set up trusts for each of your children to hold assets for their benefit. You may also want to set up trusts for children who aren't minors but still may not be capable of handling large sums of money; the trust documents can specify the age at which the child would be entitled to those assets. (After you've set up the trusts, check back with an estate planning attorney to confirm the wording of any beneficiary designations that relate to these trusts.) Alternatively, you could leave all the assets to your spouse with the understanding that he or she will take care of the children's financial needs.

Meanwhile, if you do name adult children as beneficiaries, it's best to keep the wording of your designation specific enough to clarify your wishes but general enough to accommodate changing circumstances. For example, rather than naming specific children, you could say "My then-living children per stirpes." That language means that upon your death, your assets would pass to any children alive at the time. And should one of your children predecease you, the "per stirpes" part of that statement means that child's share of your assets would pass to that child's children.

As you name your beneficiaries, you should also be aware of designations that could be problematic. Think twice about naming a special-needs individual as a beneficiary, because transferring assets directly to the disabled individual could affect his or her eligibility for government-provided benefits. In addition, if the person is mentally disabled, he or she may not be able to manage the assets. If you're in a position to transfer a large amount of assets to a loved one with special needs, first consult with an attorney who specializes in estate planning. That person may recommend that you set up a special-needs trust. If the special-needs individual already has a special-needs trust, you could name the trust as the beneficiary.

If your beneficiary already has a large amount of assets, you could end up creating an estate planning headache for him or her, or compounding an existing one. That's because any inherited assets will be included in that person's estate, and if the taxable estate is above a certain threshold at the time of his or her death, his or her heirs will owe estate tax. (These issues don't pertain to husbands and wives, who won't owe estate tax on assets inherited from a spouse.)

And while there's nothing inherently wrong with leaving assets to elderly individuals, IRA assets, in particular, may be best left to a younger person who may be able to stretch out the IRA's tax-saving benefits over his or her lifetime.

Finally, resist the urge to be vague in the hopes that the individual to whom you leave the assets will know your wishes and distribute them accordingly. That person may not know your wishes or could decide to simply keep the assets; legally, he or she would have that right. You may also complicate his or her estate planning efforts, as those inherited assets would count as part of that person's estate even if they were ultimately distributed to others.

Next Steps

► Once you've arrived at your beneficiary designations, plan to discuss them with your loved ones—ideally before you've filed the paperwork. This is particularly important for your largest assets. That will give your loved one a chance to alert you to any circumstances that might argue against naming him or her as a beneficiary.

► Also, plan to review your beneficiary designations on a regular schedule, ideally as part of an annual review of your finances. Major life events, such as a marriage, a divorce, the birth of a child, or the death of a loved one, may require that you make changes to your designations. By the same token, you'll also want to review your beneficiary designations if you or your employer have recently switched retirement plan or insurance providers, as the beneficiaries you specified with your previous provider may not automatically carry over to the new one.

36

Create a Personal Legacy

LIKE MANY CHILDREN, I can thank my parents for giving me a good financial start in life. My sisters and I always took it for granted that our parents would cover the cost of college, and careful financial management was the rule in our household. My father, a lifelong stock market junkie, taught me about investing and even told me about a fast-growing little company called Morningstar back in the early 1990s, before it was my employer.

Thankfully, my parents are still alive and well. But when they're gone, I know that their legacy for me will be much greater than a financial one. They raised six children, including one with special needs, with grace and joy, and from them I learned that family can help you sail through the stormiest seas. I've already rhapsodized about my mother's ability to make the best of any situation, and I can thank my Dad, a former business owner, for showing me the value of conducting business with the highest level of honesty and integrity.

I could go on and on, but the larger point isn't about my parents. Rather, it's that each of us, whatever our life stage and whether we have children or not, can leave a legacy that extends far beyond our financial wherewithal. While I've devoted this book almost entirely to helping you create a financial plan, we all know that all the money in the world doesn't amount to a hill of beans if you didn't help those you love, and learn a few things yourself, along the way. That's why I wanted to devote the final chapter of this book to leaving a personal legacy—a nonfinancial one. And one of the best ways to do that is to take a few moments to communicate your belief system and your important life lessons to your loved ones.

Of course, we convey our values in the way we live our lives. But a personal legacy—often called an ethical will—can also help you communicate your belief system to your loved ones. In essence, this document says, "This is what's important to me. This is what I stand for."

In contrast to a regular will, which is a legally binding document that communicates how you would like your physical possessions to be distributed, a personal legacy isn't a legal document. It's there only for your loved ones—or even you alone—to see.

In fact, the beauty of a personal legacy is that there are no set parameters, so you can shape it to suit yourself and your family. It can be as simple as a few bullet points stating your core values or as long as a book that lays out all your major life experiences. You decide who sees your personal legacy and whether they see it while you're alive or after you're gone. It can take the form of a written document, a video, or an audio recording. You can create a personal legacy at any life stage. Your personal legacy can include details about your spiritual or religious beliefs, but it certainly doesn't have to. A personal legacy is for religious and nonreligious individuals alike.

I've provided a Personal Legacy Worksheet (Worksheet 36.1, available for download at www.morningstar.com/goto/30MinuteSolutions) to help you get started, but you shouldn't feel limited by it. Rather, think of it as a way to get your creative juices flowing. Don't think of this as a document that you complete once and never look at again. You should feel free to update it and refer to it as time goes by.

To create a personal legacy, you'll need:

▶ Time to think clearly

Start the Clock

Step 1

Start by dating your personal legacy and also specifying who should see it. Also, bear in mind that you don't have to call it a Personal Legacy at all. You

Worksheet 36.1

Personal Legacy

PREPARED FOR: _____ DATE: / /

You'll Need:
- Time to think clearly

LEGACY

Values and Core Beliefs

_____
_____
_____
_____
_____

Major Life Achievements

_____
_____
_____
_____
_____

Special Individuals/Impact

_____
_____
_____
_____
_____

Other Information

_____
_____
_____
_____
_____

Print your worksheet at: www.morningstar.com/goto/30MinuteSolutions

might instead call it a "Legacy Letter" or "A Letter to My Loved Ones." (See? Everything about a personal legacy can be customized—including the name!)

Step 2

Jot down what you consider to be your values and core beliefs. Try to be as specific as possible. For example, rather than simply saying "Honesty," you could say "Honesty: I have always tried to be truthful and trustworthy, in my work and in my personal life. It is the quality I have valued the most in my wife, Ellen, and my close friends, Al and John."

Step 3

Document the achievements and contributions for which you hope to be remembered, in your personal life as well as your work life. Also document important life experiences, and explain why they were significant.

Step 4

Next, note the individuals who have had the biggest impact on your life, and say why they were important to you.

Step 5

Is there anything you'd like to clarify for your loved ones—any decisions you made or actions you took that your friends and relatives might not have understood at the time? Your personal legacy gives you a chance to explain and/or apologize if you would like to do so.

Step 6

Finally, when you've completed your personal legacy to your satisfaction, you can do a few different things. You can store it with your other estate planning documents so that your loved ones can read it after you've gone. But you don't have to wait: You can also share your personal legacy with your loved ones now.

You may also find that referring back to your personal legacy helps provide a worthwhile sense of perspective during uncertain financial times. This book aims to help you create a financial plan that you can feel comfortable with even though the stock market, the economy, and your portfolio will ebb and flow over time. I hope it has done that. Ultimately, though, the meaning you derive from your life and the impact you have on others will far outweigh your financial assets. Referring back to your personal legacy can help remind you of that fact.

About the Author

CHRISTINE BENZ is director of personal finance for Morningstar and editor of *Morningstar PracticalFinance*, a monthly personal finance newsletter geared toward individual investors. She also writes a weekly column on Morningstar.com, "Improving Your Finances." She was co-author of *Morningstar® Guide to Mutual Funds: 5-Star Strategies for Success*, a national bestseller published in 2003, and author of the book's second edition, which was published in 2005.

Christine began her career at Morningstar in 1993. She has served in numerous roles on the company's fund analyst team: analyst, team leader, editor of *Morningstar® Mutual Funds*™ and *Morningstar FundInvestor*, and director of fund analysis. She began focusing on personal finance in 2004, launching Morningstar.com's "The Short Answer" column.

Christine received her bachelor's degree in Russian and East European Studies and Political Science from the University of Illinois at Urbana-Champaign.

Index